Selected Letters of Paul Hindemith

Books by Geoffrey Skelton

Wagner at Bayreuth: Experiment and Tradition
Wieland Wagner: The Positive Sceptic
Paul Hindemith: The Man behind the Music
Richard and Cosima Wagner: Biography of a Marriage
Wagner in Thought and Practice

Translations

Wagner Writes from Paris   (with Robert L. Jacobs)
Cosima Wagner's Diaries

Selected Letters of Paul Hindemith

Edited and Translated from the German by
Geoffrey Skelton

Yale University Press
New Haven and London

Published with assistance from the Hindemith Foundation.

Designed by Deborah Dutton
Set in Monotype Joanna by Marathon Typographic Services, Inc.

Printed in the United States of America by Vail-Ballou Press, Binghamton, New York.

Hindemith, Paul, 1895–1963.
    [Correspondence. English. Selections]
    Selected letters of Paul Hindemith / edited and translated from the German by
Geoffrey Skelton.
        p.   cm.
    "Index of Paul Hindemith's works": p.
    Includes index.
    ISBN 0-300-06451-9 (alk. paper)
    1. Hindemith, Paul, 1895–1963—Correspondence.   2. Composers—Correspondence.
I. Skelton, Geoffrey.   II. Title.
ML410.H685A4   1995
780'.92—dc20
    [B]   95-17335
                                                                            CIP
                                                                            MN

A catalogue record for this book is available from the British Library.

The paper in this book meets the guidelines for permanence and durability of the Committee on
Production Guidelines for Book Longevity of the Council on Library Resources.
10 9 8 7 6 5 4 3 2 1

Contents

Acknowledgements

For permission to select, edit, and translate the letters contained in this book I am indebted to the Hindemith Foundation, which holds the copyright to all the composer's works, including his letters, and in particular to Dr. Giselher Schubert, director of the Paul-Hindemith-Institut, who allowed me complete freedom to make my choice from all the letters preserved there. Dr. Schubert and his staff gave me much valuable help at all stages of preparing the letters for publication. My task was further aided by the presence in the Institut of the material belonging to the Paul Hindemith Collection at Yale University, of which I have made very considerable use.

In the course of my work, I consulted the following publications and wish to acknowledge their help: Dieter Rexroth, ed., *Paul Hindemith Briefe* (Fischer: Frankfurt, 1982); Andres Briner, Dieter Rexroth, Giselher Schubert, *Paul Hindemith: Leben und Werk im Bild und Text* (Zurich/Mainz: Atlantis/Schott, 1988); Luther Noss, *Paul Hindemith in the United States* (Champaign: University of Illinois Press, 1989); the Schott Verlag (Mainz) publications *Paul Hindemith: Zeugnis in Bildern* (1961); *Paul Hindemith: Die letzten Jahre* (1965), *Paul Hindemith:Werkverzeichnis* (1985); various articles in the *Hindemith-Jahrbuch*, in particular Claudia Maurer Zenck's detailed account of Hindemith's relations with the Nazis, "Zwischen Boycott und Anpassung an der Charakter der Zeit" (*Jahrbuch* 1991/XX).

With the exception of Figure 15, all photographs come from the Paul-Hindemith-Institut, Frankfurt am Main, and are used with the permission of the Institut. For Figure 15, I wish to thank the Paul Hindemith Collection, Yale University Music Library, New Haven, Connecticut.

Editorial Practices in the Letters

Despite his reluctance to write them, Hindemith's letters contain many more words than there is room for here, not least because, once he had made up his mind to start, his pen was apt to take over, resulting in exhibitions of high spirits, lively narration, robust argument, and even, on occasion, a rather choleric temper. To preserve as much as possible of these qualities, I have preferred, in the letters I have chosen, to omit passages that are either repetitive (such as many of the frequent and sometimes lengthy apologies for not having written earlier) or of no particular interest generally (instructions regarding proof corrections, details of dispatch, and so on). As a general rule, I have omitted opening and closing forms of address to each correspondent after their first appearance, except when they reveal some change of relationship or some of the facetious inventiveness in which Hindemith took such delight. All such deletions are indicated by ellipses in square brackets, thus: [. . .]. Other ellipses are Hindemith's own.

All the letters apart from those marked as having been written in English were written in German, and the translation is my own. In these German letters Hindemith occasionally made use of foreign words or phrases (usually English), and these are printed with underlining. The letters in English have been reproduced exactly as Hindemith wrote them, since they provide an accurate picture of his progress from a rather comical beginner's English to the complete ease shown in the letters to Cox and others during and after his thirteen years of residence in the United States. Spelling errors that are clearly mere slips of the pen or typewriter I have corrected without comment.

In his love of word play Hindemith was apt at any moment to go off into flights of fancy: he invented words ("ornithography"), distorted metaphors ("when the egg is ripe"), used phonetic spellings (naming himself "Semischäcksbier" in tribute to his own skill as a writer of librettos), and so on. Rather than deaden the effect by devices such as [sic] or footnotes, I have left it to readers to recognize and interpret these little jokes for themselves. That may sometimes take a moment or two, but I here give an assurance that they are not misprints.

The majority of the letters were written in Hindemith's clear and firm handwriting, which only very occasionally (and particularly in the letters to his wife while waiting for her to join him in America during the Second World War) shows signs of haste or agitation. With increasing frequency, he took to using a typewriter during and after the years in America. In both cases, whether handwritten or typewritten, additions or erasures are as few and far between as mistakes or corrections. Hindemith tended always to write his letters, long or short, in one solid block, indicating changes of subject only by a dash after a period. In the interests of easier reading I have used these as an excuse to start a new paragraph in the longer letters.

Hindemith frequently failed to supply an address or a date at the top of his letters. By consulting the notebooks in which he kept a fairly detailed record of his daily activities, the Paul-Hindemith-Institut has succeeded in providing the missing information, which is printed in square brackets. When Hindemith did supply them, addresses and dates were written in several different ways over the years. Since the style here is not important in itself, I have standardized for the sake of clarity. I have shown the address in full only on its first appearance, afterwards indicating it only by the place name. These authentic dates and addresses have no square brackets.

Hindemith did not use a consistent style to indicate the title of a musical or literary work: sometimes it is placed within quotation marks, but usually it is not differentiated at all. In both the English letters and my translation of the German ones I have followed Hindemith's inconsistent practice; in the linking passages, however, I have observed normal publishing conventions. Hindemith spelled some personal names, particularly Russian ones, in the German way. For ease of identification, I have in most cases changed these to the traditional English spelling without comment.

Introduction

"You are well acquainted with my standard opening of letters," Paul Hindemith wrote to Oscar Cox, his friend and lawyer in Washington, on 7 February 1954, "accusing myself of having not written earlier—so that I can spare you that old routine." The usual excuse was pressure of work. It is seen in the opening letter of this collection; in the letter to Carl Schmidt of 11 November 1934: "As always amid much work, I find my way to music paper more readily than to a writing pad"; in the letter to Emma and Fried Lübbecke on 6 December 1939: "There was a lot of work here, since the little springs of composition were flowing fast, and the clearing work in the garden also took a lot of time"; and to Cox in a letter of 5 April 1958 (not sparing him the old routine this time): "Its author has resumed the life of a composer and is producing his sounding blueberries by the thousands." He could even lightheartedly turn the excuse to his own advantage, as in his letter to his publishers Schott of 16 June 1928: "You have heard nothing of me for a long time. I hope you have noticed."

The letters in this selection prove by their contents that the excuse was no empty one. Throughout his life, Hindemith was a man of action. Besides being a composer, he was simultaneously a concert violinist and viola player, orchestral conductor, teacher, and writer of opera librettos and textbooks. His letters, when he found time to write them, were factual rather than reflective, yet seldom unrewarding. Once committed to the task, his innate desire to communicate provided a generous flow of news and opinions, frequently enlivened by the sharp wit with which he observed his fellow creatures and the jokiness with which he sought at the same time to protect himself from them.

Though outwardly convivial, Hindemith was an intensely private person, guarded in the expression of his emotions, and he firmly resisted any attempt to publicize the details of his life. The number of people in whom he confided were few, and there was none, except for his wife Gertrud, with whom he was ever fully open. This statement is—and can only be—based on the evidence contained in the letters that have been preserved. His relationship, for instance, with his mother, to whom he was closely attached, remains undefined in the absence so far of any of the letters he was known to have written to her. But from his correspondence with others, it is clear that chief among his intimate friends was his publisher Willy Strecker who, together with his brother Ludwig, ran the firm of Schott in Mainz. Next on the list would probably be Oscar Cox, in the letters to whom Hindemith reveals an unusual amount of emotional feeling. With both of these men, the existing business connection ensured that the flow of letters remained fairly unbroken (despite excuses). Hindemith's correspondence with Emma Lübbecke-Job, the pianist who did so much to promote his music at the beginning of his career, though spasmodic, stands out for the fact that it was maintained throughout his adult life.

The chronological arrangement of Hindemith's letters in this book provides a biographical framework to which only a few details need to be added concerning his life before the first letter and after the last. Descended from a family of carpenters and saddlers in Silesia, Paul Hindemith was born in Hanau, near Frankfurt am Main, on 16 November 1895, the eldest child of Robert Rudolph Hindemith, a painter and decorator, and his wife Marie Sophie Warnicke, a farmer's daughter. His musical talent appears to have come from his father's side of the family, as he himself speculated after meeting a previously unknown uncle and three cousins during his first visits to America. His accounts in his letters to his wife of his joyous music making with these unlikely partners will be found later in these pages. Robert Hindemith appears also to have been something of a musician, possibly a frustrated one. Despite the family's poverty he took care to have his three children trained musically from an early age: Paul as a violinist, his daughter Toni as a pianist, and his younger son Rudolf as a cellist. The children even appeared in public on a few occasions, billed as the Frankfurt Children's Trio and accompanied by their father on a zither.

After two years of study with Anna Hegner, a respected concert violinist, Paul was awarded a scholarship to the Hoch Conservatorium in Frankfurt on her recommendation. He entered the Conservatorium in his thirteenth year after having completed his elementary school education. His teachers were Adolf Rebner, a concertmaster at the Frankfurt Opera (violin), Arnold Mendelssohn (composition), and Fritz Bassermann (conducting). Before long he was joined at the Conservatorium by his brother Rudolf, who was admitted at the age of ten.

Their father being too proud to accept financial help from better-off neighbours, the two boys played in taverns and cinemas to earn money while still studying. There were, however, well-to-do music lovers in and around Frankfurt, such as Carl Schmidt and the Ronnefeldt family, who showed their interest in the boys through hospitality, commissions, and introductions to friends further afield. Among these was the Weber family in Switzerland, with a letter to whom this selection begins.

It ends at Christmas 1962, a year before Hindemith's death in Frankfurt on 28 December 1963, with a card to Darius Milhaud, the French composer who had been a friend and active ally at the musical festivals of the twenties in Donaueschingen and Baden-Baden. Hindemith remained active to the end. His last public appearance was in Vienna, where on 12 November 1963 he conducted the first performance of his final composition, the Mass for mixed chorus a cappella, at the Piaristenkirche. If he relaxed at all in his last years, it was to delegate the writing of letters almost entirely to his wife, who was as proficient in English and French as she was in German. As a result, Hindemith's correspondence with Paul Claudel on the oratorio Ite, angeli veloces and with Thornton Wilder on his opera The Long Christmas Dinner was conducted almost exclusively through her.

Gertrud Hindemith died on 16 March 1967. There were no children of the marriage and in her will she directed that the entire Hindemith estate be devoted to establishing a foundation to aid and promote music, most particularly contemporary music, in Hindemith's spirit. To carry out these aims, the Hindemith Foundation established the Paul-Hindemith-Institut in Frankfurt am Main. Among the institute's tasks was the collection, preservation, and annotation of both Hindemith's and his wife's correspondence. All the letters printed in this book, with the sole exception of those to Edith Sitwell (the property of the British Library), were chosen from this collection.

The Letters

In order to earn money while still studying at the Hoch Conservatorium, Hindemith accepted an engagement in the summer of 1913 as first violinist in a small band formed to entertain visitors on the Bürgerstock in Switzerland, above the Vierwaldstättersee. During this time, he stayed at the home of the local physician in Aarau, Dr. Gustav Weber, who was a great lover of music. Hindemith and the Weber family became close friends.

Hindemith's teachers at the Conservatorium were now Adolf Rebner (violin) and Bernhard Sekles (composition), who had succeeded Arnold Mendelssohn.

The pupil in Friedberg, some twenty-five miles north of Frankfurt, was Wolfgang Schmidt. His father, Dr. Carl Schmidt, a professor of philology, was not only a good pianist, but also a promoter of concerts in the vicinity, at which both Paul and Rudolf Hindemith frequently played.

To the Weber family   Frankfurt
                                                    27 December 1913

Dear Frau and Herr Doktor,

A curse lies over my activity as a letter writer. So far I have never been able to write a letter with a clear conscience and always have to begin with apologies for the long gap between one letter and the next. And so it is today. I last wrote to you 3½ months ago, and since then I have never ceased being annoyed with myself for not doing so again. But with the best will in the world I just could not. How often have I thought of you, knowing you would be cross with me for not writing! You must surely have thought often enough that I had forgotten you. But that would be impossible. If all my thoughts had been letters, you would have had plenty to read. But enough in this style. I shall now tell you all that has happened to me and what I have been doing during the time I have not written.

After Bürgerstock I went, as you know, with the band to Lugano. I thoroughly enjoyed myself there. The lake, the lovely scenery, the Italian bustle, and the journey through the Gotthard made such an impression on me that I should have been glad to stay on even beyond 15 Sept. Our conductor was still very satisfied with me. He came to the railway station to see me off and gave me a large bottle of Chianti. I got on very well with the other players, and I was very sorry to have to leave, for among them were some really nice and kind people. Our band in Lugano was worse than on the Bürgerstock. We had 4 new players, since 4 others had left. The new 4 did not play as well, however. The cellist made a hash of everything, and the horn player could no longer lip properly. Then, despite the constant rain, we had to play out in the garden most of the time, and of course, on account of the damp, the instruments were never in tune with each other. And then the snapping of the strings! At every concert at least one of them snapped, and that had a very depressing effect on one's musical mood. Throughout the summer I have had to send for E strings, 25 Marks' worth from here alone (50 sets of 3 = 150 strings!), and despite that I still had to buy some in Lucerne and Lugano. Otherwise, however, it was splendid.

I returned home on 16 September and on the 17th was back in the Conservatorium, having prolonged the holidays by 2 weeks. Then work really began. I have a great many lessons: violin, piano, counterpoint, composition, instrumentation, orchestra, and chamber music. Herr Rebner was very pleased to see me back again. I have learnt quite a lot so far: the complete Mendelssohn concerto, a concerto by Theodore Dubois, the big C major sonata by Bach, and practically the whole of Wieniawski's Ecole moderne. I am now playing the Beethoven concerto. I am tremendously pleased that Herr Rebner allows me to play such a masterpiece, and I shall spare no effort to be able to play it well for him after the holidays—at any rate better than the girl at those conservatory examinations in Zurich. If I played like that, he would certainly throw the music at my head. He says he is very satisfied with me and is nicer and more friendly than he has ever been in all the long time I have known him. He is now getting me to play all the big concertos in succession (Dvorak, Brahms, Tchaikovsky, Saint-Saëns etc.). I am much looking forward to the coming year. It will of course mean extremely strenuous work and demand a great deal from me, but I shall face it bravely and work hard. I want my teacher to go on being satisfied with me. His praise makes my work easier, and his kindness and friendliness mean more to me than if he were to give me money (which says a lot, coming from a musician!). My profession is giving me more enjoyment than ever, and I live entirely for music. Admittedly, that is not without its occasional unpleasantnesses. Not so very long ago Herr Rebner made a terrible scene and bawled me out good and proper because, during an evening recital, I had not played exactly as he wished, though it hadn't seemed bad to me. But that gives me no reason to doubt his friendship. You will see from this what he expects of me, and I am happy that he makes such big demands. In this respect I value him more than any of the other teachers. Also in his manner of playing I prefer him to most of the well-known virtuosos.

Our dear Professor Mendelssohn has been ill since October. I am now getting counterpoint and composition lessons from Herr Sekles. He is very pleased with what I bring along and praises it to the skies. Just now I am working on a trio for clarinet, horn, and piano. It is giving me a lot of headaches, for the differing qualities of the instruments give scope for some very unusual effects. There really are problems to be solved (acoustical ones and so technical ones as well). I look forward to the moment when I can hear the piece played. I have done only 2 movements so far. Progress is very slow, because it is very difficult work. For the wind instruments (and for the horn in particular), it is very difficult to play. Sekles likes the piece enormously. It is harmonically very interesting, and that impresses him. He always addresses me as "Herr College," because I now bring him finished compositions, whereas until recently all my work had been uncompleted. I don't know why this is. For some time now I have been moving with my composing in a completely different direction; I shall be interested to see what comes of it. In counterpoint we are doing 2-voice fugues for the piano. With Sekles this is rather boring. Prof. Mendelssohn is better at explaining things, he helps us and works alongside us, as if he himself were still learning. I hope he comes back in the New Year. He is suffering from gallstones. I have learnt a very great deal from him.

He has given me some sensible advice and taught me to profit from what I have already learnt and make use of it. He has always been so nice to me that I am very sorry to have my lessons with him interrupted by illness.

Now I must go and get changed for The Miracle. I'll write more about that below. I'll continue writing in the morning. Till then, adieu.

28 December 1913

Yesterday I went to a performance of Vollmoeller's "Miracle," which Max Reinhardt is now presenting in the Festhalle. If you ever get a chance to see it, do not miss it! One can hardly believe it is possible to keep control over such immense masses of players. I was completely bowled over and would never have believed that anything so brilliant and so grandiose could be done on a stage, or rather in an arena. The whole gigantic Festhalle has been transformed into a colossal church. All the lamps have become church lanterns and all the windows church windows. Church bells ring out at the start, and the whole hall becomes as black as night. Then the sound of the organ and nuns singing. Stupendous lighting effects, a procession lasting ¾ of an hour, wonderful music, and a rich display of people, costumes, and scenery! And how well the actors act! I came out of the hall reeling and have only this morning returned to my senses. It sweeps one right off one's feet, and one forgets it is all just theatre. I shall go again, come what may, even if I have to pay 20 marks for it. On 1 January we are having Parsifal here. I'll see if I can find a sympathetic soul to buy me a ticket. If not, my own purse will have to bear the burden.

While on the subject of theatre: something on the lighter side. I am playing in the Neues Theater as concertmaster for an operetta. "Filmzauber," utter nonsense from beginning to end, yet funny and charming. This evening for the 17th time! I shall soon be sick of it. We play the whole thing by heart and prick up our ears only when a new joke is cracked above our heads. Maybe you have already heard the music: at least the numbers of truly classical beauty: "Unter'n Linden," "Kind, ich schlafe so schlecht," etc.

I have already played in a very large number of concerts. I can't send you any programmes, partly because I myself have none, partly because there would anyway be too many. [. . .] I also took part in some wedding celebrations in Bad Nauheim in October, another similar affair two weeks ago in Friedberg, and then Christmas festivities in Niederrad. That's about all. You will now understand how little spare time I have and forgive me for not writing to you for so long. I had to attend all the rehearsals for the concerts and could not afford to neglect my own studies and works.

Then the many rehearsals in the Neues Theater and the trials with my own pupils. Of these I have 3 here and one each in Friedberg and Nauheim. In fact, they all work hard, and in particular the young lad in Friedberg gives me great delight with his earnestness and willingness. All the same, I am always glad when a lesson is over. There have been times when I haven't known whether I was standing on my head or my feet. I was out and about all day long and hardly ever got home before midnight. For 3 whole weeks I haven't even seen my father or my sister. It really was high time for the Christmas holidays to arrive. Not that I got tired or weary or nervy. On the contrary, I have felt very well throughout. But one begins to be a stranger to oneself and in many respects one to some extent loses the connection between one's inner and outer selves. As I said, I was really glad when the holidays came. On Christmas Day, I lit the stove in my room, put all rugs, quilts, and pillows within reach on the floor and placed boxes of cookies and fruit beside them. Then I buried myself in the cushions and read. I felt like a sultan. For the first time in ages I was once again Paul Hindemith. Just now I am reading the Arabian Nights. I find the glittering fantasy and the old-fashioned style of these stories very fascinating.

We had a very nice and happy Christmas. A young Swiss was with us on Christmas Eve. He is playing the harp in The Miracle and so cannot travel to Basel for the holidays. As presents I got the Beethoven quartets, a piano score of Tristan, a wallet, a toilet case with brushes, combs, and mirror, and a whole lot of little practical gifts besides. Rudolf was given a gun, a pair of boots, books, underwear, overcoat, and various other things. I made a whole number of purchases. Potatoes for my mother, books for my father, material for a dress for Toni and books for Rudolf. All in all, we were very happy and content.

The greatest achievement of recent months has perhaps been the establishment of our Conservatorium club "Urian." It has 6 members (each always madder than the rest) and our main aim is to amuse ourselves. 3 are Swiss and the rest German. Best of all are the club gatherings, which are held in the digs of the various members. Dress: dinner jacket with light trousers. Complete ban on alcohol during sessions. Just water and mint pastilles. We also make music, but only such that specially prepared ears can withstand. Best of all, ears stuffed with cotton wool. We have perpetrated a drama with music, which we will perform in the New Year. You too are cordially invited. But please bring aspirins with you. [. . .]

Well, that's it for now. Rudolf has lapsed again, they are shooting for prizes next door, and I can't miss that. People are already wondering why I haven't given a sign of life all afternoon. So I'll stop now. [. . .]

With many warm greetings to you and all acquaintances in Aarau,

Yours,

Paul Hindemith

Hindemith was still pursuing a busy life as student, performer, and teacher when war broke out in August 1914. His father volunteered at once for service in the German army, and the task of supporting his mother, brother, and sister fell on him. In June 1915, Hindemith started work as a violinist in the Frankfurt Opera orchestra. The musical director was Ludwig Rottenberg, his future father-in-law.

Playing in (and soon leading) the opera orchestra was only one of his many musical activities. In addition to his solo appearances, Hindemith also played in the Frankfurt Museum symphony concerts, of which Willem Mengelberg was the permanent conductor, and as second violin in the Rebner string quartet led by his teacher.

Of Hindemith's early compositions, the Trio for clarinet, horn, and piano mentioned in the previous letter was labelled Opus 1. The two mentioned in the following letters were the String Quartet, Opus 2, for which he was awarded the Felix Mendelssohn-Bartholdy Foundation Prize, and the Concerto in E-flat Major for violoncello and orchestra, Opus 3, which was first performed in Frankfurt on 28 June 1916 with Maurits Frank (cellist of the Rebner Quartet) as soloist and Hindemith conducting.

To the Weber family   Frankfurt

5 September 1915

[. . .] I am about the only one of my relatives not yet to have been called up. One uncle is with the engineers in Russia, another with the territorial reserves in Silesia; one cousin is in the Argonnes, another has just been called up in Cologne.

Father is now in the neighbourhood of Souain in the Champagne district. So far things have gone well with him. From the beginning of the war until October, he was with an outpost outside Namur. From there he went to Lille, where he took part in the street fighting. Then until winter he was stationed north of Lille facing the English. There he rescued a patrol that had gone astray and was awarded the Iron Cross. From Lille the regiment was moved to the Champagne district, where he still is, sometimes here, sometimes there. At Whitsun, Father was given 12 days' leave. You can imagine our joy when the bearded reservist arrived, quite unexpectedly. True, he was fabulously filthy, and his uniform was stiff with "dugout mud," but he was healthy, merry, and cheerful, which is the main thing. He looked better and fresher than ever before, a sign that the war is doing him good. His greatcoat was much shot up, and he had brought with him some shell fragments that had drilled holes in his trouser legs. His present position seems not exactly an ideal summer resort. [. . .]

I have not yet been enrolled in the ranks of the fatherland's defenders, for which I am not sorry. I have in fact been twice summoned to a medical but was deferred on account of general physical weakness and a heart defect!! Probably there will be more medicals before long, and I have no hopes of being put back yet again. That doesn't please me at all, since I have just taken up my post at the opera house here, where I have been engaged up to 1921. This year as a first violin and from Sept. 1916 as 2nd concertmaster. That's pretty good, isn't it? So far I am greatly enjoying my operatic activity; but I am a patient person and am waiting till I get fed up with it. For me the past school year has been a time of the most strenuous work. In spring I played the Beethoven concerto with orchestra in the large hall here (Frankfurter Tonhalle), with great success. But it meant I was left with a lot on my plate: not long afterwards there was the prospect of a composition evening at the Conservatorium, at which my quartet was to be performed. Since it was only half completed, I had a fabulous amount of work still to do if I was to deliver it at the appointed time. I succeeded, but only at the sacrifice of every available minute. Every evening I sat writing notes until 2 or 3 o'clock. I had to write the score and all the parts myself, since no copyist was prepared to take on the huge task in so short a time. After these nights of hard labour, which left me with shaking bones and a buzzing head, came the nerve-racking rehearsals. Leaving aside the fact that each part was difficult enough in itself, playing them together was so incredibly difficult that we needed an unholy number of rehearsals to get it right.

By sheer bad luck the II. violinist was called up a week before the performance, so Prof. Bassermann took over this part himself. In consequence, we spent the week rehearsing for dear life, and on the evening of the concert it clicked more or less. It was a big success. Admittedly the reviews were miserable, but the audience, as well as all the experts, was highly delighted. The two conductors from the opera were also there, and a few days later my letter of engagement was in my pocket. But it did not leave me unscathed: I had to spend 3 weeks in bed, since I was totally done in. Work like that again?—no, I couldn't stand it. Until last month I was still feeling in my head the evil effects of those days, but now I am back to normal.

In June I played the Brahms concerto in the Cons. to colossal applause. Even Herr Rebner was delighted, which he otherwise never is. When he was called up a week later, the honourable but unwelcome task of taking all his lessons fell on me, and I did that up to the beginning of the vacation. He has now returned. I find the vacation extremely welcome. After all, it was a bit much too much work. Besides the concerts already mentioned I also had a number of more modest performances in town and out, not to mention the terribly many charity and soldiers' concerts one is duty bound to take part in. And then there are still my 6 pupils in Friedberg and the operetta in the Neues Theater every second or third evening; more than a packhorse could keep up for long, and I have made a firm resolve not to work so awfully much in future. [. . .]

To the Weber family   Frankfurt
                                              Whitsun holidays 1916

[. . .] I hope you are keeping well and in good spirits. I take it the war is not causing you too many difficulties. At any rate it must be much pleasanter living in dear and lovely little Switzerland than here. I too would rather be there; but I haven't the slightest prospect of that within the foreseeable future. I can't leave here under any circumstances, first on account of my job in the theatre, second because I am classed as an infantryman fit for active service. (!) In the latter capacity I should by rights have reported to Mainz on 1 May, but the theatre appealed yet again. The appeal runs out at the end of this month, and then I shall probably have to join the Prussians, unless I have the colossal luck of being deferred once more. In Mainz I would have gone to the regiment where my father was.

I wrote you in my last letter that my father had been posted missing. We had news 3 weeks ago from the Red Cross that he died in battle on 25 September 1915. We had in fact come to that conclusion a long time ago, when there has been no news for half a year (since September), one is bound to reckon no more will come. He was here on leave last year in May, and that was the last time we saw him. He returned then to his position (the so-called witches' cauldron in the Champagne district). He wrote regularly, always very cheerfully, until we received his last letter, dated 12 September. Then the big French offensive began. The position he was in at that time was taken by the French, and our first thought was that he had been taken prisoner. [. . .] In the end, two comrades from my father's company were located in the prison camp at Etampes, and they swore on oath that they had seen him lying dead beside the dugout. So now there can be no more doubt, though we still lack official confirmation. I have written to Etampes in the hope of receiving more details, but as yet have had no reply.—The war has torn a painful gap in our midst!

But enough of so sad a subject. You too surely have had your fill of it, and it is therefore quite unnecessary for me to lament and parade my grief before you. The war in itself is sad enough, and the best thing one can do is to set up a "music-hall of humour" against these present times; that helps in many ways. I have been successful in achieving it, and so am not suffering at all in these dismal times. On the contrary! I have not allowed myself to be got down, have been gripped by a quasi-raging will to work, and have brought off several fine things. If it doesn't bore you too much, I will tell you a bit of what I've been doing.

To start with, what is at the moment most on my mind is composition. My string quartet, with which I won the Mendelssohn Prize last autumn, will very probably be performed in Vienna some time this year. I hope it comes off! If I am still here or am back here in the autumn or winter, we intend to play it again here too. At the end of last year and the beginning of this, I completed a further opus, a big cello concerto with orchestra or, more exactly, a symphony with cello obligato. That was a real grind! It is to have its first performance here in the Conservatorium on the 26th of this month. The cellist Frank (Rudolf's teacher) will play it. It is admittedly very difficult but sits well for the cello. The orchestra sounds excellent. I'm willing to bet the reviews will again be miserable, but that doesn't worry me. Sekles, my composition teacher, wants to help me get it published. It is an unfavourable time for such things, I know, but maybe it will come off. [. . .]

I have a large number of plans lined up, and I hope I shall have time in the next 10 years to carry them all out. I have also not neglected my fiddling and was busy with that as well. A lot of concerts (solo as well as quar- or more-tet) are the best proof of that. Karlsruhe, Pforzheim (twice each), Saarbrücken, Heidelberg, Nuremberg, Bamberg, Freiburg—those were about the main places in which I or "we" were. "We" means the Rebner Quartet, in which I played II. violin. In Karlsruhe I played both times in the Schlosskirche in the presence of H.R.H. the Grand Duchess Luise, and each time I was granted lengthy audiences. One of the concerts in Pforzheim was a big solo concert, in which I loosed off the Mendelssohn concerto and the Ciacona. Brilliant reviews laced with fine epitheta such as "majestic display," "captivating," "deep insight," "sparklingly light," "brilliant achievement," "height of rare ability," "powerful impression," "infectious verve," and so on.

In March I passed my audition at the theatre and am now permanently engaged as I. concertmaster. In the audition they made things *very* difficult for me. To start with, I was called to the director's office without being given any idea what I was wanted for. There, *completely unprepared*, I played for the director and the two conductors the 1st movement of both the Brahms and the Beethoven concertos, the complete Mendelssohn concerto, and the Chaconne, which of course gave the gentlemen a great surprise. On the following Thursday I passed yet another audition, at which not just the above-named, but also the Amsterdam conductor Wilhelm Mengelberg (director of the Museum concerts here) and a large number of our orchestral players were present. I played Mendelssohn, Brahms, and Bach. All went well, but Mengelberg, a man with red hair whom I thoroughly dislike, was utterly opposed to giving me the position, "because I was much too young." I have heard that he had another fiddler secretly lined up for it. However, when some extremely difficult passages from Salome (which I had never before seen) were put in front of me and I played them straight off by sight, he couldn't of course object any more. At the moment I am doing the same work as the second concertmaster, but after the summer vacation I shall be moving up and alternating with the other I. concertmaster, Hans Lange. The theatre work is very strenuous, particularly in winter, but I very much enjoy it. On top of this, there are, every second week, the Museum concerts with their never-ending rehearsals. So there is little chance now of taking things easy. If you bear in mind that, besides all this work, I have been studying, giving lessons to 3 pupils, rehearsing with the quartet, and still finding time to take a serious interest in nonmusical matters, you will see that my days are filled with work from morning till night. [. . .]

Well, now I must stop. I am really tired after so much writing and, besides, Mother is calling me to tea. I must not miss that, since I am already feeling hungry again (here one is now always hungry!). [. . .]

> Among the friends of his own age with whom Hindemith made music during his spare time while awaiting his induction into the army, Emmy Ronnefeldt and Irene Hendorf were the two who shared his interests and in whom he most closely confided. Emmy was the daughter of a well-to-do Frankfurt family who took an interest in the Hindemith brothers after their father left for the war. Irene was a fellow student at the Hoch Conservatorium, studying the piano. Emmy Ronnefeldt cut out what she described as "the purely private passages" in the letters to herself and her mother before releasing them for publication.
>
> Hindemith's Three Songs for soprano and orchestra, Opus 9, were not performed until 1974. The Quintet in E Minor was never completed and was probably destroyed in the air raid that damaged his last home in Frankfurt, the Kuhhirtenturm, during the Second World War.
>
> Sekles's Die Temperamente was an orchestral work. Else Gentner-Fischer was a singer at the Frankfurt Opera.

To Emmy Ronnefeldt [Frankfurt]
May 1917

[. . .] I was surprised with Sekles recently. I showed him my songs with orchestra (2 are finished) and do you know what worried him? That the songs are too free in form and bear no resemblance to "usual" Lieder! And these are our modern musicians! Something written from the depths of one's soul, with not a thought in hell of Lieder forms or such-like rubbish, something a little bit unusual—this makes them nervous! I want to write music, not song and sonata forms!! Of course, if I write logically and my thoughts just happen to come out in an "old" form, that's all right. But in 3 devils' name I am not bound to keep on thinking in these old patterns! And I have the feeling that it's precisely my new songs that, through their lack of restraint, are more genuine than Sekles's Temperamente, for instance. With all respect to my teacher! I'm coming more and more to the conclusion that it's high time I shook myself free of all this conservatory nonsense. What ties me to these people, after all? Tradition, and nothing else. When I really want to know something, there's nobody who can help me, nobody to whom I can talk seriously about music, because none of them has any ideals left: their whole art has turned into mere handicraft. And now even my own teacher comes along and is unwilling—or unable—to understand what I'm trying to say. So what am I still doing there? Yes, it really is a thankless affair. One tries to pin down on humble paper the sweetest kisses of Frau Musica and, when one thinks one has conjured up a vision of eternal bliss, what do these blockheads hear? Not music, but just notes, bars, dynamics, forms and such-like trivialities. The trouble with our music is that it lacks music! And all I want to do is to make music. I don't care a damn if people like it or not—as long as it's genuine and true. [. . .]

To Irene Hendorf [Frankfurt]

[24 May 1917]

Stuttgart, 20 December 1902

Honoured Herr Rosenthal!

On my last visit to your house on the 14th of this month I absentmindedly permitted myself to leave behind both my new sunshade and a jar of pickled gherkins. Since my wife has now become aware of the absence of these articles from her pantry, I herewith politely request you . . .

Beg pardon, dear Irene, it's just that I have opened my guide to letter writing at the wrong page. However, please make no mistake, in anno 1902 this man really did leave umbrella and gherkins behind (I have it in print, can be seen at any time). Well then, listen. I have rehearsals every day until next Thursday and am always busy in the evenings, so the music making is off. But Friday would be fine, then we could really get our noses stuck into it. Are you coming to one of the Schwarz guest performances here? If so, we can talk everything over then. Otherwise, you can perhaps write me again? I fear this music making will have to be the last for some considerable time, since I am becoming more and more convinced I shall at long last have to report for military service the week after next. (Shall I then have the Schubert sonata played to me?) It is possible in this case that I may be prevented from taking part in the Mainz concert: that would be an awful shame. I'll be happy if it turns out otherwise (but don't expect it).

Now I must quickly tell you what tremendous joy you gave me on Monday with the quintet, and I thank you many times for it. Unfortunately I can't make you any high-sounding speeches, you know that—but you also know what I mean when I say little, don't you? Imagine that I might have sent you a huge bunch of flowers, or a pound of toilet soap, or 50 pounds of potatoes—or imagine I might write an ode to you or compulsively feel a madly beautiful piano piece on to paper—or God knows what. And, having imagined that, feel thankful for having got none of it! Instead I send you tears, handshakes, kisses, and other attributes of gratitude (very warmly felt), as many as you can stand. (NB! Can you stand much?) And if at any time I can do you a favour, . . . etc., in the same long familiar strain.

So farewell, you faithful soul, and be glad that you are not here, for in the past few days I have broken out in a cannibalistic lyrical rash that today has reached fever pitch. (Always dangerous for fellow creatures and other people.) It comes from writing songs. The third is almost finished in sketch form, the second completely finished.

Auf Wiedersehen.

Your Paul

NB! (Hindemith)

To Emmy Ronnefeldt   Frankfurt

Sunday, June 1917

[. . .] I finished my songs precisely at Whitsun, begun at Easter, completed at Whitsun—is that a good omen? Sekles, now that he has seen them as a whole, is absolutely delighted with them. He declares the orchestra masterly. I am really proud of this opus. There are three songs. The last one is a march. Youth marches out, thrones are toppled, prisons smashed, barricades built, prisoners freed, a frightful racket raised—incidentally, a marvellous poem of real power. I believe the music combines worthily with the text. The orchestra is very large: 8 horns, 2 harps, 5-man percussion, & a whole host of other pretty little things—a truly respectable score. — At the conclusion, the singing voice has to scream continuously—terrific, isn't it? Nothing for musical people. Tough constitutions required!! A singer with two sets of lungs. Sekles declares the song would need at least "3 desks" of sopranos to sing it. Still, for the time being that is not the case. Frau Gentner is now looking through them. Since, worse luck, I am only an infernal amateur in matters of vocal technique, I have asked her just to assess their singability. But she will sing them to me some time. Without orchestra, of course, I shall just fill in (substitute orchestra!) on the piano. [. . .]

What are all these clever dissertations you've written about composition lessons, etc.? I am not obliged to show Sekles my things, nor do I have any need for it. But one does have to have at least one person who understands, if not the emotional side of things, at any rate the technical side. I may have a very tough stomach, but I can't stuff just anything into it. Joy over a successfully completed work can come on one with the force of an eruption—and, rather than burden some ignoramus with it, I prefer to go to the teacher with whom after all I grew up musically, even if maybe he doesn't quite know what I'm aiming at.

Incidentally, regarding "craftsmanlike"—you are confusing that with "technique." All art needs technique. Without it, no art. And that, for better or worse (mostly worse!) one has to learn. — A composition lesson is nothing but a free lecture in counterpoint, harmony, and form. One must make use in one's works of all the things one has learnt in these separate compartments (that's to say, it would be more correct put the other way round), & in a composition lesson you just get your knuckles rapped if you have written something clumsily or incorrectly. (Incorrectly does not = against the rules! There is an aesthetic rightness that is not bound by rules—though in fact all rules have basically evolved from aesthetic principles. And until one has mastered technique to the extent that one can write down everything one feels in one's heart, a lot of water will flow down the Main. I suppose I can declare with an easy conscience that I have been at this stage since about the summer of last year. (Of course, technique develops further with time, and anyway everyone changes his views and also his feelings to a certain extent.)

And then: yes, the views of "sensitive laypeople" are of course quite nice. But what is the more desirable: an emotional audience that weeps and rolls its eyes without knowing why; that is possibly carried away just as easily by horrible kitsch dressed in sober robes as by serious works of art? Or a so-called expert audience that hears, God help us, nothing but harmonies, forms, and all the rest of that junk? Though the one is as objectionable as the other, I still prefer the latter (personal opinion, of course), so long as the laypeople lack a wider "artistic understanding" and the "experts," despite their knowledge, preserve the necessary degree of naiveté. — But audiences are not going to change, and it is therefore not very "appropriate" to stake out claims and to link weighty arguments to them. I write exactly as I choose, and I don't give a damn at the moment whether people like it or not. To be true, genuine—that is the ruling principle!! And that's that. I must be off to the theatre. Mignon, ugh! [. . .]

On 13 August 1917, Hindemith was called up for military service in the German army. He was placed in an infantry regiment for training, with the rank of musketeer. His application for a transfer to a military band was granted, and on 16 January 1918 he joined another infantry regiment, stationed at Tagolsheim in Alsace, as a drummer. The commanding officer, Graf von Kielmannsegg, was a great music lover, and he soon had Hindemith busy forming and training a string quartet with other members of the band, to play for his private pleasure.

To Frau Ronnefeldt

Sender: Musk. Paul Hindemith
1.Ers.Bat.I.R.81
6 September 1917

Dear Frau Ronnefeldt,

I have been wanting to write to you for a long time, but it "didn't work." That is to say, I have now become so well trained in Prussian laziness that I could be a corporal at the very least. All the same, I am still just a very ordinary Landsturm [territorial reserve] recruit and as such hop around the circus (alias the barrack square) day by day, tracing the most amazing bow sweeps. I get a lot of fun from it (please don't think I have gone crazy, oh no, the sergeant major has not yet got me that far), and I believe that in time I shall become quite a good soldier. During the first week, in which I found it terribly difficult to accustom myself to this pyramidal malingering, I slept here in the barracks and made the discovery that bedbugs don't bite me. There are masses of them here. [. . .]

But now I am sleeping at home and thus get the chance to eat 2 breakfasts and 2 suppers. [. . .] I am still doing the theatre work (without rehearsals, thank goodness). With that I manage to ward off a total decay of my inner self. I do in consequence have to get up very early, but I have got used to that fairly well. Usually just after 4 o'clock. Formerly I had no idea that clocks functioned that early, but each morning my alarm assures me to the contrary in very robust fashion. Yesterday I was about to be carted off to France; I appealed, however, because I have been here only 3 weeks. I probably won't be staying very much longer; I reckon another 3-4 weeks. In the meantime, I'll try hard to get myself sent to a military band. I imagine life there would be very much pleasanter than in a dugout. [. . .]

To Emmy Ronnefeldt

28 November 1917

[. . .] I am still hoping my transfer application will be granted: it should come anytime now. And when that is in hand, I may sail off at once, perhaps in a few days' time. Even if the application is turned down, I can be posted at any moment. The comrades who were called up at the same time as or after me went off last week—to the Champagne district! It is solely thanks to my application that I was not with that transport. So please keep your fingers crossed for me, I myself haven't the time, and anyway the fingers of my army gloves are so huge that I can't cross them by myself, I'd need an aid squad of at least 2 men for that!

With every one of my superiors, from the captain to the corporal, I am on the best of footings (my own, of course). My captain grants me all kinds of concert leave straight off without a murmur, the lieutenants are constantly questioning me about theatre affairs, and the rest (from sergeants downwards) are being continuously supplied with theatre tickets. Recently I sent one of the vices to a Museum concert. He wasn't very keen at first, but when he read on the ticket that the seat cost 5 marks (of course it cost me 0 marks), he felt most sweetly tickled. As Bruckner's very long Romantic was to be played that evening, I thought he might be giving me a few hours' extra drill next day. Apparently, however, Schapira's decolleté and her fiery strumming on the piano touched a sensitive chord in his vice-soul, for next morning, despite my unpolished belt, he declared it had been really good and he had also seen how busily I'd been fiddling. Since then my rifle drill has been wonderful, my boots are never muddy, and (as had always been the case before) I no longer drew attention to myself while throwing a hand grenade, whereas before I never discovered the correct fingering and never threw it more than 20–25 metres. I hope to become a lance corporal soon. And that will be very necessary, for if I have to pay for all the many theatre tickets, I shall no longer manage on my 3.30 Marks per decade. Should I not be promoted in the foreseeable future, I shall have to put in for a wage increase.

Over the next few days, I shall no longer be a soldier, since I have my "contractual" exemption for the Museum. Besides that, I have been granted 4 days leave from Sunday, as I have concerts in Friedberg and Karlsruhe, this time real ones in fact. In consequence, I am in extremely good spirits and am sleeping twice as much as before. Besides that, I have finished the third of the piano pieces. It sounds terribly degenerate, has neither time signature nor key, nor harmony in the accepted sense. If I go on working in this genre, I shall end up one day in a territory beyond good & evil, where it will no longer be clear whether what I have written is a higher form of music or just a substitute for music. The things give me great joy, all the same. One of the pieces is 9 bars long. My present great ambition is to write one consisting of just 3 bars, theme, development, coda. Conciseness is the sign of the master! In a piece still to come, you will have to reach inside the piano and pluck the strings; in another, the lid of the piano will be slammed shut, always at the point where I have allowed a clear major chord to slip through unobserved. So that one's music sensitivity will not be offended. Wait, this idea must be brought into being right away, a theme has just occurred to me. Stop, stop, stop!

Next time a bit more sense. [. . .]

To Dr. Carl Schmidt   Alsace
                                                                        19 January 1918

Dear Herr Doktor,

Now at last I have time to reply to your letter. Unfortunately I did not get a chance to work out the passage you sent me; I had rather a lot of duties in the barracks. In the meantime, however, I have moved up to the front. Here I am living like a pig in clover. Hardly any duties. True, we are stationed in a front line village, but the trenches are a full 3 km away. The artillery is shooting all day long, but not in our direction. Captive balloons, planes, machine-gun fire—there are more than enough of those around, but here, in spite of them, we live quite peacefully side by side—until one fine day the Frenchies will have the bright idea of heaving a bomb into our farmhouse. Officially I am a drummer in the regimental band, but my main task is playing quartets. My partners are unfortunately not first-class, but they are very keen and make a tremendous effort. I also give them lessons in harmony. I live in a shack with a very nice set of companions, mostly from Oberhessen. The place sounds like a town pipery. Music coming out of our ears. Practising all day long. The curious tonal mixtures that can be heard there. Tuba, piccolo, viola, flugelhorn, clarinet. If the war continues in this style, I shall be very happy. But it will surely turn out differently. The regiment will probably be moved in the next few days—to a hotter spot.

With warm greetings to the entire Schmidt household

Yours,

Paul Hindemith

Res.Inf.Reg.222, Regimental Band

Apologies for writing this letter in such a disorderly and muddled way—the music buzzing around one's ears drives one crazy.

To Emmy Ronnefeldt   6 February 1918

[. . .] The journey to the front brought all kinds of work and upset with it. (I left on 16.I.) [. . .]

To replace the cancelled "offerings" [for the Ronnefeldt silver wedding], I have written a string quartet (though in fact it is not yet finished), which I want to dedicate to your parents. I don't know whether your father will like it, but I believe it will give your mother some pleasure. In my own opinion it succeeds very well. Here I am recovering the fabulous will to work that back home more or less deserted me in recent days. For the piano pieces I shall have gradually to find my way back into the world of the piano. I am rather out of touch, for here we play only quartets and brass band music. The former I find very refreshing. My fellow players are by no means first-class, but they are making hair-raising efforts, and through these and the many rehearsals I have with them, we are producing reasonably good music. The count, our regimental commanding officer, for whom we always play, is delighted. He is extraordinarily kind to me. The day before yesterday he took me with him to Mülhausen, and throughout the journey he kept up a wonderful conversation. He is a fabulous man. In Mülhausen he gave me a volume of Nietzsche, and he also invited me to visit him in Weimar when he is on leave. I am glad that I have been sent to this regiment, for here I live a fine life. In the band I bang the big drum with skill and enthusiasm. I am assured that this instrument has never before been handled with such precise rhythm. The duties here are not terribly demanding, I have a lot of free time and can work for myself as I choose. And it is not so terribly dangerous here either; admittedly the French are constantly shooting at the batteries, which are very close to us, but as yet they haven't fired on the villages themselves. Perhaps, however, a few stray shells may one day land on our little village. We are 2½–3 km behind the front. [. . .]

Hindemith's first compositions to appear in print were the Three Pieces for cello and piano, Opus 8, which Breitkopf & Härtel published in 1917. The concert at which Rudolf Hindemith played them took place at the Hoch Conservatorium on 6 March 1918, and the programme included the first part of the uncompleted quintet.

Emma Lübbecke-Job, the pianist in both these works, specialized in contemporary music, and she took part in many first performances of Hindemith's works. She and her husband, Dr. Fried Lübbecke, an art historian, lived in Frankfurt and became Hindemith's lifelong friends.

The string quartet that Hindemith was currently writing as a silver wedding present for the Ronnefeldts was his Opus 10. It was given its first performance by the Rebner Quartet on 2 June 1919.

To Frau Ronnefeldt   21 March 1918

[. . .] I was pleased with all the nice things you wrote to me about my compositions. When one reaps such warm and genuine praise, one at least knows that one has not been working in vain. And I had my doubts about the quintet often enough after Sekles, Rebner, and others found nothing in it to please them. Oh, these masters! All the same, I learned something from it all: just to keep on writing as I have to; never to give way; to make no concessions. It is difficult, because it means many people will not go along with it; but never mind, they don't matter, as long as a few loyal souls remain who will stick with one to the last. I am sure that Rudolf played the cello pieces very well; after all, he knows from me how the things are to be tackled; and Frau Lübbecke is also useful in this sort of music. I should so much have liked to hear the quintet because I wrote it with great enthusiasm and because it is the first of my pieces to be worked without reference to traditional forms (that so very famous "chamber music style"), leaving room for thoughts and feelings of all kinds. Your quartet will not proceed so inconsiderately. It is much better behaved. A wicked rock has been blocking my way in the final movement for quite some time, and I can find no way round. I shall just have to wait until somehow or other the way ahead drops into my mind. I am still hoping that you will be able to hear the piece before the year is out, and that you will find pleasure in it; it is a gay piece. [. . .]

The two works for violin and piano are part of Hindemith's Opus 11.

To the Schmidt family   9 May 1918

[. . .] I am sitting in a bullet-riddled English village in the most splendid weather, have nothing to do but enjoy life, and am consequently feeling extremely well. But we are still active in some ways. Though we seldom make music now, we have more time for stealing, sleeping, and eating, all activities that leave one very hungry and tired. A comrade and I have fixed up an extremely comfortable little room for ourselves in a relatively little damaged cottage. Just imagine how grandly we live: we even have curtains over our—admittedly very decrepit—window; we also have a milk-glass lampshade that turns the murky candle glow into a cosy and, above all, even light. But the most refined article of furniture in our cabin is the chaise longue, an old cot mattress which, covered by a blanket, is the envy of all visitors to our Eldorado. The entrance is the only thing that is not aristocratic: it leads through our donkey stable. We have a mule that pulls our music waggon [. . .] Until recently we had two peasant horses, but someone fetched them from the stable during the night; we then obtained the mule by the same method; but we need another.

I have finished writing the violin sonata I began in your house; there was still one movement to do. If I can get some music paper in the next few days I shall copy it out and send it to you. Altogether I have composed quite a lot: a big string quartet, and now I am busy on a sonatina for piano and violin. [. . .]

To Irene Hendorf   26 May 1918

[. . .] On our journey to this district after Easter, we sat on our waggons blaring our melodies out over the countryside from morning to night. And each time we stopped at a station, the people were beside themselves: they cheered, showered us with cigars by the boxload. We came near to causing a few disasters, however: a tunnel was within an inch of taking off, blown to bits by the force of our notes, and one man almost demolished a level crossing with his motor horn. But despite all tricks of fortune we arrived here in one piece, spent a month swarming through one godforsaken hole after another, and finally landed up in a former English village, where we have been for the past 4 weeks. The beauties of nature are scarce here, but there are rather more artificial ones: countless shell holes and here and there a house of some kind that has survived with only minor damage. Our regiment is primed for action, but we are getting ready for a rest period before long; for us life begins then; we can make music again day and night. Things here are not exactly harmless, however. Only yesterday an airman—who saw us rehearsing and appeared not to approve of our "old" interpretation of the Parsifal Prelude—tried to drop a bomb on us; a weighty affair, but it didn't do anything, giving up its ghost about 100 m away and just sending us running for dear life. And a few other amusing tricks of that sort. In our last billet, our driver got one in the side of his head—it has healed now—and on the same afternoon, a shell splinter weighing about 3 pounds landed on the ground beside me. There are air fights all the time, day and night. But we here haven't been fired at yet, a fact I find not uncongenial. On the whole it's a very tolerable life—relatively speaking, of course, for after all it's wartime. [. . .]

The songs offered were probably part of Hindemith's Opus 18 collection. The piano pieces, already mentioned in his letter of 28 November 1917 to Emmy Ronnefeldt, were later collected under the title "In einer Nacht," Opus 19.

To Irene Hendorf   5 August 1918
Dear Irene,

You must have had a bad sunstroke or be feeling tremendously dissatisfied, since you raise such a racket. Anyway, many thanks for your long letter, which made me very happy. The reviews—like everything in any way papery at the moment—have gone the way of all flesh (to quote Lessing), for I have been lying in the sick bay for the past week with colossal diarrhoea, i.e., not lying, but running, and all sorts of things are going the way of all flesh. Now, however, I am so far recovered that I should be set free with a blessing in the next few days.

Now to the point. Why are you so much against giving a piano recital? One singer or one instrumentalist, that's all right, but two of this breed—that looks horribly as if you are begging pardon for being there too. — You're not usually like that! So get your Frau Westphal—a singer is always a better draw than a scraper—and let her twice sing three songs in the course of your giant world-city programme, then the problem will be solved to everybody's satisfaction. What exactly were you thinking of with all the Beethoven cello sonatas? For heaven's sake, one of those is quite enough! Besides, I am sure that you two, you and Rudolf, would not perform them in the spirit of Beethoven, and that would of course be a big mistake. Choose a programme that suits you, one with which you will capture "the heart of the public": a Brahms Rhapsody, Chopin waltzes or etudes, a Liszt rhapsody or the Hungarian Fantasia. — You have choice enough; I am not all that well primed on the subject, you must yourself know best. If you want my songs to be sung, I have two for contralto at home, ask Rudolf to give them to you. [. . .] They won't be quite your style, however, they're too delicate for that. Have a look at them, anyway, for they are singable. Do what you like with the piano pieces. Put them on your programme or get them published. I've no idea what effect they would have played together, but I believe that in their present state, with some still missing, they would sound all of a muddle. [. . .]

On 28 July 1918 Hindemith wrote in the diary he kept during his military service: "In the morning, terrible news. Our count has died in action. — What a blow it is for the regiment, the band, for me myself! Who can replace him?" Then on 15 August: "The big event: the band was introduced to the new colonel, Grimm. [. . .] We have been lucky again. [. . .] A worthy successor to our beloved Count."

To Frau Ronnefeldt   20 August 1918
    [. . .] Recently, when our dear Count died so suddenly, we were all in a mood of deep depression. No one knew what would happen next; we were left hanging by a thread with our quartet. But now all our worries are over. The count has a worthy successor, a colonel who in civil life is court intendant in Gera and knows a lot about music. Everything remains as it was. He has quartets played to him, and, since he is familiar with the entire chamber music repertoire, he arranges his own programmes. He is a very attentive listener, so playing for him is a pleasure. — Now to tell you something amusing. I have been made a corporal. Not on account of bravery or any other of my military virtues, but just because the last time we played quartets for him our colonel amused himself by "giving me a stripe." If the war goes on long enough, I'll maybe finish up a captain! [. . .]

To Emmy Ronnefeldt   28 September 1918
    [. . .] It's not easy writing in a dugout, it's too cramped and too wet, and all day long one's ears are ringing with the sound of eternal gunfire. Outside, shells are flying around our heads. Mornings and evenings we go to Douai to play to which-ever of our regiment's companies is taking a rest. We have to march at the double, since the street is under constant fire. Everything gets shot at here, nowhere can one live for 2 or 3 days in the blissful knowledge of not hearing this beastly noise. In fact we're no better off than the conscripts in the trenches. You can't imagine how sick and tired I am of this life. How long does this wretched existence have to go on? Will this stupid breed of idiots never put an end to this devilish war? A pity I'm not religious, or I should long ago have declared war on God. These damned people who keep the war going should be sent here for a few weeks' summer holiday, then they would soon learn.
    But enough of this grumbling, it won't do any good. [. . .] Recently I have got back again to composing, after having had absolutely no ideas since June. The day before yesterday I completed the first movement of a sonatina for violin and piano and am now working on the last, but I haven't got the middle movement yet. The piece will sound very al fresco. Very big and thick, sweeping brush strokes. The

other sonatina, on which I was working during my leave, is also not quite finished; it's just that I can't find the right approach to this interrupted work. I want to write a whole series of these sonatinas, which in fact = small sonatas, since they are too lengthy for sonatinas. Each one is to be totally different in character from the one before, in form too. I want to see whether in a series of pieces I can extend the expressive possibilities—which are not very great in this kind of music and with this combination of instruments—and bring them closer to the horizon. Many years will pass before I finish this work—if I live to see it, or keep my health. I believe it will be an interesting task. But I am sorry for the poor people who—attracted by the poster that two enthusiastic musicians, no longer quite right in the head, will paste on the walls in twenty years' time—will buy tickets and then imagine they can sit back and enjoy themselves.

. . . Concert Hall

12 Sonata Recitals   1–12 Febr. 1938

I	II	III
1. E-flat Major	5. Sonatina, variations	8. In three-voice counter-
2. D Minor	on a single note	point (would-be)
3. No particular key	6. F Minor & A Major	9. With light and colours
4. Dorian	(mixed)	etc.
	7. With drum beat	

[. . .] I have sent quite a few pieces of music home (from Douai), piano pieces, piano concertos, and things for piano duet. There is a lot of music lying around in private houses and music shops. It is a shame to see it all just getting dirty and unusable. Altogether it is a shame, the way everything is being destroyed here; I should be quite glad not to have to watch it all happening! [. . .]

The following letter was written on notepaper with the letterhead of a lawyer in Douai, Paul Godefroy. Hindemith crossed "Godefroy" out and wrote "Hindemith" above it.

To Fried and Emma Lübbecke   5 November 1918

My dear Doktor Lübeckes,

I must write to you more often, so that I shall at least learn how to spell your name properly. As it is, I never know whether two b's or two k's are necessary. If I have today sinned against ornithography, please be thankful that I have at least not written it with a ÿ. (This by the way.) Are you very cross with me for never having sent word at all? I have found it so difficult (since some time past) to write letters, it costs me much effort to summon up the energy to write even the most vital ones to my mother. And most of the time I have no writing desk either. In the former haylofts—you can have no idea how many haylofts there are in northern France and Belgium—my drum always served in this capacity. But when one sits in front of it, one's legs go to sleep up to one's collar. We are now living in splendid comfort, however. A small school hall provides our living quarters, and we lie, some 30-man strong, on the floor like the creeping things in the "Creation" recitative. Just now the entire army is engaged in going to sleep, while I am enthroned on the seat of a child's school desk, writing by the light of a candle. I had in fact intended to write to you at noon today, but, since there were some unusually lively goings-on among my underclothes, I had to conduct the "daily inspection" and lay a lot of poultry low. I have now developed quite an impressive finger technique.

For some time I have had the feeling that it would be much nicer playing sonatas and trios at home than having to sit here "enjoying" life. I don't know whether this is a correct point of view. Our present way of life has of course many advantages: one travels the world free, one sees and experiences splendid things, one "learns to be tough," and, above all, one is part of the so-called Great Times. But why is one never satisfied? Many a conscript in the trenches—though there are not many in the trenches now—envies us on account of our comfortable life. But wait a while, soon—! In the coming days, our band is to be reduced in numbers. This reduction, as all of us fairly confidently predict, is almost certainly the prelude to a complete dissolution before long, and then we shall be setting out in corpore to meet the Tommies. My intention at the moment is to make a smart "about turn" halfway. I can only hope that the armistice for which we all (and particularly I) long will prevent me from doing that.

Germany seems, however, to have multum many men to spare, since it is taking so long to decide whether to put an end to the whole business. By rights the eager warmongers and Vaterland party members should now be sent to hold the front themselves for a change. Of course I know nothing at all about politics, and for that reason have in the past few days become a keen social democrat. When the war ends, I too shall be inscribing Liberté, Egalité, Fraternité on my banner. So don't be surprised when one day I come to your house and declare your clay zoological garden to be mine from now on. (Between ourselves: I'm not quite as brutal as that!) Infected by the democratic bacillus, I shall from now on compose only bright red pieces. I have now completed a sonatina (yet again), the first movement of which is so left-wing and radiates so much bolshevism that on listening to it the whole right-wing loudly cries "shame" and rises from its seats, but that does not worry the composer Hindemith. The other sonatina that received its first performance in your sacred halls when I was on leave is still not finished, but all the same I have decided to dedicate this piece to you (perhaps it will spur me on to write the missing part of the last movement before very long). So when, towards the end of the war year 1920, a huge crate arrives at your door, you can think at once to yourselves: "Aha, here comes Paul Hindemith's sonatina!" But maybe the stretta of this war will now come to a swift end, and then I myself shall be able to call on you, but of course deloused, washed, and combed. I shall bring my own mug and artificial honey, so you will have no need to worry about feeding me. And if it grows too late in the evening and I am too lazy to go home, I'll pinch a bundle of straw from somewhere or other and lie down in the piano. Here, unfortunately, I have no piano to sleep in, but all the same I expect to sleep soundly, this eternal retreat-offensive makes one rather tired.

Goodnight wishes from your

Paul Hindemith,

who would be very glad if you would one day write to him.

Hindemith was released from the army early in 1919. He at once resumed his old position as concertmaster at the Frankfurt Opera and rejoined the Rebner string quartet, this time as violist. At a concert in the Frankfurt Saalbau on 2 June 1919, he played in performances of the string quartet he had written for the Ronnefeldts and of the uncompleted quintet, in which Emma Lübbecke-Job played the piano part. She also accompanied him in performances of the violin and viola sonatas from his Opus 11.

The success of this concert led him to offer the works to the publishing firm of B. Schotts Söhne in Mainz, of which Geheimrat Ludwig Strecker had been head since Richard Wagner's time. The reply he received came, unknown to him, from the Geheimrat's two sons, Ludwig and Willy, who had just joined the firm and were eager to bring it more up to date.

To the Schott-Verlag   Frankfurt

3 July 1919

Dear Herr Geheimrat,

I received your letter of 1 July yesterday. My pleasure over your words of appreciation was indeed very great, but still greater was my astonishment over the remaining contents. I am fully aware that in times like these it is very difficult to publish large and serious works and that publishers cannot live by their ideals alone (though one cannot regard as ideal the principle of making honorary payments of not more than 100 Marks to composers who have not yet made "a great name" for themselves in order to be able to use these to produce the greatest rubbish which, however, always sells well). I think I can assume that you also well know how difficult it is for a composer to believe in his ideals when he learns that for a work on which he has laboured for weeks and months with the greatest care and love he is offered the paltry sum of one hundred marks. The sum of 100 Marks does not pay even for the music paper and copying of the parts, let alone for the time and trouble of composing the work. Your proposal suggests to me a considerable contempt for intellectual work that I am not prepared under any circumstances to accept. My ambition to see myself in print is not as great as that. My sole interest is to publish the piece before next season, because it will often be played. As you know, there is almost no good modern chamber music to be had, and that is why I allow myself to think that this quartet might well help to fill a "long-felt need." I could achieve this very well by publishing the piece myself, a method that would certainly be of greater advantage to me. I have so far held back from this, however, since I wish to avoid taking on more work, and in my opinion it looks better when a piece is brought out by a large publisher. Yesterday I happened to speak with the owner of one such firm, and he at once offered me 500 Marks for the quartet—without having seen the work, simply on the strength of my recent concert. Should you be prepared to raise the "honorary payment" very considerably above this sum, I am ready to agree to your proposals. Otherwise I must ask you to return the score to me as soon as possible, so that I can send it to this other publisher. With many thanks for the trouble you have taken in considering my compositions, I am

> Yours sincerely,
> Paul Hindemith,
> Concertmaster

The Strecker brothers raised their offer to 1,000 Marks, to cover the Opus 11 sonatas as well as the quartet, together with an option on all future works and an assurance of extra payment in the event of reprintings. Hindemith found this acceptable.

Pressure of concert work that year led to Hindemith's offending one of his early sponsors. The work enclosed as a peace offering was the Sonata for unaccompanied viola, Opus 11, No. 5.

To Dr. Carl Schmidt   Frankfurt
                                                              23 August 1919
Dear Herr Doktor,

You must be in a real rage with me, or at least be feeling very annoyed. And you are right. It is disgraceful of me not to have been in touch with you. [. . .] I did indeed mean to write to you for your birthday. Besides that, I had promised to make you a present of some music. As I have said: disgraceful—but I believe, if exactly the same situation had recurred and I had had so many ideas and such a will to work, I should again have been just as neglectful. In point of fact, I journeyed to Holland with the firm intention of dedicating to you the first major piece I should complete. I send it to you herewith, hoping that it will give you pleasure. Everyone so far to whom I have played it likes it very much—I too am satisfied with it at the moment. Before very long I shall find my way to your door, armed with a viola, and play it for you in all its uncivility. (Close the windows!) I cannot play it well, for it is so horribly difficult. Since I was unable to play J. S. Bach's Ciacona to you, but did not wish to leave you entirely without a ciacona, I have taken the liberty of serving one up for you in the sonata's last movement. Would you rather have a cleanly written copy of the piece? With the sonata I send you belated but well-preserved good wishes for your birthday. You can be sure that I should dearly have liked to be with you on that day.

"Our" concert on 8 July was our (the Rebner Quartet's) concert in Marburg. I can remember quite clearly mentioning "our" concert. I told you that I would be coming from Marburg. As member of a group through which I earn a (for me) considerable sum each year, I cannot throw all our joint concerts together to the winds. (Then everyone could try it on; and then where should we be?) Since I could not put off to another day the Marburg concert that had already been moved to the 8th—why I don't know—I wrote to you at once, asking whether you could not change the date of your concert. The strike took care of the remaining muddle, as you know. There is one thing I could have done: written to you soon after, but— see above. —

One other point I must put right: the whole affair had nothing to do with any nerviness on my part. By that time, the pressure of work had ceased, and I had recovered from the severe winter long before. And on the Sunday I spent at your house I was not conscious of being irritable. I could more easily admit to such a thing now, after I've been working so hard. Beside the enclosed sonata, I have written a one-act opera, songs with string quartet, songs with piano, and a large cello sonata. Schott in Mainz has bought from me the string quartet, two sonatas for violin and piano, as well as the one for viola and piano. The quartet will be appearing shortly.

You of course know Meisel, our second violinist, who was in the Friedberg garrison. It seems he is giving 120 chamber music recitals there. Yesterday he told me he wants to play my quartet at one of them, since I am very well known there, and he also wants to introduce novelties. I cannot of course stop him, since the piece is no longer mine, but I'm hoping it will be too difficult for him. Should I laugh or should I cry?

I shall be coming to your house shortly. To break in the sonata and to try Herr Rossbach's grand piano. Till then, warmest greetings to you and the whole family, and do not be cross with me, I am sure you know that, even when I don't write (since I have a growing horror of words through all my dealings with music paper), I am always your
    Paul Hindemith

The compositions sent to Schotts that had given the Strecker brothers "so many headaches" were mainly those Hindemith mentioned in the foregoing letter to Dr. Schmidt. The Cello Sonata, Opus 11, No. 3, was given its first performance on 27 October 1919 by Maurits Frank and Emma Lübbecke-Job, the Three Hymns by Walt Whitman, Opus 14, by the baritone Helge Lindberg on 26 February 1920. The new quartet was the String Quartet in C Major, Opus 16, which was launched at the first music festival in Donaueschingen on 1 August 1921 by the Amar Quartet which Hindemith himself established especially for the occasion (violins: Licco Amar, Walter Caspar; viola: Paul Hindemith; cello: Rudolf Hindemith).

To the Schott-Verlag   [Frankfurt]

11 April 1920

Dear Sirs,

I am very sorry that you are having so many headaches on my account. I had no intention of giving you any nuts to crack, and I must give you the firm assurance that there is nothing at all "crackable" in the pieces I sent you—it is all music of the truest and most natural kind, not in the least bit "forced." (All the same, I do understand your point of view.)

Why are you so astonished? I have not changed, I am still writing just as easily as before, and the difference between my earlier and my present things is not basic, it is only a question of degree. I could not write in this way before, because I was still too undeveloped technically (and personally). Added to that, the pieces you already know were almost all written at the front, and it is obvious that in such conditions, cut off from all decent music, one has not much chance of developing musically. All the "alarming" features you don't like in my new music can be seen in the other things, though incomplete and clumsy, and of course obscured by all kinds of formal rubbish. Worth noting in this connection are: the fugato in the first movement of the quartet, whole passages in the second movement, in particular the variation in A major, and, in the last movement, the last ⅘ stretto in the finale.

In the smaller (E-flat) violin sonata, the second movement; in the other one, the beginning and end of the first; in the viola sonata, the first variation and the fugato in the finale. It is all much more developed in the cello sonata, which you heard here last autumn and which (should you want to take a look at it in this regard) Frl. Hendorf, Mainz, Albinistrasse 6, can give you. The sonata for solo viola also tries hard to be intensive music but often falls short. In the Whitman Hymns I have almost succeeded in pinning down the things that have been going around in my head from the start. But they still cling in many places to all sorts of old-fashionedness. (Atavism is a tiresome illness that can only be cured by patience, hard work, and a lively and ever ready power of invention!) A one-act opera ("Mörder, Hoffnung der Frauen"—text by Oskar Kokoschka) stands on the same level. A series of piano pieces has already turned out much better, and, in my new quartet, and above all in the new songs, I have now achieved for the first time what I always wanted but couldn't bring off.

Next Thursday (the 15th) Frau Lübbecke will be playing the piano pieces here in the small Saalbau at 7 o'clock. I should be very pleased if you could come and hear them; I believe that you will then be convinced through the "evidence of your ears" that I haven't changed at all, that the Hindemith you know stands in all his health and strength before you, that it is only on paper that the things look so wild, that there are no nuts to be cracked, and that the pieces—if you listen with an open mind without stipulating what it is you want to hear—will please you very much. (The songs you do not like have been sung here and in Stuttgart by Lindberg with great success.) [. . .]

To the Schott-Verlag   Frankfurt
                                                    Wednesday [End February 1922]

[. . .] I am glad that you like the cello sonata; I still like it myself. I note with satisfaction that my things are getting better and simpler (high time, too).

I am not sending you the contract yet. Could you not raise the payment for these pieces a bit and, as with my previous things, grant me a share of the profits from the 2nd printing onwards? Composition now involves me too in big expenses (the present bad times are unfortunately forcing me to learn a little accountancy!); the cello sonata and the new quartet, for example, have just let me in for almost 2,000 Marks in copying fees for score & parts (and that is not even dear). If I were to take into account the fact that, in the time I spend writing, I could be doing more profitable work—giving lessons, etc., which in any case I shall have to do sooner or later—I should already be filing for bankruptcy. This is not a reproach to you; but I cannot go on laying out my own money. From my slowly oozing fame I can't even keep myself in music paper (one Mark per sheet, God help us, I shall now write nothing but duets for two violins). [. . .]

At the time of the following letter, the cellist in the Amar Quartet was Maurits Frank. The two one-act operas, Mörder, Hoffnung der Frauen and Das Nusch-Nuschi, were first staged on 4 June 1921 in Stuttgart under Fritz Busch and then on 26 March 1922 in Frankfurt under Ludwig Rottenberg together with a third, Sancta Susanna. The other works mentioned (where not clearly identifiable) are: the piano suite ("1922," Opus 26), the symphony for small orchestra (Kammermusik No. 1, Opus 24, No. 1), another set of songs (Des Todes Tod, Opus 23a), the ballet (Der Dämon, first performed in Darmstadt on 1 December 1923), the fairy play (Tuttifäntchen, performed in Darmstadt on 13 December 1922).

To Emmy Ronnefeldt   [Frankfurt]

                                                                [September 1922]

Dear Emmy,

[. . .] A pity you are not around to see the new zest we are bringing into musical
life here. The spirit of enterprise has seized hold of me. Last year I finally left the
Rebner Quartet, but in May I founded a proper quartet of my own: the Amar
Quartet. We play only modern music and are kept very busy. In the summer we
played at both the Donaueschingen and Salzburg festivals—with very great success.
We are off soon to Denmark and Czechoslovakia and in the winter to Paris. At both
the above festivals I once again succeeded in scoring over all the other composers,
and since then my affairs have been blooming beyond all expectations. All over the
place my things are being performed—my operas are to be done in Dresden,
Prague, and Kiel and have already come out here. Publishers are falling over one
another to get me, and I am making use of the favourable constellation to pick out
the one who will pay me the most, and then I shall get out of the orchestra and
spend my full time composing and playing in the quartet.

But my finest achievement has been to establish a "music community" here in
Frankfurt. We play modern music at Zinglers in the Kaiserstrasse (once every 2 or
3 weeks) before an invited audience of about 80: a purely musical gathering
without any financial complications. The audience pays nothing, the players get
nothing, and the very small expenses we settle among ourselves. So here at last we
have got music for music's sake! Personal ambition has no say in the matter, and
there are no newspaper reviews. And the best thing of all: none of the Frankfurters
is allowed in!! I have had a lot of trouble about that, for they all seem to think they
ought to be there. Nothing doing! And then, on top of this, we (the quartet) are
shortly to give seven musical evenings devoted exclusively to brand-new chamber
works from all countries. We're even doing some Russian ones never heard anywhere in Europe before. Great, isn't it? I must think up all sorts of new ideas like this
before very long—it's urgently necessary.

I've discovered a new sport: I'm playing the viola d'amore, a magnificent
instrument that has been quite forgotten, and for which very little music exists. The
loveliest tone you can imagine, indescribably sweet and soft. It's tricky to play, but
I play it with great enthusiasm and to everyone's delight. [. . .]

What else have I done this year? A lot of orchestra, a great many concerts, a lot
of touring. And an awful amount of composing: a song cycle Die junge Magd with
six instruments, a piano suite, a symphony for small orchestra, a wind quintet, a solo
viola sonata, a sonata for viola d'amore and piano, the Marienlieder, another set of
songs with two violas and two cellos, a sonata for viola and piano, a ballet (to be performed on 1.12 in Darmstadt), a solo cello sonata, and a Christmas fairy play that is

to be done here and in five other theatres. Most of these things are being published, too. I've got a chronic mania for work, and doubt if I'll ever get rid of it.

Rudolf is in Vienna, having recently returned from America. We never hear from him. [. . .]

At the time Hindemith wrote the following letters to his publishers, Germany was in the grip of rising inflation, and the German Mark was worth only a tiny fraction of its present value. Die tote Stadt (The Dead City) is an opera by Erich Korngold (1920).

To the Schott-Verlag   Frankfurt

3 1 October 1922

Dear Herr Dr. Strecker,

[. . .] I have in front of me the contracts I have made with you so far. They show that in 19 19 I gave you four chamber music works for a total sum of 1 ,000 Marks. Additionally, you took on the preparation of my operatic material without the slightest risk to yourselves, since I bore all the expenses myself. (You couldn't have experienced that very often. In my view, you probably wouldn't have covered your costs either with "Die tote Stadt" or with Sekles's opera. Furthermore, you have received in the spring 4 things (chamber music works and songs) for a total of 10,000 Marks, and, more recently, another four larger and smaller compositions for the same sum. On top of all this, you have an option on all my compositions for the next ten years (and for this you have not paid me a single penny!)

The fact is that for a relatively small sum you have been "stocked" by me with a host of pieces, of which some are already selling well and most are often played, at any rate more, or just as often, as the other new chamber works you publish. Added to that, you know as well as I do that this is only the beginning and that I am well on the way to becoming very well-known and being played very often. So in the course of the next few years you will not only be covering your costs but probably also be doing good business with my things. I am very unskilled in financial matters and until recently knew nothing about fees and royalties, etc. All the more reprehensible is it that you have taken advantage of my ignorance to palm me off with miserable royalties. How does this behaviour match with the fine words in the introduction to your catalogues? Does it come under the heading of "bighearted-ness" and "idealism"? I say nothing about the fact that you paid me poorly for my first things. I was unknown and you could not know what might one day come of them. Nor will I dispute whether it was honourable of you, at a time when I was having to struggle like mad in three separate professions in order to earn enough to live on, to charge the entire cost of preparing the operatic material to me — it was a risky undertaking, that I admit, though it might be thought that you could have shown at least as much confidence in it as I myself. But, after I had last year had successes enough, and then more recently had registered successes that were completely beyond dispute — thus opening up a prospect of many performances and in consequence increased sales — after all this, for you to offer for a further 4 pieces the same sum (a sum that at the time could have bought only about a third of a new suit!), that is conduct of a kind I do not wish to discuss further, since, now that I have seen what other publishers are prepared to offer me, I consider it quite out of the question.

I have here, from three large publishing houses, offers that show beyond all doubt that you have — to put it mildly — been making a complete fool of me, and I can, I suppose, assume that you would have continued along the same lines if I had not made a move. So, to cut a long story short: if you outbid by a considerable amount the highest of these offers, I shall be happy to stay with you. Should you not feel inclined to do this, I shall be released from my contract, since other publishers are offering me more and in consequence will receive the compositions on conditions less loaded in their own favour. At the same time, I draw your attention to the fact that two of the offers will enable me to give up my job at the theatre and thus release me from the shackles that greatly hindered my composing activities. I can then work free and untroubled for myself—and you will get some idea of what I can do, once given time for it, after having seen what I produce when harnessed like a harvest horse from morning until late into the night. From now on it is all the same to me who publishes my things: I am well enough known, as you are aware. The time is past when a publisher must go to a lot of trouble in order to get my pieces performed. Certainly the publication of my first pieces was a risk for you, but you got them cheaply enough. Once you had seen that the pieces were successful, you should have paid me a royalty such as other publishers are offering me now. The agreed proportion of the net profit (20%) that comes to me is a trifle not worth mentioning. If I wished to live on that, I should need to have 1,000 pieces in your publishing list, each of them selling 1,000 copies per year.

A few days ago I saw a contract one of my friends, an instrumentalist who some years ago hoped to make a career as a composer, had made with a large publishing firm. This contract, made in 1919, gave him a fixed monthly salary (continuous) of 500 Marks, to be adjusted in line with any eventual currency changes, and, in addition to that, royalties on each separate work. Nothing has since been heard of this man as a composer, for, having himself realized he would never be one, he gave up and terminated the contract. The work on the strength of which he received this contract was no better than those early works of mine that you published, and it was hardly ever played; today it is already almost totally forgotten. In return for royalties he was obliged to do the same as I, that is, to submit all his future compositions to the publisher for a number of years. Now please compare this offer with the offer you have made me—!!! So once again: if you are interested in receiving further compositions from me, I must ask you to make me an acceptable offer. It might be to your advantage not to set this too low. I shall have no hesitation in leaving you if your offer is lower than the highest I have so far received.

Incidentally, the payment of an extra sum for the compositions supplied this year I should consider, not as a special act of kindness on your part, but simply as the fulfillment of a moral obligation.

To end with: do not be unduly angry with the somewhat unaccustomed tone of this letter. I too have now discovered that, in matters of money, friendship has no place.

As always, with best wishes
> Your
> Paul Hindemith

To the Schott-Verlag   Frankfurt
                                                10 November 1922

Dear Herr Dr. Strecker,

[. . .] I have received your letter. I am quite aware that I was rude. Apparently I was not rude enough, otherwise you would probably have taken the whole matter a bit more seriously. You have not refuted the reproaches I made, so they still remain—except for the one concerning the share of profits. I did not approach other publishers, as you suspect, but received the offers without any instigation on my part. These offers are not bluffs (as you appear to assume), and nobody is scattering figures around just to impress me and then in the end not to pay up. I hereby inform you that agreement with one of these publishers is as good as settled, I am waiting only for your reply. As previously mentioned, this agreement will give me the opportunity of devoting myself entirely to composition, so you can reckon roughly the sum in question. If you are interested in continuing to receive compositions from me, I request that you let me know by Tuesday what you are prepared to offer. I cannot wait any longer and am by no means inclined to miss an opportunity that assures me a good living and with it liberation from encumbrances of all kinds. I stress emphatically that it is not my intention to leave your firm; on the other hand, as things now stand, one large publisher is as good as another as far as I am concerned, and the one I like best is the one that pays the most. The present times, I believe, force everyone to adopt this egoistical standpoint, and besides, I have learnt, not least from you yourself, that one must keep an eye on one's own advantage, and I should deserve a thrashing if I didn't do so. If by next Tuesday you have made me an offer better than the one now before me, I shall remain with you;

otherwise I shall without hesitation go over to one of your rivals. That is my final decision, and I have no intention of entering into further negotiations.

Warm greetings for now,

Your

Paul Hindemith

To the Schott-Verlag   Frankfurt

19 January 1923

Dear Herr Dr. Strecker,

I am very pleased that the contract is now in order. It is a pity that this could be achieved only at the cost of a lot of bother, and you will probably not be able to forget that it was I who caused the bother. I do not of course intend to try to convert you to my point of view—which I outlined to you in my earlier letters on this subject—anymore than I can accept your view of it. But you must not think I do not appreciate the fact that you have now reached this agreement with me. I am fully aware of the value of the concessions you have made. But I do ask you to recognize that I too have made concessions, by turning down at the end of December an offer that would have given me, besides the same subsidiary terms, a regular monthly salary (in whatever currency I choose) of around double what I shall receive from you. I found it vexing to have to negotiate music like a sack of potatoes, and I signed your contract despite those brilliant other conditions and despite the objections you raised up to the end. I hope we shall both profit by it. You can be assured that my work will not let you down. I have handed in my notice at the Opera and hope to be free by the end of next month. [. . .]

The annual music festival at Donaueschingen was the brainchild of Heinrich Burkard, musical director to Max Egon Fürst zu Fürstenberg, on whose estate it was held. After the first festival, at which Hindemith's second string quartet was played, Burkard invited him to help run the festival. The following letter was written some time in 1923. Emil Hertzka was head of the Viennese music publishers Universal-Edition. Both Schönberg and Webern attended the festival in 1924.

To Heinrich Burkard   [Frankfurt]

[1923]

Dear Heinrich,

I've heard from Hertzka that Webern has a new quartet ready. Write to him at once and reserve the first performance rights for this summer. Hertzka himself didn't put it over properly, so you must arrange things with Webern yourself. How is it with the Schönberg Serenade? If you don't get it, then at least try to get the new Wind Quintet. Leave no stone unturned: we must at all costs have something by him as well as Webern. Particularly the Schönberg you must get without fail.

If you have these things, Donaueschingen will be morally way above all this year's other music festivals.

So, my lad, get stuck in, or you're for it!!!

Yours

Baule

The one-armed pianist Paul Wittgenstein commissioned a concerto for piano, left-hand, and orchestra from Hindemith (as he also did from other contemporary composers, notably Ravel). Hindemith's concerto apparently did not please him, however, and he never played it. Nor did he return the manuscript, which is assumed to be in the hands of his heirs. The Concerto (Opus 29) remains unknown to this day.

The "watchtower" Hindemith wished to (and eventually did) purchase was the Kuhhirtenturm, built in 1490 and located in Grosse Rittergasse in the Sachsenhausen district of Frankfurt. It was severely damaged by bombs in 1943 and restored in 1957.

To Paul Wittgenstein

Frankfurt,
Leerbachstrasse 9
4 May 1923

Dear Herr Wittgenstein,

The score of the last three movements of your concerto will be sent off to you tomorrow morning. I still have not been able to write out the first, since I have a terrible amount of work to do. So that you will not need to wait so long, you will be receiving what I have already written out, about 80% of the whole. I hope you will be able to read my handwriting without too much difficulty. It is my habit to write all my scores in pencil, since I always have to make many improvements while working. I expect to have it all done by the end of next week. I should be very sorry if the piece should fail to please you—it may perhaps sound to you rather unusual to start with—I wrote it with much love and like it very much myself. [. . .]

Now I have a great favour to ask. Could you send me part of the fee you quoted for the piece soon after you receive the things I am sending off tomorrow—about half? For the complete sum I am having an old watchtower converted into a home. Work on the building can start as soon as I put down a sufficient advance. Now is a very favourable time to start work, because the exchange rate for dollars is very high and building materials and wages have not yet risen so rapidly. If you could send me part of the money soon (not changed into marks or crowns, if at all possible), it would give me the chance of building fairly cheaply, and I should not be averse to that. Please do not be angry with me for burdening you with these unpleasant business matters, but there is no avoiding it.

For now warm greetings.

Yours,

[Paul Hindemith]

The following letter, written in Freiburg and undated, accompanied the three movements of the concerto mentioned above.

Dear Herr Wittgenstein,

With this you will be receiving the last three movements of your piece, and I hope that, on looking through the score, your alarm will subside. It is a simple, completely unproblematical piece, and I am sure that in time it will give you pleasure. (To start with you may be a little horrified, but never mind that.) You will understand the piece at any rate—if you have any doubts, I am always here to give you precise information. When you have studied the piano part from a technical point of view, I shall be very willing to go through it with you musically. I believe the piece will prove playable. I am now busy writing out the remainder, it will be finished in perhaps a week, and then you will get the score and the solo part.

Till then with warm greetings and good wishes for much enjoyment on your first reading of the score,

Yours

[Paul Hindemith]

PS Please wait with the sending of the cheque until I let you know the best way of dispatching it, I must first make enquiries.

The Allgemeiner Deutscher Musikverein was a long-standing music society in Germany that organized festivals of new music. Hindemith was eager to compose a full-length opera, and the Strecker brothers made a number of suggestions for possible subjects, including Faust to a text by Bertolt Brecht. Their and Hindemith's own efforts came to nothing, however, until the middle of 1925, when Hindemith decided on Cardillac, with a text written by Ferdinand Lion based on a tale by E. T. A. Hoffmann. Franz Blei wrote the text of Das Nusch-Nuschi.

The new quartet was the fourth, Opus 32, first performed by the Amar Quartet in Vienna on 5 November 1923.

To the Schott-Verlag   Bremen

4 April 1924

Dear gentlemen,

Thank you very much for your letter. The idea of a competition seems to me a very good one, and I shall of course be willing to referee it along with others. Do you think there will be many interesting entries? After my thorough experience of refereeing in Donaueschingen, in Salzburg, and at the Allgemeiner Musikverein, I have become pretty sceptical. At the moment I am convinced there are no more undiscovered talents (not in Germany, at any rate), the discovery business has been pretty eagerly pursued and quite a few have fared better than their abilities justify. If the competition proves me wrong, you will have done a very great deal for modern art, for then new people with new things will really have been found. So once again: I am with you, send me as much as you like, I'm not afraid of a bit more work.

The problem of opera texts has again been very much on my mind recently, and I can tell you in strict confidence that (first) there is a prospect of my getting a brand-new libretto from Romain Rolland (I think I shall be able to see it in Frankfurt in the next few days) and that (second) Franz Blei has promised me one very shortly. One or the other should surely be worth something? I'll write again as soon as I know. Can we not wait until then? Should neither be of any use, we can always go back to one of the other gentlemen. A South Seas subject, or indeed any other theme with very pronounced exotic colouring, seems to me somewhat dangerous. One can never get entirely away from those eternal and very cheap exotic musical effects that are a European invention anyway and always suggest (to me at least) an attempt to find a way out of the cul-de-sac in which modern opera is stuck—a weak attempt at that—and it is my opinion that one should attack the problem with all one's strength and without being scared of destroying things that are already rotten anyway. As far as I am concerned, an opera can be set in a factory, in the streets of a large modern city, in a railway train, or anywhere else you like (I am not of course restricting the action to such places, all I am trying to say is that I don't think a good opera has to contain a heavy shot of romance), it doesn't have to be naturalistic, veristic, or symbolic. The main thing is that one should be able to write some real music for it—and I think I could do that now. If neither of the two above-mentioned things is suitable, then let's just start work with one of the writers you mentioned; somehow or other we must find a way.

I haven't been very industrious lately. For some months now I have been carrying around a hidden flu, or something like it, and in consequence have been pretty stupid. However, as soon as I've seen the doctor in Frankfurt next week and also know about the librettos, I shall start work at once, either on an opera or the long-planned chamber symphony. In the following days, you will then get my new quartet at last, sent from home; I think you'll open your eyes wide when you see it. I still consider it to be very good (and have done so for a pretty long time). Wherever I go, I find my things being played, so the chamber music side is well under way. All that is missing now is a good opera, and that must come before the year is out. [. . .]

Willy Strecker wrote to Hindemith on 7 June 1924: "Quite by chance we heard that you have just been married. Why did you keep from us this joyful occasion?" There was no reason for failing to inform his publisher beyond the almost obsessive desire of both husband and wife to guard their privacy. The wedding took place at a registry office in Frankfurt on 15 May 1924. Gertrud Hindemith was the younger daughter of Ludwig Rottenberg, musical director of the Frankfurt Opera. She had received some training in singing and in acting but did not pursue a career in either after her marriage, preferring to place all her considerable talents at the service of her husband.

The piano concerto was Kammermusik No. 2, Opus 36, No. 1, and the first performance was given in Frankfurt on 31 October 1924 with Emma Lübbecke-Job as soloist and Clemens Krauss as conductor (not Hermann Scherchen, a conductor with whom Hindemith quite often worked).

The string trio Amar, Hindemith, and Frank played in Salzburg on 6 August 1924 was Hindemith's Opus 34.

To Willy Strecker   Obergurgl (Tirol)

                                                    15 August 1924

Dear Herr Strecker,

Now that I am at last far away from all music, all music festivals, and all music makers and am sitting in Gurgl, partly snowed in, partly drenched in sunshine, I have time to write my long overdue reply to your letter. [. . .] It will make it easier for us both if I deal with each point separately.

(1) Financial statement. I was very astonished—though certainly not unpleasantly—to receive so much money from you. From the papers enclosed I see—after some effort, for figures are obstinate creatures—that my things are being performed and sold relatively often. A fact that for you too will certainly not be unpleasant. I believe that publishing my things will shortly bring you financial rewards. Publishing is for you, I suppose, (as composing is for me) a pleasure in itself—but when it brings something in at the same time, it is of course doubly enjoyable. So I wish both you and myself continued good fortune. There will be no lack of cooperation on my side. At the very least you will be receiving enough things to print. That brings me to

(2) The piano concerto affair. For the moment the piece as three-month embryo is promised to Scherchen. So far I have completed only one movement, but I should be able to complete the rest in time for the performance at the Frankfurt Museum (beginning of October). There are special circumstances attached to this piece: I should like to reserve it for one season for Frau Lübbecke in Frankfurt. She took an

interest in my things when nobody else cared a damn about them and played them when it wasn't as easy as it is now to get Hindemith on the concert platform. I should like to show her my appreciation for that, and my idea is: the piece will be wildly in demand, and she would then have to play it everywhere. [. . .]

(5) Have you read anything about Salzburg? I, thank God, nothing at all. Here in this paradise there are no newspapers. The trio was a very big success. Not just with the German clique, but in general—which particularly delighted me, for I do not subscribe to the view that German music is an exclusively German affair. We shall be playing the piece in the coming winter in Paris and Rome, where we now have several engagements. We three players enjoyed the piece too and played it well. [. . .]

With warmest greetings from your
Paul Hindemith
—and from my wife too

To the Schott-Verlag [Frankfurt]
2 April 1925

Dear gentlemen,

[. . .] You talked recently in Wiesbaden about a fantasy for salon orchestra based on "Tuttifäntchen." I have been thinking about this and ask you please not to publish any such thing. This piece is really of only very limited interest. Apart from the fact that it consists of children's music that would be too vapid for the general public, the music itself is just an accompaniment to happenings on stage and as such completely lacking in a character of its own, barely effective without a stage. My main objection, however, is this: I am firmly convinced that a big battle over new music will start in the next few years—the signs are already there. The need will be to prove whether or not the music of our day, including my own, is capable of survival. I of course believe firmly in it, but I also believe that the reproaches made against most modern music are only too well deserved. Enemies of the new music will use all possible means to attack it. A piece such as "Tuttifäntchen" would provide a welcome opportunity for mounting an attack on me and on the new music, since an arrangement for salon orchestra can reflect nothing of what emerges on stage. People will have good reason to say (since in such cases everything gets generalized) that young musicians have no sense of style and no feeling for substance and effect. I am of the opinion that in the next few years the utmost orderliness will be called for in such matters, and I myself will do all I can to achieve it. Therefore I must ask you, if it is at all possible, to suppress the publication of this piece. It is in any case hardly likely to be a brilliant business proposition. The music is surely too naive for general use. You will, I hope, have noticed that in all my recent things

I have been striving for the highest degree of purity and orderliness, and it is of great significance to me to see some slight recognition of my efforts coming from outside. I beg you, if at all possible, to avoid anything that might stand in the way of that. I hope you share my point of view. Otherwise everything is in order. The piano concerto is said to have been a big success in Prague. That pleases me a lot, for—despite your dislike of it—I still consider it a good piece; at least as good as the cello concerto. The performance under Zemlinski was, I hear, extraordinarily good. [. . .]

Hindemith wrote to Brecht about Ludwig Strecker's idea of a Faust opera, but received no reply. So the search for a suitable opera subject continued.

To the Schott-Verlag   Frankfurt

20 June 1925

[. . .] I have received your opera synopsis. Unfortunately I am not at all happy with it. It is the precise opposite of what I mean by an opera, for all sorts of reasons that would take me too long to set down here. In practical terms, what weighs against it is its extraordinarily strong resemblance to "The Masked Ball" and many other operas, the themes of which he has just dressed up in modern clothes. In that way an opera text is not of course difficult to invent, and there are quite enough of those around already. For that reason (though not alone for that reason), there is no such thing as modern opera. With the best will in the world one cannot give the things that are being performed in theatres as contemporary opera today the name of modern opera. It is the same old sauce over and over again, just stirred around a bit differently. With any luck my continued efforts to find a text will soon be crowned with success. Brecht, a lazy devil, is out, but I am corresponding with a whole lot of other people and am hoping for results soon. [. . .]

The Donaueschingen music festival was still of major importance to Hindemith.

To Heinrich Burkard   Frankfurt

1 July 1925

Dear Heinrich,

Scherchen is coming. He costs only 400 plus free travel and free accommodation. So a bit cheaper than Szell. [. . .]

Schlemm is nothing; we played his things through yesterday. He knows nothing yet. There's music enough in him, but he has an awful lot still to learn. A performance of such immature things would be of no use to anybody. I don't want to go through the trouble we had with Winkler again: one invites someone along so that he can revise and improve a piece under supervision, and then one finds he's not capable of it, because he has been taught nothing right. You can't make up for the neglect of several years in three weeks.

Today at last I returned his piece to Serck and told him in a letter that the piece is simply bad, and he should learn to write well and tidily in a proper craftsman-like way before producing atonal and other japes of that sort. Just to put you in the picture in case you get an enquiry from him.

Where are we living in D'eschingen? Can you find accommodation for Rudolf (perhaps with Himmelsbach or similar) with a yard where he can keep his dog, a young St. Bernard which he cannot leave here by itself? It is well behaved and housebroken and a nice animal. [. . .]

Till Tuesday, greetings from us all to you all,

Yours,

Paul

Hindemith was in Duisburg for the first performance of his Concerto for orchestra, Opus 38, which took place there on 18 July 1925 under the direction of Paul Scheinpflug. The other compositions mentioned are: Piano Music, Opus 37; and Kammermusik No. 4, Opus 36, No. 3, for violin and orchestra, which was first performed in Dessau on 25 September by Licco Amar under the direction of Franz von Hoesslin.

The "chords" probably had something to do with the Kammermusik No. 2 for piano and twelve solo instruments, first performed by Emma Lübbecke-Job the previous year.

To Emma Lübbecke-Job   [Written in a train]
                                                              19 July 1925

My dear Emma, your birthday has just begun. I have just woken up, and my first deed this morning is to send you my very warmest and best wishes. I very much hope that Schaffner has sent you the little book. If so and, after looking through it, you don't know what it is all about, they are the new piano pieces—part of them at any rate.

I am now on my way home after a tiring tour. I arrived early yesterday in Duisburg after an all-night journey and spent the whole morning rehearsing. In the evening the new orchestral piece had its first performance. It is good. Sounds right. The success was very big—some hissers, of course, but as a result the applauders all the keener. The orchestra played with great enthusiasm, and Scheinpflug conducted nicely too. Good as it was, the performance was not yet all it should be (that is to say, I shall be highly delighted if all further performances are even half as good), this kind of playing and ensemble technique is still too new for the players; they play everything in the Wagner and Strauss manner, which of course means what should be light, elegant, and flowing becomes heavy and ponderous.

I shall be seeing you at the end of this week. Will you let me know when you arrive? I'll do the chords when you're here. At the moment I still have a lot of writing to do on the violin concerto. Afterwards I should be able to complete the second movement.

The rocking here is terrible, it's almost impossible to write. [. . .]

The cello concerto (Kammermusik No. 3, Opus 36, No. 2) was given its first performance in Bochum on 30 April 1925; the following letter refers to its first performance in Berlin.

To Willy Strecker   Torrentalp [Switzerland]
                                                              25 August 1925

[. . .] Regarding the cello concerto in Berlin: I should of course prefer it to be done there as I had thought, i.e., that my brother would play it. Could not Oskar Fried be talked to about this? I do not know Efrem Kurtz; but after the experiences I have had with almost all instrumentalists, it can be assumed that he does not at the moment possess the proper playing style for my things. Since practically all musicians have been brought up in the tiresome romantic manner, full of rubato and "expression," they almost invariably play my things wrong. For that reason it would of course be better (particularly in Berlin) for the pieces to be first heard in an authentic form—after that everyone can do as he likes.

Have you reached agreement with Hoesslin? I studied the violin concerto with Amar a few days ago. He will play it very well. [. . .]

The first part of 1926 was devoted to the composition of Hindemith's full-length opera Cardillac. The first performance was fixed for 9 November 1926 at the State Opera in Dresden, with Fritz Busch as conductor.

As soon as the opera was completed, Hindemith set about composing his Concert Music for band, Opus 41, for the Donaueschingen festival, which that year was featuring works for military band. It was played there under the direction of Hermann Scherchen, to whom it was dedicated.

The mechanical music pieces, which were composed directly on rolls for a mechanical organ, were featured at Donaueschingen in 1925 and included the Triadisches Ballett, for which Oskar Schlemmer devised the choreography and sets.

None of the other works mentioned in the following letter (apart from the set of violin studies) was completed.

To the Schott-Verlag   Carqueiranne, near Toulon,
                                             Hotel Beau Rivage
                                              18 August 1926

[. . .] Since Donaueschingen I (or rather we) have been travelling around quite a lot. We have seen something of southern France and now have more or less settled down here by the sea. This vacation tastes fine after the winter of hard work— I intend to stay here some time yet. Has anything important happened? [. . .] Have there been any more takers for Cardillac? There's nothing about it in the newspapers here—Petit Marseillais, petit Provençal, petit Var, and other petits—backward sheets. [. . .]

I myself have done nothing worth mentioning. I've done 1½ violin studies— there will be 10 or 11. The whole thing will then be a series of "systematic studies in contemporary violin techniques" and will contain studies of moderate difficulty that should give today's violinists what the studies of Rode & Gavinies gave previous generations. I am doing the things on the side (they are hardly compositions anyway, more like pure construction work) and you will be getting them complete sometime in the autumn. I have promised Klemperer an orchestral piece, which I'll start after this pause for breath. Then I want some time to do a concerto for string quartet and orchestra! [. . .] Probably no suite or anything like it can be made out of the Donaueschingen mechanical music pieces. They would need a lot of tinkering with, and in that time I could be writing something new. I can use a piece from the organ ballet in a string quartet I want to have ready for a first performance in Berlin in the spring.

Could you sanction a sizable advance on the expected proceeds from Cardillac? (If you do, you'll of course be cutting your own throat: I shall get used to lazing about, stay here, and write nothing more.) I'm thinking of about 1,000 Marks.

Enough for today, it's too beautiful for writing letters. [. . .]

To Emma Lübbecke-Job   Kurhaus Frutt am Melchsee
                                             13 September 1926

Dear Emma, you're getting an answer straight away. Today for the first time the weather is bad, and there is nothing better to do than to write letters. Music notes as well perhaps, but I now have nothing at all in my head. During this whole vacation I managed to complete only 5 (in words: five) violin studies.

Play on the 29th, yes, I'll do that of course with pleasure. But what? We have played my two viola sonatas twice already at Epstein's, the one solo sonata has also been on the programme three (or perhaps even four) times. And the rest of the viola repertoire we have also gone through twice. I feel we would be the first to laugh if someone else kept mounting the platform with the same pieces. I consider it inadvisable to give ourselves away (for that is what it amounts to) to that extent.

I have a sonata for viola and piano by Siegl at home, but it is so lala, and even with that we would still be 3 pieces short. What I myself would most prefer would be for nothing of mine to be done for once (you could then perhaps play the Honegger sonata with Rudolf); the Epstein people have already heard so much of me, and I am beginning to feel rather embarrassed by appearing always as a propagandist for my own things. — It begins in time to look slightly comical and might give the sort of impression a circus strongman laboriously lifting up a cardboard cannon ball makes. Don't you agree?

If you manage to find some other pieces, you can count on me. If there really is no other way, I will even play yet another solo sonata of mine. But only as a favour to you. I did once play one of them (in Dresden) in the first concert of the season— but it is too risky to make such experiments when one has played nothing for 2 months. So what do you think? There is no time to write. You can tell me at home what you have arranged. [. . .]

[Postscript] Enclosed an example of our much developed "pictorial art." We have about 7 dozen little pictures—something for you to look at! [. . .]

Hindemith's growing desire to close the gap between composer and audience led him to see in the musical youth movement led by Fritz Jöde, a Berlin music professor, a possible medium through which to work. Jöde's Musikantengilde (Musicians' Guild) held its first "leaders' week" in Brieselang in the autumn of 1926, and Hindemith attended it.

To Fritz Jöde   Baden-Baden—Frankfurt
                                                            12 October 1926
(the train is rocking so much, I hope you can decipher all this)
Dear Herr Prof. Jöde,

Brieselang now lies several days behind us. Have you, on looking back, been assailed by doubts of any kind? Or have you only now, looking back, become really enthusiastic about our joint "coup"? I the latter.

Rarely in my whole musical existence have I been so full of hope and confidence. I am of course as much aware as you and many others of the hostility, misunderstanding, stupidity, and malevolence that will confront us. What does that matter, however, in connection with so important an undertaking? We must meet soon to discuss the purely technical means of carrying out our plans. As soon as I am in Berlin I shall ring you. [. . .]

I feel that you should soon approach various composers with very detailed requests to compose music suited to your purpose (I myself will within the next few days have completed a small orchestral suite which Höckner in Bieberstein is to get—and besides that I shall certainly have part of the ensemble-playing book done in time for Donaueschingen). I found the convention extraordinarily interesting; it confirmed in every way my ideas about the youth movement and its working together with music—contemporary music. Several things struck me, the modification of which in Donaueschingen will surely be to the advantage of your work.

I found that the lectures were addressed almost exclusively to professional musicians, and a musical layman could hardly get more than vague conceptions from them. As most of your members are laymen, care should be taken to be as understandable and factual as possible. In this regard Erpf's lecture was very good, but, because of the confusion caused by Kaminski's trick of making everything look ridiculous, it did not have the effect on all those present that it should have had in view of its importance. Can one not have lectures submitted in advance? I feel that nothing should be left to chance.

Lectures on purely practical problems were unfortunately much outnumbered by theoretical expositions. I do not think there is much point in providing people with information about church modes (which are in fact only—or almost only—of historical interest) instead of explaining more modern views of musical matters (in the manner of Kurth, for example) to them. Most important of all, comparatively little time was given to instruction in purely technical matters . . . A kind of seminar (about 1 hour daily) should be set up for the leaders, where they would receive more detailed instruction in conducting and producing; people from the listening group should come forward and conduct, so that the others can learn from their mistakes.

The unremitting air of enthusiasm in which the community is wrapped strikes an onlooker as somewhat curious. My feeling is that enthusiasm is a rare and precious substance, and one should not demean oneself by applying it to everything down to (for example) food . . . But I am sure that a lot of such slightly comical accretions will fade away when once people see that they—like all of us—are just part of a larger happening. You know that it was in order not to give my support to this false enthusiasm that I did not put in an appearance on the morning before my departure; I ask you once again to view my nonappearance in the proper light.

My general feeling is that modern music showed up quite well at the convention. Now that your people have come into closer and more extensive contact with it for the first time, I hope the prospects of working together in Donaueschingen will be very favourable. Maybe some of the diehards will fall away—but of course they were bound at some point to be left behind. The others will recognize that something is being done here to revitalize music from top to bottom for us all, and they will be all the more eager to support the movement. Do not delay too long in writing your scene-setting article for the Donaueschingen programme. I shall be writing mine in the next few months so that we have time afterwards to discuss things thoroughly and make changes where necessary.

Filled with the highest hopes, I send my regards to you and all the others.

Yours,

Paul Hindemith

The much respected, but conservative, Austrian musicologist Heinrich Schenker took exception in his 1925 yearbook *Das Meisterwerk der Musik* to a remark made somewhere by an unnamed music theory teacher that "were Beethoven to be composing today, his musical language would be closer to that of Hindemith than of Clementi." Schenker responded that, if Beethoven would write today like Hindemith, "he would be as bad as the latter." And he added, "If today a composer existed with Beethoven's capabilities, he would doubtless compose like Beethoven." Hindemith, in his current state of sensitivity about the worth of "modern" music, could not let this go unchallenged. It is not known which of his quartets were sent with this letter. Schenker's reply (printed in the *Hindemith-Jahrbuch* 1991/XX along with Hindemith's letter) amounted to a proposal that they should simply agree to differ.

To Professor Heinrich Schenker   Frankfurt

25 October 1926

Dear Herr Professor Schenker,

I have discovered my name on the last page of your yearbook and, however "bad" I may be in the times in which the Lord has chosen to place me, that fact leads me to write a few lines to you (I had meant to before this). What I wish to say to you is not that I am vexed, for I am not. Since you know that I am bad, I am entitled to assume that you are familiar with some of my music, and I cannot be vexed about that. In regard to myself, I can tell you that I am a keen and grateful reader of your books. Grateful, because in them, for the first time, I find, properly stated, all that a good musician hears, feels, and understands in his musical activities; because in them one sees displayed the basic principles of musical creation which, as you so rightly keep on saying, have been valid from the beginning and will always remain valid. And for the music of our day, these are just as important as for any other time in the past. You have my word for it that, before I knew even a single sentence of your writings, I had always tried—and please do not laugh—to observe these basic demands. Some of my attempts may have come to grief, in many pieces they are perhaps not as clear as they should be, in others they are possibly obscured by a disorderly mass of external factors. (It takes a long time to reach the point of being able to express properly all one wants to say.)

With this letter I enclose the scores of two of my quartets; if, after overcoming your preliminary and subsequent uneasiness, you examine them as I hope you will with the same care and thoroughness you would give to a Scarlatti sonata, I am convinced that you will find in this music your "Urlinie" [fundamental line] and, together with it, musical reason and logic and confirmation of your teachings. I cannot take the liberty of comparing myself with Schubert, but I do ask myself whether I might not vary the final sentence on page 200 of your yearbook to the extent that, if contrary to expectations you dismiss this music as meaningless, the blame should not be placed unconditionally on me alone. I am not of your opinion that music died with Brahms, and I am also not yet old enough to believe that our times are worse than any previous times—I should then be putting myself in the position of someone who allows a railway train's right to move, yet at the same time demands it should do so on four legs, since wheels do not occur in nature. What is worse is perhaps just this: that the best brains occupy themselves with complaints that things are no longer as they once were. All we have are descriptions, discussions; but where is the positive work? Is it not better to attempt to produce music, even at the risk of going astray ninety-nine times out of a hundred, rather than just write about it?

I earnestly beg you not to believe that I subscribe to your theories for any reasons of self-interest; and please do not fear that your teachings are being misunderstood or distorted by me in a cheap show of enthusiasm. Be assured that both here, and in all the music that I either write or play, I am striving above all for clarity and honesty. If we cannot reach common ground in words or musical notes, I hope on some occasion, by playing a Bach violin sonata to you, not only to give you pleasure, but also to prove to you that musicians still exist today. And finally I beg you to read this in the same dispassionate spirit in which it has been written. Try to maintain the tranquillity that prevents one from despising or even hating one's fellow beings; the tranquillity and the boundless love of music that impels me to undertake anything—even this perhaps hopeless written attempt—that serves to remove misunderstandings, smooth out differences, and promote ways of working together, not against one another.

With the deepest respect and friendly greetings,

    Yours sincerely,

    Paul Hindemith

Cardillac was staged in several other German opera houses immediately after its premiere in Dresden on 9 November 1926. Hindemith went alone to the production in Oldenburg where he wrote the following letter to his wife, the first known to exist.

In Hindemith's letters to his wife Gertrud, he addressed her in his customary fashion (as subsequent letters will show) by a nickname, in this case Pushu, and signed himself similarly. These nicknames, as well as the words Mashmu and Bushbei in this letter, were part of a private language, the meaning of which can only be guessed. Hindemith often addressed and drew pictures of Gertrud in the form of a lion (not lioness), in deference to the fact that she was born on 2 August 1900 under the zodiacal sign of Leo. As in this letter, the term lim was extended to include the household pets.

Werner Ladwig was the conductor of the opera in Oldenburg.

To Gertrud Hindemith [Oldenburg]
28 November 1926

Dear Pushu of my heart, so that you will know where Yijak is, I send you the enclosed scrap of newspaper. I am slowly beginning to feel very alarmed: am I already imbecile enough to justify these excruciatingly boring forms of public recognition? Tomorrow there's to be a big official spree with prime minister, long speeches, and potato salad—all on my account. Worst of all is that a right-wing organization has declared itself "solid behind Cardillac." It is being debated in all seriousness whether I should not be awarded the Oldenburg medal for artificial honey. To top it all, Herr Landmann's letter. Yijak doesn't take at all kindly to all this. He wishes he were sitting with his lions somewhere in a little house far away from it all. [. . .]

Mashmu, my little friend, Ladwig has just come to fetch me. I want to explain some things in Cardillac to him. Tomorrow I shall be shown the stage set—everyone declares the production will be magnificent. After the experiences I've had I am sceptical.

Greetings, my old house lion, and many, many
little kisses
from Yijak
with empty Bushbei

By 1925, the Donaueschingen music festival had become a major international event and had outgrown the little town in which it had begun. The three organizers (Burkard, Hindemith, and the Bavarian composer Joseph Haas) were searching for a new site. Hindemith favoured Frankfurt and asked the director of the Frankfurt Fair, Otto Ernst Sutter, to draw up a set of proposals for a German Chamber Music Festival to be submitted to the city authorities. The four dots (Hindemith's own) in the second paragraph of the following letter refer to this projected festival.

To Otto Ernst Sutter [Frankfurt]
5 January 1927

Dear Herr Sutter, thank you for your draft. I find it very valuable, particularly in relation to the economic aspects of the matter. I have a few remarks to make on the following points.

First of all: . . . . should adopt and carry on the endeavours and traditions of the Donaueschingen music festivals. This is right. The Donaueschingen tradition is that the music committee (Haas, Burkard, and I) pick up ideas that today lie in the air (chamber symphonies, madrigals, chamber operas, mechanical music, music for young people) and start putting them into practice. The liveliness that has so far been characteristic of Donaueschingen is insolubly tied up with the ability to make quick decisions and the easy mobility of a committee made up of just 3 persons. A music committee of 7 means the death of the festival. There might be some sense in it if one could still reckon—as one could some years ago—that, of the round 1,000 submissions made each year, as few as 3 pieces were usable. That is not the case. We have in consequence increasingly shifted to a policy of setting up certain musical guidelines and then inviting younger composers to carry out the new ideas in company with us. An idea that has proved to be the only practical one. But it can be carried through only when the music committee exercises strict objectivity (as we have done) and makes use of its personal relationships with all young composers to encourage them in their compositional work. Only in this way can one avoid getting just rubbish. I am firmly of the opinion that, in this special case, standards will fall without a certain initiative that seven people can never hope to possess. The juries of the Allgemeiner Deutscher Musikverein and of the International Society demonstrate each year that many-headed music committees achieve nothing. Let me illustrate this with two examples of great importance to us:

I. Mechanical music. Mechanical music has today become a matter of vital concern. Open any music periodical and you will find this view confirmed. So the idea occurs to someone that the time has come to write not just about mechanical instruments but for them. Someone else familiarizes himself with all the technical problems, another negotiates with the factories, yet another gets other composers interested, shows them how to handle the instruments. What does a multiheaded committee do? There are no performances at all, since mechanical music is, for 99 out of 100 musicians, like a red rag to a bull. Or, at the very best, a motion is forced through to the effect that mechanical music be produced—: you can depend upon it that the response will be so feeble that the whole thing will collapse.

II. The youth movement. The most important question in the musical life of today, the relationship between people and art, can only be tackled through personal contacts. I have set the ball for this relationship rolling and have brought Jöde and his whole circle over to my side. With a music committee behind me, I should never have succeeded. The question of the youth movement's place in music and in the projected festival in particular could under no circumstances be resolved by a "music committee." Ask the whole set of "professional" musicians here whether they have any idea of what the youth movement is aiming at!

So, in short: I shall cooperate only if the artistic organization remains exactly what it has always been. Without additions, without subtractions. Not out of personal vanity, but because I know that it is only in this way that festivals make sense and can survive for any length of time. We must remain, as we have always been, completely uninfluenced in the choice of programmes and participants. Whenever one of three people has a good or a new idea, it is not difficult to convince the other two. But one against 7: that is hopeless. So let enough confidence be shown in the existing arrangements to ensure that they continue exactly as they are, otherwise we shall take our proposals elsewhere. [. . .]

Rudolf Hindemith had left the Amar Quartet, of which he had been a founding member, once before and had then been replaced by Maurits Frank. Rudolf returned, however, and so this was the second time Frank, now a cello teacher in Prague, was being asked to step in. Kapser was the nickname of the second violinist.

The negotiations to move the Donaueschingen festival to Frankfurt came to nothing, and Baden-Baden was chosen instead: the first festival there, with the three directors unchanged, took place in the summer of 1927.

By this time, Hindemith had accepted a position teaching composition at the Staatliche Hochschule für Musik, one of the state music schools in Berlin, and in October 1927 he and Gertrud moved there permanently, though keeping the Kuhhirtenturm for their frequent visits to Frankfurt. Hindemith's mother and sister continued to live there.

To Maurits Frank

[Frankfurt]
12 April 1927

Dear Mau,

You will probably be surprised to receive such urgent news so suddenly. I'll make it as short as possible.

You will surely already have heard that we are once again facing the breakup of our quartet, that is to say, we are now as good as broken up. The cause of it you can well imagine: you know us three and you also know Rudolf. He has gone completely off his chump: fools around more than ever, declares he can no longer stand being with me and Amar. Besides that, he has the crazy idea of becoming a millionaire without having to work much, and he is also seized by a pathological ambition that cannot be satisfied by playing in a quartet. One day he wants to form a jazz band, on the next he wants to become a music director, and other larks of the same kind. Apparently he is now to become a teacher of jazz music at the Hoch Conservatorium (apparently he himself and others see him as an authority in this field). It is to be hoped that this worthy calling will suffice for his ambition.

I have no wish to begin again with a new cellist, at the risk of being let down once again in two or three years' time. And so we have decided all three to give up quartet playing and take steady jobs. Amar intends to remain here as a teacher, privately to start with, then from the first of January at the state music school to be opened here. Kapser has several prospects that should be decided soon. And I myself am going to Berlin. The news of our breakup has aroused great regret everywhere.

We have had many letters asking us to keep on playing. We have as well a crowd of engagement offers for next year, so we must after all stop and consider whether something as good as this should be allowed to disappear from the face of the earth without a murmur. One could have a steady job and play quartets for one's own amusement: just concerts that one can enjoy oneself and that pay well and a few tours abroad. That could be a very pleasant life. Would you like to join in? We are used to playing together and therefore could spare ourselves unnecessary work. We three and presumably you too are now older and more rational. You will surely manage to avoid clashes now. With a dash of goodwill that ought to be possible. And when one is not together day and night as in former times, there is less chance of friction. All of us would just have to make a real effort. [. . .]

For our quartet activities the prospects are as follows: first we would be playing in the Frankfurt international festival. Two quartets by Vogel and Beck. After that the Donaueschingen festival (now transferred to Baden-Baden), with quartets by Berg and Odak and ensemble pieces in which unaccompanied violin and cello will be needed. A tour of twelve concerts has been offered us in England (can be extended, if pursued seriously, this is just the preliminary enquiry). Four concerts in Petersburg have likewise been offered (state-supported), and there is also an enquiry from Moscow. On top of this, there is another big Italian tour (our fourth). So far we have of course committed ourselves to nothing, since we had already broken up. It would be a very great pity if all these nice things went by the board. In Germany itself we should only need to play the few large cities. We can leave out Peine, Oelsnitz, etc. As I see it, we would need to set aside about three months each year for playing. As far as I am concerned, October, January, and May. During the rest of the time, we could meet once or twice a week to rehearse for future needs. [. . .]

Let me know at once whether you are willing in principle, so we will know whether to take things on or finally break up. [. . .]

Maurits Frank rejoined the Amar Quartet, which continued for two more years.

The 1927 festival in Baden-Baden featured miniature operas, one of which was Hindemith's Hin und zurück and another Darius Milhaud's L'enlèvement de l'Europe. Hindemith had persuaded the Musikantengilde under the leadership of Jöde and Hans Mersmann to hold their "leaders' week" that year in Baden-Baden at the same time, and he joined in their activities.

The inclusion of "cantatas in chamber style" in the festival of the following year was designed to create a still greater cooperation with the youth movement, and Milhaud responded to Hindemith's invitation with his "Cantate de l'enfant prodigue," as well as some children's pieces and music for a news film. The Theremin-"Ätherwellen" instrument was similar to the electronic trautonium.

In addition to composing and teaching, Hindemith was also busy with concerts: his first visit to Russia was in December 1928.

To Darius Milhaud (written in English)   [Berlin]

[January–April 1928]

Dear Milhaud, do you remember this little collection of compositions "Das neue Werk" you saw last summer in Baden-Baden, containing little pieces for song or instruments for the "musikalische Jugendbewegung" (Youth-motion(!!!)) for schools, dilettants etc. etc.? Please have the kindness and send me anything to complete this collections. (It is edited by Schott—you know). I would prefer Instrumental-pieces for two violons, alto & 'cello, singular or orchestral, also to be (ad libitum!) completed by flutes, oboes, clarionets or bassoons. The execution of these pieces for the string-players (for the winds too!) must be very easy!! Only first position!! Intervals not too difficult. Only the easiest double-tones. Short pieces, I think six or seven. Will you do it? Ich would be very glad, Jöde & Mersmann (the other Editors) and Schott too. Please write me some words about it. — Have you anyone new composition which is possible to be executed while the next Baden festival? We want to play organ pieces (organ solo or with other instruments), cantatas in chamber style, film-music, little operas (like last year) and compositions for the Theremin-"Ätherwellen"-instrument. Or do you know a young composer, who can work such compositions?

We had been in Russia for four weeks and there they all told about you. When are you coming to Berlin??

With the kindest regards for you and Mrs Madeleine.

Yours   Paul Hindemith

(Excuse my very bad English!!)

The viola sonata was Opus 31, No. 3 for unaccompanied viola, which was not published during Hindemith's lifetime.

To Gertrud Hindemith   [On tour]

[11 March 1928]

Dear good Pushu of my heart, my best friend, I think so much and lovingly of you and send you many little kisses. Good beast, I love you very much. Are you well? It is not nice, alone like this, eh? I go around feeling very bored. It was quite pleasant in Basel. Heinrich Burkard travelled with me from there to Freiburg, the train was packed, because people were returning from the Leipzig Fair. In Basel there was an immediate rehearsal, then I lay down for a short nap and then practised. In the evening my playing was not exactly first-rate, but it was at least respectable and by Swiss standards people were very enthusiastic. Afterwards the entire orchestra mob sat around for a while; I soon went home, I was very tired. The viola sonata is not as good as the other one and is much too difficult; one can play it well only when one is feeling abnormally keen, and that doesn't always happen on stage. I won't play it anymore but will just write another one when the occasion arises. At any rate, I shall be a bit more cautious in the coming days and practise the Windsberger properly; if that doesn't go very well either, I shall maybe lose my nerve and then play worse and worse. I'll get down to it for an hour this evening, after I arrive in Augsburg. And I think I shall travel overnight from Weinheim to Aachen. That way I'll gain a free afternoon in which I can spend a few more hours practising. It is urgently necessary. [. . .]

> The opera was Hindemith's *Neues vom Tage* (English title: *News of the Day*), for which Marcellus Schiffer, the librettist of *Hin und zurück*, was writing the text.
> In Paris, Hindemith played his Kammermusik No. 5 for viola and large chamber orchestra, Opus 36, No. 4, of which he had given the first performance in Berlin on 3 November 1927 under Otto Klemperer. Nadia Boulanger, the French composer, was famous as the teacher of many distinguished musicians.

To the Schott-Verlag

Berlin W30
Berchtesgadenerstr.4
16 June 1928

Esteemed Mr Publishing Firm, dearest sons of Schott,

You have heard nothing of me for a long time. I hope you have noticed. The reason for it lies in all the work I am doing with the sweat of my brow to keep you satisfied. My opera is approaching the end of its first act. I hope to be able to send you the complete score ready for printing in ten days' time. Appearances suggest that the thing will continue to turn out well. I have done more work with Schiffer; we are continually coming upon further splendid ideas; we give each other the impression of being Goethe and Beethoven working together on Egmont. The text of the second act will also be settled next week. Regarding the first act, I have consulted a canny lawyer. Some things will be altered, but only two or three sentences, the rest can stay put. The whore you wanted will be removed with many thanks. In the fifth scene, Frau Laura will now appear in the bathroom without any hint of eroticism. Herr Heuss will find it deadly boring. Have you any objection? The whole thing will be an opera for families and people wishing to start one. In comparison, Cardillac will seem a highly obscene affair. [. . .]

Koussevitzky in Paris was a very great success. He did the piece very well indeed, was full of praise, and wanted to take me with him to America at once. I am in no such hurry. Your brother was also at the concert, I saw him for only a moment afterwards, for a terrible number of people were talking me into the ground and I was, at the same time, in great haste to get away. Of the ladies so often expected, only Mlle. Boulanger was there. She wears glasses, was very nice, and, just as promised, I did her no harm. [. . .]

Diaghilev had been trying to persuade Hindemith to write a ballet for his company since 1926. Hindemith finally accepted a commission for "No. 27," the subject of which is not known. But the large number of compositions completed in 1928, including the opera Neues vom Tage as well as a large number of choral and instrumental works for youth groups and amateurs, had temporarily left Hindemith in a dry spell. Diaghilev continued to press him until his death in August 1929 brought the project to an abrupt end.

To Serge Diaghilev   [Berlin]
                                                            2 January 1929

Dear Herr Diaghilev,

[. . .] I have been trying for some time now to write the ballet, but there is nothing doing. At the moment, there is nothing doing. For several weeks I have been completely written out; not a single note is coming into my head. You yourself know there is no point in trying to force oneself to work. Perhaps, in order to deliver the piece as arranged, I could write a score: you would then be receiving the dull-witted routine work of a hack, which would be of no use to you and even less to me. I do not need to assure you that I am still awaiting with the greatest interest for the moment when I can begin work on the ballet. However, I do not know just when I shall again be capable of writing any respectable music. It may be in three days, perhaps only in three months. In any case I must ask you not to reckon on my having it ready for this year's season. I find it extremely unpleasant to have to tell you this, but in the present situation there is no other way. Please postpone my work till your next season. Should you at all costs need a novelty for this spring, I suggest you approach Bohuslav Martinu, Paris XIV, Rue Delmabe 11, whom I consider to be very well qualified and who can write some good music for you in the shortest possible time. If you wish to do "No. 27" with him, I must of course send you the script. Should you still wish to do a ballet with me, I should prefer to keep the script until I begin to write.

Please do not be too angry about this change of plan, which I find very embarrassing, and please understand the reasons for it, against which I am helpless. [. . .]

Hindemith made his first visit to London in order to play the solo part in the first performance of William Walton's viola concerto. This was played at a Promenade Concert in the Queen's Hall on 3 October 1929 under the direction of the composer. Sir Henry Wood, one of Britain's foremost conductors and director of the Promenade Concerts, had already performed some of Hindemith's own works there and would later conduct others.

Edward Clark was the head of the music department of the British Broadcasting Corporation. Walter Leigh was an English composer who had studied with Hindemith in Berlin.

Marko (no longer alive) and Alfi (mentioned in subsequent letters) were the Hindemiths' schnauzer dogs.

To Gertrud Hindemith [London]

[2 October 1929]

Dearest Pushu, kisses. Yashny. I miss you very much and wish I were already back home. I am alone and a bit stupid and sad. I have just come from the rehearsal (evening around 7); it should have been early this morning but wasn't because other things were being rehearsed. In this way—because I stayed to listen—I at least got to know the famous Sir Wood and now know for certain that he cannot do my viola concerto. I shall talk to Clark about it tomorrow. Walton is conducting his concerto himself. It won't be up to much. So far he has had only one rehearsal in which he managed to play the first movement just once. The orchestra is bad, consists mainly of women, and English ones at that. Nothing but super Anni Giesekings. And at the concerts themselves there are not even seats. The audience stands around—smoking permitted—and can do as it likes. Notices all over the place: Please don't strike matches during the music. One can really feel homesick for Zwickau or Bielefeld. Really one can play here only in order to earn a few pounds. It has nothing at all to do with music. Since these Promenade concerts are solidly sold out, however, a big need for music must lie somewhere in these people. I shall play as decently as I can, but not much—I believe—will come of it. This evening I have arranged to meet my pupil Leigh. We are going to some revue or other.

The crossing was quiet—with the help of a few tablets. There was no room in the hotel despite the telegram, and so I am now living in the Royal Palace Hotel in Kensington High Street, expensive and not particularly good, like everywhere here. I shall be glad to get away. For Pushu: just now, as I was going through Hyde Park, I saw our little car. 8/38 Mercedes, our colour exactly and our chassis, only no Pushu inside it. And this morning I saw two Markos on a lead, but not as handsome as our dear dead black one.

Dear good creature, farewell and consider yourself embraced and beloved with all my heart by your

Paul

The "theatre of mystery" was Maskelyne's in Oxford Circus.
Emma Lübbecke-Job was coming to join Hindemith in a concert that included the Trio for piano, viola, and heckelphone, Opus 47, first performed earlier that year.

To Gertrud Hindemith [London]

[4 October 1929]

My good old fellow, your little letter arrived this morning—many thanks. I have now one concert behind me, it went well and was a good success. After it came a reception: at the home of that terrible lady pianist from Salzburg who once played a duet there with the comical lady cellist Harrison. It was terrible. All the English greats with the exception of Shaw were there. I left very soon. On the evening before last I went with my pupil Leigh to a revue (nothing special), and after this I shall be going with him to a <u>theatre of mystery</u>: I am really looking forward to that: feats of magic will be performed there. Great! This morning I was at a rehearsal of the London String Quartet, four good and honest souls who played me a quartet of mine (op. 10) very nicely and very respectably. And now I have just eaten in an Ital. restaurant in Soho with Leigh. Tomorrow I again have a few musical engagements, the day after I have to rehearse with Emma, who will have arrived by then, and then I shall soon be allowed to return home to my Pushu. This morning I went for a walk in the park (<u>Kensington garden</u>). That is a park for lions: dogs everywhere, mostly very handsome. I also saw the two Markos again—but they are much too fat. Tomorrow I have arranged to meet Fini (who comes from Frankfurt, I've known her for ages) and her husband for golf somewhere in a weekend area. London is very nice again. But I am still very glad to be returning home soon.

Warmest of greetings, and give Alfi a paw. For you, good and loving little kisses and a half-hour or so of strokings, Yashny and Bashbei.

> Your
>
> Paul

Morales has not been identified. *Bitter Sweet* is an operetta by Noel Coward.

In addition to using their private language, Hindemith addressed his wife now and again in the respectful second-person plural form, sometimes mixing it with the intimate second-person singular usual between married couples. This occurs in the closing sentences of the following letter, but it is impossible to reproduce convincingly in translation.

To Gertrud Hindemith   [London]

[6 October 1929]

Dearest dear one, I should so much like to be with you, and I am awfully much looking forward to Wednesday, when I can at last return to you. I like it well enough here, and, now that I am getting along better with my fragmentary English and also understanding better, I could be content if I had not so great a longing for home. Yesterday I went with Morales to an operetta—"Bitter-sweet"—which must be one of the biggest examples of kitsch ever to have been hatched from a human brain. It has already been played hundreds of times, it is totally booked up for weeks in advance, and through Morales's influential connections we were given the director's seats. The usual lousy music, an excellent half-French soubrette, the others rather boring and the tenor weak. But well produced, and the staging also very good. But absolutely not the Berlin style: utterly bourgeois and with not a trace of glitz. The audience full of enthusiasm from the beginning to "<u>God save the King</u>." The plot, the moral of which is roughly that one shouldn't choose a musician over other bridegrooms, seems to have been written straight from an Englishman's heart. After the performance I dined very well with Morales and then went through the touching experience of changing from summer to winter time, awed by the inserted extra hour which, however, I had forgotten by this morning and thus got up an hour too late.

Today we rehearsed from 11 till 2. The heckelphone player, a nice man who is tremendously keen, cannot have too much rehearsal and, courteous like all the English, never stops thanking. (We'll start at B—<u>thank you</u>—you were ¼ too late—<u>I'm sorry, thank you</u>—we must repeat the movement once again—<u>thank you</u>.) but apparently he has never in his life had anything to do with barline changes, and so we needed three times as long as with us at home. All the same, I have the feeling that all this trouble bears better fruit than our way, when everyone wants to get things done as quickly as possible. Altogether I have now seen a lot of English musical life. In some respects astonishing things. It is surprising, in view of the, in some respects, truly incredible love of music, that more has not come of it. It seems to have been shunted onto completely the wrong track. Emma played very well. Apparently they arrived yesterday evening, and she rang me here early in the morning.

I had lunch with Clark at Mr. Cooper's house. He is secretary of the London Symphony Society and wants to arrange a concert performance of the scene with the Lady and pantomime from Cardillac. [. . .] The food was excellent and totally English (leg of mutton, a kind of green sauce, very large green peas—mulberry-tartcakepuddingpastrypie) and afterwards we sat round the <u>fireplace</u>. And now I have been for some time back home, have changed four strings on the viola d'amour, written a letter to Pushu and now will perhaps be going down to dinner or off to bed without it. What would you advise? My buttons vote yes, the pattern on the carpet no. Consider yourself ardently embraced and extraordinarily beloved. One loves you very much and one's single burning desire is to be back home with you soon and to take you in one's arms. Goodnight, dear one.

Your   Paul

Eduard Reinacher was a German poet, three of whose poems Hindemith set to music in 1922 as a cycle for female voice, two violas, and two cellos (*Des Todes Tod*, the "dances of death" to which he refers in the second letter). The new work was wanted for a summer festival in Berlin, the new venue of the original Donaueschingen festival after two years in Baden-Baden. It did not materialize; instead Hindemith composed his children's opera *Wir bauen eine Stadt* (English title: *Let's Build a Town*).

To Eduard Reinacher [Berlin]
[April 1930]

Dear Eduard,

[. . .] Here on the Jungfernheide on 22 June there is to be a large gathering of about 5,000 people from all over Berlin—music lovers, amateur singers—who are coming together to make music for themselves. I have been asked and I want to write something for it together with my composition class, but I have no text. Can you write one for me? It is a question of just a short piece. [. . .] The most suitable subject would be a discourse on some matter of very general application—gratitude, love of music, etc.—and perhaps of a moralistic nature; something so obvious and easy to grasp that 5,000 people can immediately declare themselves in agreement with it. [. . .]

Yours,
Paul Hindemith

To Eduard Reinacher [Berlin]
[14 April 1930]

Dear Eduard,

My thanks for your quick reply. I find both Amundsen and the Six-Day Cycle Race excellent; they are very fine pieces. Only neither is really suitable for the projected purpose. Amundsen because it is too much in the nature of a report, whereas for an event like this, one needs something in which the participants are at the same time involved in the action—this is the only way to achieve singing of the necessary directness. The snag with the cycle race is that it cannot be made completely clear by means of song alone (one cannot gather from it what is happening at any one point), and, added to this, only a single person can be used as a singer almost throughout. The main point of the whole ceremony (or whatever one likes to call it) is that several thousand people are being given the opportunity to work in a common cause. The third piece is basically not unsuitable, only I do not believe that matters dealt with in such minute detail can have any sort of effect in so huge a space, and certainly not in the open air. The clash of two points of view is of course good. But it would be better to treat the chorus in opposition to the soloists. Singing against each other is without doubt one of the main attractions of a clash between soloists and chorus.

You have also used far too many words in this piece. You must take into account the fact that music stretches words like rubber and thus multiplies the piece by at least twenty. The very short, precise language you used in your earlier dances of death is far more suitable. The best language for music is always the shortest and least ornate. Everything that has not been said is said by the music. That is a good division of labour. So you can be very sparing with your adjectives and save them up for better occasions. I myself should prefer a somewhat meatier theme than this one. [. . .] For events of this kind, didactic themes are best. Discussions about some purely human or national virtue, or something or other of that kind. The soloists could teach the chorus and the latter talk about their teaching, or the other way round. You need not set too much store on great poetic beauty. About the most important point here is that maximum clarity should be achieved with as few words as possible.

Are you prepared to try again? Do not be impatient. It is certainly not so easy to produce such things. It took me a very long time to do it in music. Once you have come to see that such things are really needed and really made use of, you will feel like me that this is one of the very few artistic endeavours still worth pursuing. You seem a bit downhearted? Maybe working on this affair will give you a little joy. I should be very glad if you would make another attempt, for I consider such things more important today than concert music or similar rubbish. And I believe that you could write the words for it, once you have got the style under your skin. [. . .]

PS: Love stories would hardly be suitable. I don't think it's a good idea to have thousands of people debating matters of love.

Hindemith had known Mrs. Elizabeth Sprague Coolidge for several years, for she was a regular visitor to the International Society of Contemporary Music in Salzburg, and his String Quartet, Opus 10, had been played at her own summer festival at Pittsfield, Massachusetts, in 1923. The result of her commission was his Concert Music for piano, brass, and two harps, Opus 49, which was given its first performance in Chicago on 12 October 1930 with Emma Lübbecke-Job at the piano. Hindemith was not present.

To Mrs. Elizabeth Sprague Coolidge   [Berlin]

8 May [1930]

Dear Mrs. Coolidge,

Frau Lübbecke has sent your kind letter on to me, thus allowing me to see exactly what your intentions are. The idea that I myself should come to America with a new piece in this coming October will unfortunately be impossible to realize. If I were to travel to America, it could only be within the framework of a sizable concert tour, for which I should then have to allow two months. That could not be done this year: I have already refused 3 offers of lengthy tours since I am overloaded with work for the coming twelve months.

It appears from your letter, however, that your main concern is for a composition from me, and there should be no difficulty in finding someone to conduct it. I could set about writing a piece for you at the end of June after the conclusion of the music festival here in Berlin. All the same, there are still certain considerations on my side. In the last few years, I have turned my back almost completely on concert music and have been writing almost exclusively for amateurs, for children, for radio, for mechanical instruments etc. I consider composing in this manner to be more important than writing for concert purposes, since the latter is little more than a technical exercise for a musician and contributes hardly anything to the development of music. In consequence, I have to regard concerts as purely a matter of business. All the music I have written for concert use in recent years owes its origin to business considerations. The idealism I willingly apply to things that seem to me urgently necessary for the further development of music is something I cannot extend to concert music. On the contrary, I must balance the one against the other.

I hope you will understand my point of view when I say to you that the fee you have suggested for a concert piece by me is too low. For a commission of this kind, I do not accept less than 10,000 Marks over here. If this price is too high for you, I shall of course fully understand. But should you contemplate commissioning a composition on the above conditions, please let me know what you would like to have (length, form, category, number of instrumentalists, etc.). The manuscript could remain your property, as requested, and I should also agree to your half-year exclusive right.

Many thanks for your kind invitation. I am married. My wife and I look forward greatly to meeting you before long. If not in America this autumn, then perhaps later or possibly when you are next in Europe.

With warm greetings, I remain your obedient servant

Paul Hindemith

On his second visit to Britain, Hindemith played his viola concerto (Kammermusik No. 5) at a Courtauld-Sargent concert in London before travelling to Scotland, where he gave concerts of his own works (sonatas for viola and viola d'amore) with Erik Chisholm, conductor and founder of the Action Society for the Propagation of Contemporary Music, and with Donald Tovey, the well-known music scholar and pianist who taught at Edinburgh University.

The "little cantata" sung by the children was Let's Build a Town.

"Waluch" in the letter of 13 November is another nickname for Gertrud Hindemith, who in her guise as lion is given masculine pronouns.

To Gertrud Hindemith   39 Royal Terrace,

                                                                    Edinburgh

                                                            [11 November 1930]

Old fellow, you haven't heard from me for several days—but that is not so bad:
I have had nothing at all from you! Maybe a nice letter is lying in London. Since no
mail is delivered here on Sundays, I haven't received it, and it will reach me only
when Willy Strecker brings it to the train on Friday. I played well in London: easily
and confidently as almost never before—the well-applied summer holidays appear
to have had the right effect—and in consequence all the people with a modicum of
understanding were genuinely enthusiastic. On Sunday afternoon I was at Henry
Wood's house in the country, an hour's drive outside London. A splendid 300-year-
old farmhouse. There were guests of all kinds there, it was all like English novels.
Tea, fire place, idle chat, friendliness everywhere—it really is rather nice and probably after a while nauseating. After the concert in the evening, Mr. Clark saw me to
the train. An extremely comfortable sleeping car (and correspondingly expensive of
course—there is only first and third class), but I slept hardly at all, for of course I
was interested in seeing where we stopped and everything else. The trains travel at
a crazy speed. In the morning I got up extra early to view the countryside. It was
very lovely to begin with: a rolling landscape, grass-covered hills of medium size
everywhere, hardly any houses or trees. It looks like one of those forlorn and dried-
up mountain ranges in middle Germany. Everywhere sheep, whose legs can't be
seen, just a very thick woollen coat with a head attached, chewing nonstop. Then
it became ugly: nothing but factories, smoke, haze, horrible houses. Much worse
than in the dreariest Ruhr district.

Glasgow is terrible. Five minutes in the street and one is utterly filthy. A place in
which I wouldn't want to be buried. On top of that, Chisholm hadn't booked me
into the best hotel. It stank rather like in Bernburg and was in every way disgusting.
Chisholm is not up to much. He plays a curious make of piano, and it took me quite
a lot of effort at our rehearsal to get him up to scratch. In the evening he then played
quite passably. The children sang their little cantata very nicely. Not as cheeky as
ours were, but more like small adults; the orchestra consisted of some six traditional
English ladies in traditional dress, growling obstinately away on their instruments.
The audience took it very bravely. Probably they couldn't make much of any of the
pieces, but they left one in no doubt that they were doing their best to be enthusiastic. Afterwards at Schissholm's place, where I sat together with some traditional
Scotsmen, who behave towards the English rather like Bavarians towards the Prussians, listened to bagpipe records and then had the nature and style of the Piobreach
(pronounced Pibrok) explained to me in quite sufficient detail.

From Tovey I received a letter with an invitation to stay at his house, and on the
strength of that I shook the dust of Glasgow off my feet and journeyed here. Unlike

the frightful city of Glasgow, it is very beautiful. When I arrived he (Tovey) was still at a rehearsal, so I went for a walk with his wife and the dog Friday. After a meal we started rehearsals together right away. They are extraordinarily nice old people, and he is an excellent musician. Not a single note had to be altered in the way he played the sonatas. He is no virtuoso of course, he played wrong notes here and there, but everything he does shows true musical understanding. In every way he reminds me of old Mendelssohn, even in his appearance and his whole manner (though he must certainly be 15 years or more younger), and she looks like a some-what squashed-up Queen Victoria. Since he likes one of my violin sonatas and is not so keen on playing piano solos, I shall once again be playing the violin tomorrow. It still goes quite well, and tomorrow morning I'll put in a bit more practice. Then I am hoping tomorrow to see something of the surroundings: an almost totally for-gotten fellow student at the Conservatorium has turned up and offered me her car. So I hope at least to see the famous Forth bridge. So I am very happy here. Just now I am sitting alone before the fire: warm in front, cold behind, the comfortable Eng-lish condition. "He" has gone to a concert, "she" is somewhere in the house. One is left completely to one's own devices, thank God. Today there are great goings-on everywhere: anniversary of the armistice. The whole population goes around wearing red poppies, a floodtide of patriotism in the evening. Just as I arrived there was a minute of silence. Everybody stood up as straight as a ramrod with doffed hat. It was boring, weird, and not at all impressive.

I shall be staying here until Thursday evening, then travel back overnight. And then, the Lord be praised, I shall soon be home again in the lion's den. With many 'Büpps. Have you been good and done your gym exercises in the meantime? I am looking forward to being able soon to join in again. I must now write a few more letters, and then I shall get down again to the Greek. I am making slow, but quite good progress and shall soon have learnt half of this first letter. It is not easy, but interesting. And I enjoy doing this fiddling kind of work. My English has also got much better. In London everyone was amazed to hear me speaking it so well, and because I am forced to speak English all the time, I am learning a great deal very quickly. I could even understand Mr. Chisholm's pitiful mumbling, God help me.

Farewell now, old lion, and consider yourself warmly loved in spite of the great distance between us. Examine the envelope carefully, I am placing many little kisses inside. One for Alfi too. With very much longing and melancholy and loving thoughts of you,

Your Paul

To Gertrud Hindemith [On a train from Edinburgh to London]
[13 November 1930]
Well now, old Pushu, here I am lying once again in the train, and, so as even

such difficult rascals as lions can convincingly be shown what a good Yijak they have, I am writing you another little letter. The Edinburgh concert was yesterday, and together with worthy Tovey I played to the delight of all present, I have in fact played so respectably throughout this tour that even the lions' brood would have been highly satisfied. Even the violin-playing passed without a flaw, but I did of course practise some studies in the morning, quite apart from the fact that we used every spare moment Tovey had, partly rehearsing and partly playing for our own amusement. My stay with these people was really nice and pleasant. I was looked after like a spoiled child, without any of that obtrusiveness one so often finds. Each night an entirely superfluous hot water bottle lay in my bed, every morning at 8 tea and biscuits were brought to me in bed to keep me cheerful (breakfast wasn't until 9), and to top it all there was a picture of a lion playing the piano in my room. He looked like Waluch when he is feeling soulful and softly stroking the keys with tenderly curved paws. I wanted to trace the picture and send it to you, but I couldn't find any thin paper, and then there was no time, for we had to make music. We were seized by a paroxysm and spent the entire afternoon and evening playing, right up to the time the train left. First Bach's six organ sonatas, divided up between piano and viola, then the three viola da gamba sonatas, then some sonatas for violin and flute, then a row of Mozart sonatas on the violin and finally an old one of mine. He is a musician through and through, though he does play everything in the style of the last century, but very well. After that he played me his conclusion to [Bach's] Kunst der Fuge. I really fiddled myself to a standstill, something I haven't done for a long time. That does one good.

This morning I went sightseeing with the old lady. The town is very beautiful, but it doesn't seem right without Pushu. I wanted to buy a few antiques for you, but I wasn't sure what, and in the end thought it a pity to waste the money, it would be better to spend it in Berlin on a nice present. Yesterday I was taken by car to the Forth bridge. It is one of the finest and most magnificent things mankind has ever made. A splendid construction that blends in beautifully with the landscape. We really must visit this region before very long.

I am always telling you about my doings, and I know nothing at all about you. That is sad, I should so much have liked to have a little letter from your dear paws. I want to be with you again soon, but there are still 4 long days before I see you again. Good old fellow, consider yourself loved with all my heart, stroked and supplied with many nice little kisses. Think of your Yijak and love him too. Goodnight, dearest.

Your Paul

The following letter was written during the turbulent period in Germany when the Weimar Republic collapsed and Adolf Hitler stood on the threshold of assuming power.

The trio for recorders was part of the Plöner Musiktag (A Day of Music in Plön), a collection of little pieces Hindemith wrote to be played by the pupils of a school in Schleswig-Holstein and first performed there on 20 June 1932.

To Emma Lübbecke-Job

Berlin-Charlottenburg 9,
Sachsenplatz 1
[After 19 July 1932]

Dear Emma, as always too late. Still, we're in a state of siege, perhaps if one writes letters one will be shot dead—who knows? But good wishes on birthdays are surely still permitted. Here then is a trio for recorders. I have tried it out with my recorder society, played it often, and found it worthy of being sent to you as a birthday present. It can also be played on flutes or any kind of woodwind, but it is nicest with recorders. What are you doing? We here are swimming around in the general swamp as best we can. What will happen we do not know; now as before we leave it to the good Lord. At the end of this week we are going on holiday, probably to Switzerland. [. . .]

In 1932 Hindemith was again in search of an opera text. Having in the previous year collaborated with the poet Gottfried Benn on an oratorio, *Das Unaufhörliche* (English title: *The Perpetual*), he first turned to Benn. The subjects foremost in his mind concerned the monastery of St. Gallen in Switzerland, the fifteenth-century German printer Johann Gutenberg, and the sixteenth-century German painter Matthias Grünewald.

Die Gezeichneten was an opera by Franz Schreker, first performed in Frankfurt in 1918.

To the Schott-Verlag

Berlin-Charlottenburg
10 October 1932

Esteemed brothers, a man of good breeding does not say "It's enough to make me throw up," but all the same it is. I sit here like a dried-up spinster. Benn just won't catch fire. By being so overcritical he gets nowhere. He is straining for all he's worth, and something will doubtless emerge, but how long will one have to wait for it? The St. Gallen affair apparently doesn't appeal to him strongly enough, and it's the same with Gutenberg and Grünewald. He is still racking his brains— one must just wait and see what happens. In desperation I have decided to lay the eggs for myself. After all, I know what I want, and these poets have never been able to write the words until I have written out in minute detail what they need to do. I have collected together a lot of material on Gutenberg. The period is interesting; all sorts of things were happening in Mainz and Strassburg around 1440, it's just that the man himself yields absolutely nothing. With the best will in the world he emits no sparks, however hard one strikes. He seems to have been a somewhat dry gentleman. It might be possible to place the art of book printing in the centre of the action, but that would need a poet with "visions"—and where are they?

Grünewald might be good, if he weren't of all things a painter. Character and aim of an opera about Grünewald would have to be his painting, and there would be no way of avoiding showing the man feverishly painting, a very poor motive for music, and in my opinion a comical one too. Do you remember "Die Gezeichneten," in which the exalted lady goes into ecstasies in front of the easel? Something like that would have to happen here too. Perhaps you will find some other subjects. I shall also be casting around in my mind.

Meanwhile, for practice and to pass the time, I have been thinking of making an opera for children that could be played as a Christmas fairy tale. I was considering a variant of the Andersen fairy story, "Little Claus and Big Claus" and had already developed it quite far, but find it can't be done after all. One would either make it as naive as it is written, and then one could not put it on the stage, or one would place it in another setting, and then the motives would no longer fit. Perhaps I shall discover yet another subject. I have a few other hazy ideas. It is a stupid condition to be in. I am fully primed and could get cracking any day with some dramatic music. As it is, I can only sit here true to the motto "Despair and don't work." [. . .]

Ernst Penzoldt was a German writer and sculptor. The opera, to be called Etienne und Luise, concerned a love affair between a French prisoner of war and a German girl during the First World War.

To Willy Strecker   Berlin-Charlottenburg
                                                         [15 November 1932]

Dear Herr Strecker, [. . .] Must this interesting picture be published? You know I am not a bit interested in publicity. The result will of course be that the picture will afterwards be used by every junk newspaper in the land as a crowd-puller, and that would please me all the less since I took precious little pride in wearing the Kaiser's nettlecloth tunic. But if you already have the block and think it must appear, well then, in God's name.

Regarding the opera prospects, I can only copy the children's game and say you're getting warmer. Penzoldt is the new favourite: he was here recently, having already sent me a detailed outline of a theme we had previously discussed. Now he is improving it, in a few weeks at the most I hope to have a complete scenario, and that you will receive at once. It is the idea I am looking forward to with a great deal of confidence. Something will certainly come of it. [. . .]

To Ludwig Strecker   Berlin-Charlottenburg
                                                [20 January 1933]

Esteemed Opera Department, many thanks for your detailed letter. I am glad that you are so far satisfied with this scanty outline. Penzoldt has meanwhile sent me the first and third scenes fully complete. As scenes for a play they are very good, but of no use for an opera on account of their dialogue. I have written to him that he should first do the scenes that are still missing in the outline. [. . .]

I am not triumphing over the lack of a love duet. Love duets will, if you like, be sung in about 6 of the 12 scenes. What I certainly am against, is that every duet between soprano and tenor must always run along the lines of "I love you" and ardent embraces. That nature requires this event cannot be denied. But whether Mother Nature requires it to be carried out in the way it is done in most operas, there I permit myself to entertain slight doubts. So triumph over the missing "love duet"? Love duets without "-" you'll find in plenty. [. . .]

I shall now see what Penzoldt sends me and then meet him again here as soon as possible. I hope the outline will be finished by the end of February at the latest, and that I can then slowly start sketching the music. I intend to do the main work during the summer. I hope to make good progress, as I fully believe I shall, so you can have the opera by the winter. It is kind of you to wish to pay Penzoldt an advance. But I feel you should not give him anything until the outline is complete; I am somewhat superstitious, particularly after the experiences with Benn. I have heard nothing from him since, and I am of course making no moves either. I have seldom encountered such barefaced cheek and have no idea what the matter is with him. I can only think that, the moment he had the money in his hands, he let his troubles run away with him, oversensitive as he is, through a psychological twist, and then projected it outwards in insolent behaviour. What can one do? There is nothing for me to attempt, but you are of course in a position to remind him that he has put 1,000 Marks in his pocket without stirring a single step. I do not want this matter to upset you more than necessary, and I therefore suggest the following compromise: at the time "Das Unaufhörliche" was published I discussed with your brother the possibility of Benn's being paid an additional fee later for his text. You can perhaps enter 500 Marks in your books for this. Then please deduct the remaining 500 from my next substantial royalty payment. Your loss will not then be a great one, and I shall regard my 500 as punishment for my gullibility towards a poet. I have been more cautious with Penzoldt from the beginning and am doing everything when we are together, so that he cannot back out. The result of this working method (which indeed costs me dear, since I have to pay his travelling and living expenses, or alternatively travel myself to him) you can see in the well-prepared outline, or such part of it as you have received. [. . .]

1. In 1914, performing with a band in Switzerland.

2. As a soldier in 1918.

3. In 1927 with viola d'amore.

4. Emma Lübbecke-Job.

5. In 1930.

6. Gertrud Hindemith in 1924, at the time of her marriage .

BERLIN-CHARLOTTENBURG 9
SACHSENPLATZ 1
TEL.: WESTEND 6268

Verehrte, leider entfernte Löwen, eigentlich habe ich Ihnen gar nichts mitzuteilen, ich schreibe Ihnen nur schnell ein paar Zeilen, damit Sie mich nicht ganz vergessen. Für Ihr Brieflein herzlichsten Dank. Hier ist nichts los. Schule hat wieder begonnen, alles ist wie immer. Hexenschuss ist ziemlich wieder vorbei. Benn zielt schwer, ich glaubs wer was. Wanda hat mir Schweinsfüss gekocht. Wann erscheinen Sie wieder hier? Grüßen Sie die werten Familien und Sie sich selbst auch.

Ihr sehr verehrter
Jak.

7. 1930: Letter to Gertrud Hindemith from Berlin in German.

8. Kuhhirtenturm, Frankfurt am Main. Photo: Georg Krämer.

9. Gertrud Hindemith, Paul Hindemith, and Willy Strecker in Basel in 1933.

10. Blusch ob Sierre in the Valais, Switzerland.

Ludwig Strecker had further criticisms and suggestions to make regarding *Etienne und Luise*, and Hindemith replied to them in an addition to a letter to Willy Strecker dated 26 January 1933.

[. . .] Now a quick note for the opera department: the public should of course have everything that gives it pleasure, I don't wish to deprive it of anything. But I believe that more is done and a greater and better effect achieved with a single well-placed chord than with truly bad theatre tricks such as this farewell pantomime. I fear this pantomime would act as a "cold draught" on account of its triteness. Apart from that, it seems we are fully of one mind. I am of course always grateful for objections, though in fact hardly any come along that I have not already had myself. And of course there should be no Hindemiths at all filling the auditorium, we don't want to conjure up an inflation in this particular article, but I am of the opinion that the composer has to know best what to set before the people. After all, a thing doesn't always taste all that good at the first go, but is all the same nourishing. And I am not just for tasting good. Since on this point we seem to be of different minds, we shall, I suppose, have, like other well-mannered men, to meet each other halfway. [. . .]

Never in my life before have I written so many letters as about this opera; my God, it should turn out well! [. . .]

Hitler had been appointed chancellor of Germany in January 1933 and was now in the process of setting up the Third Reich.

Hindemith, having disbanded the Amar Quartet, had now formed a string trio with Szymon Goldberg (violin) and Emanuel Feuermann (cello); they gave the first performance of his second string trio in Antwerp on 17 March 1933.

The quintet appears in Schott's catalogue as Drei Stücke für fünf Instrumente (Three Pieces for Five Instruments).

Hindemith's plan to write a series of songs on texts by German lyric poets was not followed in any orderly fashion, and of those he mentions as completed most were destroyed in the bombing of the Kuhhirtenturm.

To Ludwig and Willy Strecker   Berlin-Charlottenburg
                                                              [10 March 1933]

Esteemed brothers, you haven't heard from me for some time. Here there was such chaos that writing was unthinkable. Regarding the opera, I send you herewith a letter from Penzoldt. The prospects for the next few weeks are of course bad, and I also have no idea to what extent it might be possible to bring out new operas in the autumn. To judge by what I now see happening in musical and theatrical affairs, I believe all the key jobs will shortly be occupied by rigidly national types. Next spring, by which time the first difficulties should have been got over, the prospects for an opera by Penzoldt and myself should be very good. Maybe not this particular text, though one cannot really know. Anyway, caution is called for, and I am in favour of shelving this particular subject for a while and seeking another. I have been looking around and have come on something that is innocuous and interesting and will this year and next be particularly topical. It deals with the building of the first railways. There are some very nice anecdotes, both in England and in Germany, from which one could easily make a comic opera. I intend to draw Penzoldt's attention to it—the subject will surely suit him well—and at the same time keep looking around myself. Let's keep hoping. [. . .]

Next Friday we shall be playing a new string trio of mine in Antwerp. Would you be interested in it? Shall I send it? In addition you could have a very small quintet for piano, clarinet, trumpet, violin, and double bass; I wrote it some years ago, recently heard it again and was astonished by its prettiness. I am writing another short movement for it and shall perform it in Kiel on the 27th. And finally I have begun a whole series of songs. 4 by Matthias Claudius, 4 by Rückert are already done—the aim is to go through the German lyric poets in sets of four. [. . .]

> The performance in England of Hindemith's oratorio *Das Unaufhörliche* took place in the Queen's Hall, London, on 22 March 1933 and was broadcast. The BBC [British Broadcasting Company] Symphony Orchestra and Chorus were conducted by Sir Henry Wood, and the soloists were Adelheid Armhold, Parry Jones, Harold Williams, and Arthur Cranmer.
>
> The performance of *Lehrstück* (the work by Bertolt Brecht and Hindemith that had caused a scandal at the Baden-Baden festival in 1929) took place on 24 March 1933 in the BBC Concert Hall, London. It was conducted by Adrian Boult; the singers were Tudor Davies (tenor) and Arthur Cranmer (bass); the comedians Harry Tate, Harry Tate, Junior, and The Other Fellow.
>
> Arnold Cooke, like Walter Leigh, studied with Hindemith in Berlin. Leigh's operetta was *Jolly Roger*, which was being performed at the Savoy Theatre with George Robey in the main role.
>
> Hindemith had a model railway in his apartment in Berlin.

To Gertrud Hindemith   Strand Palace Hotel,

London

[23 March 1933]

Dear Pushu, here at last is a half hour in which I can write to you. It is a frightful grind; I am on my feet all day long and have no time for anything at all beyond the various rehearsals, performances, and conferences. I wanted to practise the Telemann concerto I am playing in Kiel, wanted to write some music too—there's no time.

The rehearsals have been going on since Monday. In the morning the orchestra alone, and immediately afterwards Wood coached Armhold in English pronunciation. In the afternoon I made changes in the orchestral parts, because the string sections were so large that a few things in the original orchestration did not sound good. In the evening, rehearsal with the chorus. I was somewhat in despair over the soloists, who really did not sing very well. Only on the following morning did I see that they were just stand-ins (students). The proper ones sang on Tuesday morning—and in fact sang very well. On Tuesday afternoon there were various discussions about the Lehrstück, in the evening another rehearsal—dress rehearsal, which went flawlessly. Wednesday morning yet another rehearsal for the soloists and the orchestra. In the afternoon I drew up the enclosed army order and, since every member of the chorus and of the orchestra received one, I had to write my name some 400 times. I returned home just in time to change my clothes. The performance, as you very rightly remarked in your telegram, was splendid. Everything went as securely and smoothly as if it had been the twentieth repeat. Some of the singers were magnificent, especially Armhold and Mr. Williams. Success very great. It will probably be repeated and the good Sir Henry also wants to perform it in Liverpool. [. . .]

Today I spent the whole morning preparing the Lehrstück parts, then had lunch with Willy Strecker, Leigh & Cooke. Then Lehrstück rehearsal up till now. This will also be very good. A wonderful tenor is singing, and the clowns' scene is being done by very well known actors, among them Tate, the most famous comedian of all. (Looks like something in Punch.) The scene will not be acted, just spoken; it is much better like that and fits well into the piece as a whole. The three people do it excellently. Will you be listening again?

This evening (immediately after this) I shall be going to the theatre—not because I particularly want to, I should prefer going to bed, but because an operetta is being performed, for which Leigh wrote the music. There is another rehearsal tomorrow morning, and, since I shall be leaving the day after, I shall have no time for my railway shop or for the theatre of magic. With all this sweated labour you have not missed much by not coming with me—though it would in fact have been worth it for the performances. So now I shall be travelling to Kiel the day after tomorrow, and there I shall have to sit myself down and spend the whole day practising this Telemann piece, which is difficult and unusual and of which I have not the slightest idea. [. . .] On Wednesday I shall be home at last, and then I should like to have a few days free of all business. Farewell for now, consider yourself well beloved, give my regards to the 24 enthusiastic listeners and to grey Alfi. (Incidentally, I saw one here today. He was black, too fat, and dirty, but all the same looked splendid.)

Your somewhat exhausted

Paul

In a letter dated 5 April, Willy Strecker warned Hindemith that Jewish teachers (including Sekles) had been dismissed and Hindemith himself was being condemned as a "cultural bolshevist" by the Mainz branch of the Kampfbund. Alfred Rosenberg founded this Nazi organization in 1928, and in the early months of the Hitler regime the Kampfbund had sole control over cultural and artistic activities in Germany.

Georg Schünemann, director of the Hochschule in Berlin since 1932, though not a Jew, was shortly afterwards replaced by Fritz Stein, a professor of music at Kiel University and a member of the Kampfbund.

To Willy Strecker   Berlin-Charlottenburg
                                                              [15 April 1933]
[. . .] You would have received a reply to your letter before now, if I had not spent all these days lying in bed with a rather painful inflamed tendon (in my foot). I am now gradually able to crawl around very slowly, and so you shall have news at once. [. . .] It really does seem as if the newspaper criticism in England consists entirely of imbeciles. I should like to be looking on when these people take their aptitude test before starting their career. It must be a curious sight. Lehrstück on the final evening was excellent. The whole audience sang at the top of their voices without the slightest embarrassment. They want to repeat this piece too before long. [. . .]

To judge by what is happening here I don't think we need worry too much about the musical future. One must just be patient for the next few weeks. With all the changes so far nothing has happened to me. Recently, just after my return from England, I had a long talk with some of the higher-ups in the Kampfbund. It was only about educational matters, but I got the impression (after having satisfied them that I was neither a half nor any other fractional Jew) that they have a good opinion of me there. Since then they have commissioned me (though not quite officially) to work out plans for a new system of teaching composition and musical theory. Since I know how mistrustful people are, and have also seen how several who have tried to curry favour have sunk without trace, I, who have absolutely no desire to curry favour, am none too eager to carry out this tidying-up operation just now. If you will leave it to me here to watch out for the most favourable time to start something like this, you can rest assured that I shall do whatever is possible. One of these days I shall of course have to get the Kampfbund to support my things officially, but it is a bit too early yet for that. In the present state of general uncertainty it won't be possible to do much anywhere, though if you are contemplating any kind of campaign or attempts at conversion among smaller cultural associations, carry on by all means. But I would consider it advisable not to show any fear or uncertainty. God knows, we've got nothing to hide.

I shall perhaps be seeing some of the higher-ups again next week, and I'll see what can be done. Here in the school there's a grand old muddle. All the Jewish teachers have had to go of course, except for one or two like [Curt] Sachs and [Carl] Flesch, who are indispensable. Schünemann too, probably, since he has ruined everything by his vacillation. There is talk that Stein from Kiel will be appointed director (all this between ourselves!). That might not be bad for our cause, though he is not exactly a model of courage and steadfastness. [. . .]

Through this wretched foot and all the general muddle I have not done any serious work in the past weeks. I did a few songs, but what I really had in mind was a big thing for men's chorus, a short of cantata with soloists and perhaps a very primitive brass band such as can be found in any village. I am looking for texts in Novalis (the Night Hymns) and Hölderlin. Don't you agree that a kind of light and harmless but still very serious piece would be just the thing for now? With the bigger things we shall have to wait a bit.

Enough for today. My foot is hurting again, I am still unable to sit up for long. [. . .]

For the subject of his next opera Hindemith had at last chosen Matthias Grünewald, and he decided to write the libretto himself. During the ensuing months, he considerably cut back his concert engagements in order to devote as much time as possible to this work. He also had promised Wilhelm Furtwängler that he would compose an orchestral piece for performance by the Berlin Philharmonic Orchestra in the coming season. In order to kill two birds with one stone, he decided that the orchestral piece should consist of a series of preludes to various scenes in the opera *Mathis der Maler* (English title: *Matthias the Painter*). The books about Grünewald were *Der Barbar* by Nikolaus Schwarzkopf and *Das Grünewald Problem* by Hans Heinrich Naumann, both published in 1930.

To Ludwig and Willy Strecker   Berlin-Charlottenburg
[11 June 1933]

Esteemed brothers, I want just briefly to let you know that I am very busily occupied with Grünewald and am gradually beginning to have hopes of producing something (keep your fingers crossed!). I should be very grateful if you could make my work easier by sending me (on loan) a chronicle of Mainz that deals in particular with this period (above all, the beginning of the 16th century, since I am concerned with the older Grünewald). There must surely be something of this kind in the Mainz city library, whereas it is difficult to find here. On closer acquaintance with the material, I am tending more and more to see Frankfurt as the scene of action, but I want to know as much as I can about everything relating to the theme. The novel (Barbar) is silly and says almost nothing of use about the man; Naumann's book, on the other hand, has made more impression on me than any other in the last 20 years. May I keep it a while longer?

For the rest, I am composing songs and, as a gymnastic exercise, have speedily composed a fairly long saxophone duet. I shall not send you the songs until the series has grown somewhat longer, so you will have a wider choice.

Best wishes,

Yours,

P.H. in high hopes

To Ludwig and Willy Strecker   Berlin-Charlottenburg
[9 September 1933]

Dear brothers, I send you herewith the sketch of the piece as it now stands. Though it is the result of many weeks' work, it is very far from being good—it is indeed not even complete as a skeleton, which I suppose is not surprising in view of the difficulty of the material. All the same, the work to come will be very much easier than the work done so far.

Please read this attempt in a spirit of goodwill. Bear in mind that I am giving you only a rough sketch of my assembled material, and for that reason the dramatic action is shown in only very broad strokes, which is particularly damaging for a subject based to such an extent on inner development. We shall be in Frankfurt again on Wednesday. We'll ring you in the morning, and I shall look forward to hearing your views when we meet. The material gains in significance the longer one works with it, and I am utterly convinced, despite the inadequacies of its present form, that I can make something worthwhile out of it. [. . .]

To Willy Strecker   Berlin-Charlottenburg
[c. 9 October 1933]

[. . .] I have once again completely redrafted Mathis. It was really a very good thing that we were recently able to discuss it thoroughly. Having been obliged to relate it all in one go, I became much more conscious even than you of the weaknesses in the previous version. The new form will be better in every way, there are now just 7 scenes. I have given the whole thing another underlying theme, but large and important parts are still lacking. I shall be going next week to Copenhagen, and directly after that I intend to spend 6 days by the sea (Warnemünde) and await inspiration. As regards the Mainz plays, I frequently came on the subject in my researches. At the moment I have no great interest in them. Since it is not to be ruled out that at a more advanced stage of the work I may be able to use something of this kind, I thank you anyway for the list of references. [. . .]

Furtwängler is to perform my pieces in February. I prefer this to December, since I think it good to wait a little while yet. I have a very strong feeling that people everywhere are sick of the bleatings of the old guard but am of the opinion they should be given time to reach a state of real longing! [. . .]

Please do not lose patience with my slow work on the opera text. It is a fantastically tricky affair, and unfortunately I have developed a pronounced inner sense of responsibility. I know for certain that I shall overcome my difficulties, but how long it will take — that I don't yet know. I am hoping to begin on the preludes in November. [. . .]

Hindemith's close working with Willy Strecker on the new opera led to an acknowledged personal friendship between them, and for the first time in their correspondence Hindemith made use of Willy Strecker's first name, though be continued for some time to sign his own name in full.

To Willy Strecker   Berlin-Charlottenburg
                                            [Beginning of November 1933]

Esteemed Willy,

There's nothing of importance to say, but I just want briefly to let you know that the "cure" in Warnemünde was crowned with fair success: I have advanced a great deal further. The whole thing now stands very nicely on its own two feet, and the draft, except for two (admittedly very important) scenes, is more or less finished. I now want to let a few days go by, then work through what I've already done again, and in the following weeks think about the two missing bits, or perhaps not until the Christmas holidays (plenty of quiet, time, and ideas are needed). I shall then send you the draft once you are back at home. Today, as a sample, just the scene divisions, which are entirely different from the ones sent earlier; all of it is much better.

1. *Chapter house.* Large male ensemble. — Duet Albrecht-Mathis.

2. *Evening in Ursula's house.* Theatre rehearsal. — Schwalb & Regina—duet Regina-Matthis—Capito, who has become an important intriguer—Ursula alone

3. *Courtyard of Mathis's workplace.* Big duet Mathis-Ursula—small chorus—duet Capito-Ursula

4. still missing. To be a big public scene with all kinds of medievalism. Followed by Sebastian's vision, for which I have some good ideas.
    Interval (was very difficult to place!)

5. *Cloisters of Mainz Cathedral.* Boys' choruses—duet Albrecht-Ursula—Albrecht solo.

6. still missing. To be another big affair with Luther as main figure.

7. *Mathis's workplace.* Mathis monologue—Mathis-Regina—Regina, Ursula, Albrecht, Mathis—Mathis's farewell.

Everything is now more concentrated and homogeneous. It will provide magnificent opportunities for making music. During the coming weeks I mean slowly to start writing the preludes. [. . .]

Hindemith's suggestion that he might write further cadenzas for Mozart's violin concertos was not taken up. Those already written were destroyed when the Kuhhirtenturm was bombed. Only the *Adelaide* ones have survived.

To Willy Strecker   Berlin-Charlottenburg
                                           [23 November 1933]

Dear Willy, I am working at this moment on the scenario; your brother can see something of it when he comes. You will get it at the beginning of next week. I have again made a terrible number of alterations, but it is gradually coming into some sort of order. I hope to begin writing the verses during the Christmas holidays. By that time I shall also have written a substantial amount of the music. I have already begun on that. If by the beginning of next week you could send me about 12 large sheets of autographic paper I should much appreciate it. The size of the score of "Das Unaufhörliche" or the other operas should be the most suitable. A few other things I need to know, as it is a long time since I last took a ride on this article: does one write with ordinary copying ink? Or is there some lighter fluid? Can one work with rubber stamps? If so, I would have some made for the ♯ & ♭ & *p f* ♩ cresc., etc., etc. It should be possible, your man in Vienna had some. Can one use inkpads with copying ink? Ink applied with stencils is of course weaker than written ink. Does that matter?

From all that I have heard here, the outlook for my things should be good in the coming spring, the point will soon be reached at which the general boredom becomes unbearable. I have been thinking whether it might not be advisable to put down a little bait beforehand: besides the Adelaide cadenzas, I have also written cadenzas for some other Mozart concertos. Might it not be to our advantage to put a volume of cadenzas to all the (7 or 8) Mozart concertos on the violinists' Christmas table? It would be no trouble, is easier to sell than original pieces, is of some use to everybody, and can be produced cheaply and swiftly too. [. . .]

To Willy Strecker   Berlin-Charlottenburg
                                           [30 November 1933]

Dear Willy, many thanks for the various packages. The transparent paper is a thousand times nicer than the autographic sheets, I am now ordering a substantial stock from Augsburg. You originally suggested preparing the score without any stamps. It is of course somewhat difficult to write equally well throughout a piece of work lasting a lengthy period of time—in my experience the notes almost always look the same, it is the accessories that change a lot in appearance; that is why I feel that stamps will lead to greater legibility. [. . .]

I have already completed one of the preludes and arranged it for piano duet too. When they're all done, you will get them at the same time in duet form. So you can, if you like, publish them in time for the concert. They will be very easy and nice to play. [. . .]

To Willy Strecker   Berlin-Charlottenburg
                                                         [12 December 1933]

Dear Willy, the stamps arrived today, many thanks. I tried them out at once, they work very well. When the paper arrives in the next few days, I shall at once start writing. By the end of this week, I should have the second of the preludes ready — it looks as if the pieces will turn out nicely. At the moment I am working on the Angelic Concert, which is being done with the aid of an old song.

I could not reply to your long letter before, there was too much to do. Am I supposed to be feeling very foolish as the result of it? I don't at all — for all sorts of reasons. Some of the things you complain about are actually in my draft already, you must have overlooked them. In the case of other criticized shortcomings, the inadequate treatment of some of the characters, for instance, you should surely have taken into account the fact that I had sent you only three scenes, the remainder being just briefly sketched; naturally quite a lot that is in fact in place was left out. And finally I feel that on several points you are in the wrong. Of course I want to produce a practical work for the theatre, but, since I am doing it, it will never turn out the same as if you were doing it yourself. You will have to change your views a little in several matters. I can't quite rid myself of the fear that you are expecting something with a distant resemblance to Die tote Stadt. This piece cannot have that, and I haven't the heart for that sort of thing. For you to show the piece in this totally unfinished state to someone who knows nothing at all about it must of course have unfortunate results — I had written the draft exclusively for you as someone already in the know. Now, looking back, I realize how rash it is to send off half-finished drafts, and for this reason mean to send you more only when the draft can stand up on its own, which will perhaps be by the end of the Christmas holidays. I have already altered a lot more things and found a mass of new ones as well. Don't worry, the piece will turn out all right. Meanwhile, to fill in time, would you not care to read Křenek's Karl V? That is an opera and a half!! Weren't people always talking about Křenek's instinct for the stage?

I shall not be coming to Frankfurt for Christmas, I should prefer to stay here and use the holiday period in order the sooner to produce results. [. . .]

To Willy Strecker   Berlin-Charlottenburg

[5 January 1934]

[. . .] I send herewith the Angelic Concert and the Entombment, the other pieces will follow as soon as they are ready, I hope the scores are usable as they are. [. . .] The Angelic Concert is the first of the four pieces, the Entombment the last, so you can have the parts drawn up, for the first piece, anyway. I had thought up a very nice Christmas present for you: together with a pupil I recorded the duets of both pieces on gramophone discs. However, the recordings are unfortunately not good enough to give pleasure to anyone who does not know the pieces at all. And since I did not wish to be suspected of writing ugly pieces, the records remained here. Next week I shall be coming to Frankfurt for a few days. If you would like to hear the pieces, I will bring them to you. You can also see a few bits of the text. Things are now becoming much clearer. I am still finding work on it as hard as ever, and I shall be happy if I manage to bring it off comparatively smoothly. [. . .]

Hindemith's visit to London included a concert with Szymon Goldberg and Emanuel Feuermann, at which his second string trio was played, and the recordings listed for the Columbia label. The eminent British music scholar Ernest Newman, at this time critic of the Sunday Times, was always severely critical of Hindemith's music.

The Arbeitsfront and Arbeitsdienstlager were Nazi workers' organizations, the Dopolavoro their fascist equivalent in Italy. Gustav Havemann, a violin teacher at the Berlin Hochschule since 1920, was, like Stein, a member of the Kampfbund. Both of them remained friendly towards Hindemith despite their political differences. HJ stands for Hitler Jugend, the Nazi organization for boys.

To Willy Strecker   Hotel Stadt Hamburg,

Lübeck

5 February 1934

[. . .] Until now I could find no ideas for the third piece, though I sweated a lot and tried all sorts of things. In the end I gave it up and decided to leave it at two pieces. Since yesterday, however, things have begun to move again, and I am working on the "Temptation." I hope to be able to finish it within a few days, and then I shall start at once on the score. I'll send you the completed sheets in batches, so you can have the parts prepared immediately. Time is already running rather short, since the performance in Berlin is on 11 / 12 March. Would you send me the score of the first two pieces before the other, so that I can give it to Furti? I want very soon to familiarize him with the pieces in their duet form.

London was good in every way, apart from the report of our old friend Newman, who in fact only gave away fabrication secrets from my manufactory and came to the pithy conclusion that the existing 12 notes of the scale offered combinations enough, and it was quite impossible to understand why a second-class German composer should not produce this and other pieces like anyone else. That is what is called <u>common sense</u>. But the reception by the audience was good, though admittedly it consisted mainly of emigrants. [. . .] We made a large number of gramophone recordings. The whole of my trio, a Beethoven string trio, I and Goldberg a Mozart duo, my solo viola sonata, cello sonata as well, and then, because they were one side short, a duo for viola and cello which I wrote in the morning between 5 and 8 before the recording and which we then served up capitally. The recordings were an awful sweat. I played my fingers into blood blisters and even exposed the nerve on one finger, which makes playing particularly pleasant.

Quite a lot is going on in Berlin. I am still "conferring" with all sorts of higher-ups in the Arbeitsfront, the Dopolavoro and the Arbeitsdienstlager. The outcome will be that I shall make suggestions for a very far-reaching musical education system for the German people and, if things continue as they have now begun and these people continue to show goodwill towards me, I hope to provide the impetus for vast plans and to cooperate in putting them into effect. I have also received various smaller commissions, which I have rejected, because the time doesn't seem to me to be right for them. Neither did I show any enthusiasm for a kind of propaganda concert Havemann wanted to promote, because I am very much against seeing my music constantly used as a cover for one bungler after another, and altogether against always presenting contemporary music separately, as if it were something extravagant and off the beaten track. They come creeping up from all sides, but I am in favour of selling my carcase dear.

I am playing here today. Yesterday was a public dress rehearsal with a large number of HJ from Plön acting as a big claque. One of the young rascals even challenged a critic for making disparaging remarks. The concert is being given in conjunction with the Kampfbund, the conductor (Heinz Dressel, very good) is a party member, all the others too, the performance will be very good. Malicious people admittedly declare that Lübeck is always 3 years behind the times, and that is why I'm being performed here now, whereas 3 years hence I'll be banned.

So, let this report from the battlefront suffice for today. [. . .]

The Reichsmusikkammer, of which Richard Strauss was president, was controlled by Joseph Goebbels. It was part of his effort to win control over artistic matters from Rosenberg. The projected Musikkammer conference in Berlin in February had been postponed.

To Willy Strecker   Berlin-Charlottenburg
[9 February 1934]
Dear Willy, before you finally vanish under the wheels of Prince Carnival, I want

shortly to bring you up to date with the news. First: "Temptation" is progressing well, I am aiming to have it finished sometime next week, but shall make a start on the score this coming Sunday. [. . .]

Lübeck was a big success, as first official concert in the III. Reich a good omen anyway. On Wednesday I had a long discussion with one of the top people in the (at the moment still voluntary) Arbeitsdienst. Our whole conversation will probably be rushed through all the newspapers at home and abroad, and I believe that this and subsequent discussions, and written proposals still to follow, will provide the basis for the most ambitious programme of popular musical education (together with appropriate composer training) the world has ever seen. One can literally have the musical enlightenment of millions in one's hands. I myself intend, as before, to steer clear of any official position, trusting to achieve all the more from the background. In particular I want to take over the composer training myself, though not as an addition to my work; I would, I hope, be able to drop my teaching at the school.

As I already told you, there was to have been a concert of new music here on the occasion of the Musikkammer conference; apparently it is not now to take place. Instead, on Sunday, 18.II., there will be a concert in which I shall take part along with the greybeards [Siegmund von] Hausegger, [Hans] Pfitzner, [Paul] Graener, [Georg] Schumann, and [Richard] Strauss; I shall conduct the Philharmonic in my Concert Music for String Orchestra and Brass. One really could not ask for more in the way of an official introduction. If the people order the orchestral material from you, please send them a good supply of violin parts (about 16–20), so that I can use a large string section. The piece must of course be finely done and stand out to some extent among the ancient tootlers—to me the contrast with the following "Eulenspiegel" is naturally not displeasing.

Furtwängler is very busy with the opera pieces. [. . .] The stamps work excellently with printer's ink.

So, that's about all. Best carnival wishes and warm greetings to the entire Committee of Eleven. [. . .]

The Mathis der Maler Symphony was given its first performance by the Berlin Philharmonic Orchestra under Wilhelm Furtwängler on 12 March 1934. With all three movements completed, Hindemith abandoned his idea of ending it with "Entombment," which he placed between "Angelic Concert" and "Temptation of St. Anthony."

To Willy Strecker   [Berlin-Charlottenburg]
[27 February 1934]
Dear Willy, so now I've got it wrapped up and am delighted to have this piece

behind me. It was a lot of work, made more difficult by the concerts and tours in between. It would all have been much easier if something had come into my mind earlier, but unfortunately such things cannot be forced. Do please send the scores to poor Furtwängler as soon as you possibly can, even if only bit by bit to start with. From tomorrow onwards I'll be making the piano-duet version and on Saturday or Sunday I'll play the pieces to him. Time for the preparation of parts is very tight, isn't it? But a lot can be done in a week. I hope all this work will reap its reward. At any rate, everyone here is looking forward eagerly to the piece; if everything turns out as I imagine, it should mean a good success. [. . .]

Franz Willms was on the editorial staff of Schotts: the epithet "religious adviser" is meant jocularly.

Hindemith conducted the Berlin Philharmonic Orchestra in a gramophone recording of the Mathis der Maler Symphony by the German Telefunken company.

Hans Meissner was the director of the Frankfurt Opera. The phrase "infamous theatre directors of those past fourteen years" refers to the Weimar Republic period before Hitler came to power.

To Willy Strecker [Berlin-Charlottenburg]
[15 April 1934]

Dear Willy, with this I am sending for your information the completed first scene. I hope you will be satisfied. From it you will gather the style of the piece. But what you will not be able to judge until after the music are the length proportions. This scene should last about ¼ hour. [. . .] Next week, perhaps even tomorrow, I want to start on the composition. The remainder of the scenario and text of the following scene will also be tackled as soon as possible. — Can your religious adviser Willms tell me when the bell in the hymn in the first scene should sound? Before, during, or after? And for how long?

I believe the Telefunken records will be good. The waxes one was able to hear were magnificent. The Philharmonic players applied themselves with much love, I conducted respectably, and the Telefunken men behaved very enthusiastically and talked of commissions. I conducted for five hours ("Paul the Paintbrush Wielder") and for three days I could hardly use my right arm.

I have not heard from London. So I'll stay here and on 5 May once more "raise the question" of my conducting activities with Mathis in Duisburg. — The Frankfurt performance, has, however, fallen by the wayside. I visited Meissner. Seems to me to be a not exactly unidle chap. Appears (like the infamous theatre directors of those past fourteen years) to promise a lot but deliver nothing, as I also gathered from indignant remarks made by old acquaintances in the opera house. He emphatically wants to do the first performance, together with Berlin if must be. My feeling is that you shouldn't give him any firm commitment yet. There will be prospective candidates enough. [. . .]

To Willy Strecker   [Scharbeutz]
                                                                [26 May 1934]

Dear Willy, I send you the second scene herewith. Considering the great toughness of this nut (it is the most difficult scene in the whole piece), I feel I have managed it pretty well. It was very difficult. I hope you will be reasonably satisfied. The music for the first scene is completely finished. If you are interested, I will send you the piano arrangement from Berlin. I have not yet written out the score. We shall be here in Scharbeutz (on the Baltic coast) for two more days, and I hope to make good progress with the third scene. After that I shall do the music for the second in Berlin. [. . .]

To Willy Strecker   Berlin-Charlottenburg
                                                                21 June 1934

Dear Willy, here at last is the third scene. It took rather a long time, but I can't move any faster in this trade, which is after all fairly new to me, and, to add to that, the more I work on Mathis, the more difficult it seems to become. The Luther letter will be sung by the chorus as a whispered parlando and should be very effective. The ensuing marriage discussion will be done as very free recitative. The words in the Mathis-Ursula duet are at one point the same as in the second scene; in the second scene I am altering the entire opening section. The duet will be cast in grand style. The choruses at the end are songs from the Reformation period. I hope you will once again be rendered speechless. No more for today.

　　　Affectionately your
　　　　Semischäcksbier
　　Please give me a truly honest opinion.

To Willy Strecker   [Berlin-Charlottenburg]
                                                                25 July 1934

Dear Willy, here is No. 5. With each scene I have told you how hard it was to do. But this time I was driven almost to distraction, it had me sweating blood. I tried out the opening section in about ten different ways. Probably no one will even notice how much hard work went into it, which is all the better of course. In contrast to the outwardly active earlier scenes, this one depends entirely on inner tension and a big musical piece, the soprano-tenor duet. The two final scenes will be much easier to do, I trust things will go quite quickly. I want, if it's at all possible, to complete them both here and then come down to Frankfurt. There I should like to go through the whole piece again with you in detail, then spend a week or so working on agreed amendments and improvements. And only after that can I begin at last on the music! That should need only a tenth of the work caused by this abnormally difficult text. I didn't hear Mathis in Leipzig, our radio bleats only local stuff. [. . .]

The Isenheim altar in Colmar is regarded as Matthias Grünewald's masterpiece.

To Willy Strecker   Berlin-Charlottenburg
                                                      [29 July 1934]

Dear Willy, this time it went a bit faster. This sixth scene exploded yesterday with a few loud bangs from morning to evening, and today I have polished it up and written it out neatly. Record work. I hope you'll be just as happy with this as with the previous ones. I myself like it almost best of all and hope soon to be admitted to the Academy of Poets. So you don't get a shock: the quasi-cradlesong from verse 38 onwards is meant as a description of the Isenheim Angelic Concert, the verses from 161 onwards of the Temptation panels. The music will come partly from the symphony.

We will talk about the suggested alterations in the 5th scene in Frankfurt. Quite a lot can be done without difficulty, but there is much with which I don't entirely agree. You regard Capito a bit too much as a villain, and I feel this view is a bit prejudiced. In fact, all that emerges from the piece itself is that he is one of those usual cunning brothers who have both feet firmly on the ground. Thus his dismissal is meant to be less a punishment than a pushing aside of a utensil that has become superfluous. Punishment is not in Albrecht's nature, for all his indecisiveness he is very aristocratic and concerns himself with trifles only to the extent his well-being requires. Riedinger and Capito cannot be present at the beginning, the scene would become too long and would lose its classical severity. The audience knows from the 3rd scene what has gone before. The Capito-Cardinal encounter will be done in recitative drawn out so thinly that more than enough will be understood. I shall start work on the final scene on Monday. It will cause no particular difficulties, so I hope to bring the work to an end by the end of the week. It will be a considerable granite block off my mind. Now, when I look back, I am amazed at the rash way in which I began this really horribly difficult task. But soon we'll be able to praise God. Just keep your fingers crossed a few more days.

For your kind words of consolation regarding the royalty statement, many thanks. They were not really necessary, for the statement is more or less what I had imagined. I even feel that, considering the very low reading of my thermometer, it is relatively good. "Mathis" will do a lot to put things right. I am glad and grateful that you are not being shortsighted, but are aware that the low point is only temporary (and probably even useful and necessary for recuperative purposes). We shall of course settle the royalty question in the manner suggested. Only I would be grateful if this time you could keep to the old arrangement. We are under some pressure and the somewhat higher sum is a great help to me. If you consider what trouble and expense we would have had with a "proper" librettist before being so far advanced with a text as we now are with ours, this concession should not fall too hard on you. True, in expectation of a text on a previous occasion we flung an unduly large sum of money into Benn's jaws (shame on him), and owing to the political climate this sum cannot be recovered through "Das Unaufhörliche" (its turn will come again!)—that is regrettable. But the new opera will of course make up for that and, besides, I am writing the opera score myself and delivering the piano arrangement complete—this will save a few thousands.

We can chat about all the other things in Frankfurt or Mainz. I am glad that I have reached the end and can soon turn my back on this paradisaical city. A fond farewell for you. If you send me another letter full of praise for the sixth scene, I fear you will soon run out of words. Never mind, you will soon be relieved of all these difficulties.

> Warmest greetings from us both,
>
> The operamanufactury

To Willy Strecker   [Berlin-Charlottenburg]
                      [31 July 1934]

Dear Willy, here at last is the final scene, and I am glad that we have come so far. Do you like it? If at all possible, I intend this week to finish composing the third scene. Next week we shall be coming down, then we'll see each other,

> In haste, affectionately,
>
> Your happy poet

Some incautious words about Hitler that Hindemith was reported to have spoken in Switzerland in the summer of 1934 led to a ban on radio broadcasts of any of his works in Germany pending an investigation.

Hindemith went to the Black Forest to continue composing his opera, which Furtwängler had scheduled for production at the Berlin State Opera in the 1934/35 season. To put an end to the growing campaign in Nazi circles against the composer, Furtwängler requested a personal interview with Hitler himself.

Franz Reizenstein was a former pupil of Hindemith's in Berlin, now working in London.

To Willy Strecker   Berlin-Charlottenburg
                  [28 October 1934]

Dear Willy, here are the second and fourth scenes; they would have arrived earlier if I had not purposely kept them back a while to dry. This has resulted in my making a whole series of additional amendments, and I now hope to have achieved worthwhile pieces. The fifth is in progress. It will also be standing on its own feet by the beginning of November. Then I shall bring it to you. I am coming myself, since I want to discuss a few things regarding the score on the spot.

Nothing has happened here. After all the recent backbiting, the atmosphere seems to have cleared indeed in the sense that all are remaining loyal to me. At any rate, despite keeping my ears open, I have heard no hint of hostile intentions. On the contrary: never before have I been subjected to such fulsome praise as has come my way in the past few days from official quarters. Fu. was not yet with HIM. Now and again I hear that it will take place very soon, but I don't pursue the matter. A few days ago, news leaked through (it leaked through Berthel) that an interview with someone else had passed to Fu's satisfaction. Anyway, he has no doubts of a successful outcome, nor have I. I am tending more and more towards the view that we should let time work in our favour, it will do better than any negotiations. Once the opera is firmly on its feet, all the better armed will we be to set out. I recently played through some of the scenes with a good pianist, it hangs together very well.

"Mathis" was recently played in Maastricht and relayed from there over the Dutch radio. The records make things much easier: the conductors use them as a model and that resulted in an excellent performance here, too. I was there, and I played together with Goldberg—by permission of the Musikkammer. On the other hand, they are making difficulties over Vienna, where I am due to play under Breisach on 5 November.

Many thanks for your London letter. Clark, who today came through Berlin on his return from Russia and is now lying on the sofa in the next room until his train goes, says the pianist for London is very good. Reizenstein is also good, but he is too pushy for my taste, and I have learnt over the years that it is better to keep him at a slight distance. So it is perhaps better that he should not play—but to make up for it I have recommended his compositions to Clark. [. . .]

"Our dear foe H." was Friedrich Herzog, editor of Die Musik, which earlier in the
year had been made the official organ of Rosenberg's Kulturgemeinde (successor to
the Kampfbund). The Kammer was the Reichsmusikkammer. The Reichswehr
(German national defence forces) had been established in 1921 as a voluntary organization; it was dissolved in 1935.

"The theory textbook" was the first part of Unterweisung im Tonsatz (English title:
The Craft of Musical Composition).

To Willy Strecker   Berlin-Charlottenburg
                                                       [11 November 1934]
Dear Willy, here at last is the final part. It took somewhat longer because I had a lot of work in the school, and besides that no ideas came for several days. I am

glad now to have the main work behind me, it was a big task; and this final scene in particular was very difficult to do. During composition I found I had to alter some words and sentences in the text, and I also found a few more misprints. I have marked them all in the enclosed book for the final edition.

I am glad you are not letting the recent backbiting upset you. It didn't mean as much as last year's. Also our dear foe H. has been silenced for the time being and the Kulturgemeinde is to be cut back to an organization purely for art lovers, with no influence on programmes. Despite this, I intend before long to see what I can do with the Kammer. At the moment, unfortunately, all the Kammer is doing is seeking to ingratiate itself with the party, and on that account one does not wish to be too active. But I am very much in credit, and the worst that can happen is that we shall have to wait a little while. The missing Benn rang me yesterday. He is apparently seeking to renew contact. After all his carefully nurtured plans have come to grief, he now intends to hire himself out to the Reichswehr.

The preparatory work on the theory textbook for next year is well under way. The plan for the first chapter is already drawn up, and it has been thoroughly tried out in practice. [. . .]

Carl Schmidt's son Wolfgang, to whom Hindemith had once given music lessons, was now working on a provincial newspaper in Germany.

To Dr. Carl Schmidt   Berlin-Charlottenburg
                                                      11 November 1934

Dear Herr Dr. Schmidt, you should have had a reply long ago. As always amid much work, I find my way to music paper more readily than to a writing pad, and in the case of these interminable breaks a few days scarcely count. I could have written to you long ago in all these years. But I heard from your sister in Mülheim (this was also a long time ago) that you were "offended." I did not manage to find out what about, but I did not want to upset you, and so the state developed into a "position." I am very pleased that you have now restored the previous position. Previously you were not so formal, and I hope this will soon vanish. It is still very uncertain whether I can play at your place this winter. On no account before the end of March. I have to complete a large score that will keep me fully occupied until then. And whether I shall play anywhere here will depend on what is decided in the next few months. If I continue to experience the kind of difficulties I have had until now, and if the efforts to wring my neck by slow degrees are successful, I shall probably be forced to look for some occupation abroad. It is certainly the last thing I want to do, but the state of musical life is already such that an honourable musician can no longer take part in it. Well, perhaps there will be some changes.

Wolfgang has not shown up again. He disappeared one night with a promise to write me a good review in his newspaper some time. That would have been at least one department ready to stand up for me! As it is, I must continue to wriggle through the morass without sponsorship. We have been doing that for some time, and my wife is giving me firm support. [. . .]

Warmest greetings to your wife and the unknown Eva, and especially to you yourself,

Yours,

Paul H., together with wife and two dogs

Fritz Stege was music critic of the Nazi daily newspaper *Der völkische Beobachter* and editor of the *Zeitschrift für Musik* (official organ of the Reichsmusikkammer).

To Willy Strecker   Berlin-Charlottenburg

15 November 1934

Dear Willy, you must be told straight away what has happened. Your various alarm signals (and those from other quarters) came just at the right time: yesterday I was with Havemann. I stirred him up with my evidence, castigated Herzog, and praised my own deeds to the skies. The result was that, faced with this utter catastrophe of a passionate patriot being forced into emigration, he sank down in utter despair and promised to do everything he could. Today it happened. To start with, there was a meeting of the Musikkammer in the Herrenhaus. Havemann spoke first, and suddenly I heard myself being placed beside Strauss and Pfitzner as the only notable composers and export articles in his remarks. After that I was taken to see State Secretary [Walther] Funk, who is the big shot dealing with our affairs in the Propaganda Ministry, and there I could hardly get a word in, for Havemann and Stein overwhelmed him with such a flood of panegyrics that my ears burned. He was already in the picture, Fu. had already been with him, and he promised to talk to the Führer tomorrow. It was true, he told us, that the latter had once walked in horror out of a concert in Munich where something of mine was played, but he (F.) hadn't the slightest doubt that everything would be all right. Outside I met Stein again, who whispered excitedly in my ear that he had heard I was to be taken to the Führer in the next few days. He must have heard wrong, for I had arranged with Funk to meet him [Funk]. As well as with him, Furtw. had also spoken to Göring. It all seems to be going splendidly. He will now definitely be going to the Führer in the next few days and is convinced everything will click. I shall be seeing him again on Friday. Then we shall see.

This little interruption will in the end prove to our advantage. Despite that, our friend [Herzog] won't be allowed to get away with it entirely. My first thought was to call on the Kammer for a disciplinary court, but after today's experiences I have dropped that idea. The aim now must be to strew poison in some of his paths. Have you an archive of reviews, or something of that kind? If so, please get someone to look through them and see whether you can find any laudatory references to me. I believe there were some during the famous 14 years. And I should like of course to see those about Mathis. Because of all these events it would be difficult for me to leave here now, so I won't come down on Saturday. Would you believe it? That other dirty swine, Stege, who has, God knows, spat enough venom himself, has invited me through Stein to talk to him about Herzog. You should have heard my scornful laughter. Lickspittle! The corrections are being done. You'll have them by the beginning of next week.

That's all for today. More follows as soon as I myself hear something. The Kulturgemeinde branches are expected to disappear in the next 2 weeks.

Greetings,

Paul

The DAZ was the Berlin newspaper *Deutsche Allgemeine Zeitung*, in which Wilhelm Furtwängler's article "The Hindemith Case" appeared on Sunday, 25 November 1934. This article defended Hindemith's right, in view of his achievements as composer and teacher, to make occasional artistic mistakes.

The text to be shown to Hitler was that of *Mathis der Maler*.

"Wait awhile, soon," is a quotation from Goethe's poem "Wanderers Nachtlied."

To Willy Strecker   Berlin-Charlottenburg
                                                   18 November 1934

Dear Willy, yesterday evening I was with big Wilhelm, we discussed the whole thing. He is in full flight and has identified himself with the matter to such an extent that he is quite determined to give everything up if he doesn't get his way. However, he has no fears at all about that, since at the moment he is in a very strong position with the top people again on account of some foreign affairs. His plan is now this: he will write an article attacking the whole shemozzle (he was already busy on it this morning, and I immediately gave him the things about Herzog you sent me to make use of), which will appear in the DAZ or some other newspaper in the next few days. He will see that it is given to the Führer, so that he'll be prepared. His visit has been fixed through Göring and Hess for next week.

It is obvious that "Neues vom Tage" shocked the Führer greatly. I shall write him a letter (F. was very taken with this idea) in which I shall ask him to convince himself to the contrary and perhaps visit us some time here in the school, where I would have the cantata from the Plöner Musiktag performed for him—no one has ever been able to resist that. F. is to give him my letter, also the text. So you need have no qualms about the outcome of these efforts. It is hardly likely that any very serious attacks will be launched by the other side, unless they just warm up all the old muck again. F. is truly and sincerely delighted with the text. The very worst that could happen (he thinks) is that he would be advised not to bring the opera out here. He would then arrange for it to be done in a provincial city and at the same time sever his connection with the State Opera, since he cannot tolerate his plans being interfered with from outside. He says there are no new operas anywhere and no sign of any to come, and this is the one opera he must do. So please be patient a while longer. Probably it all looks much more dangerous to you, since all you can do is stand around waiting to see what new event arrives to overtake the previous bad news. The many messages of consolation, sympathy, and anger I am receiving from all sides prove to me how tragically the matter is being taken everywhere. I feel that does no harm. People are being stirred up and, once we have gnawed our way through, our victory will be final.

The corrections will be sent off on Monday or Tuesday. I haven't yet begun on the score. The weariness I felt after the long and concentrated work has now been joined by a semi-suppressed flu that takes the form of a sleeping sickness, and it has left me quite incapable of work over the past days. Wait awhile, soon.

Affectionately,

Yours,

Paul

In his article, Furtwängler had incautiously asked, "What is to become of us if political denunciation is to be applied in the fullest measure to matters of art?" The result was to unite the entire Nazi regime and its supporters against Hindemith and himself. Goebbels joined in the attack in person. Furtwängler was obliged to resign from his positions as musical director of the Berlin State Opera and Philharmonic Orchestra, and any idea of staging *Mathis der Maler* in Berlin had to be shelved, at least for the time being. Hindemith applied for and was granted a leave of absence from the Hochschule and went off to Lenzkirch in the Black Forest to orchestrate the opera, now complete in piano score.

Johannes Schüler was a conductor in Essen who had performed the *Mathis* Symphony in a concert on 20 November.

To Johannes Schüler   [Berlin-Charlottenburg]

[November/December 1934]

Dear Herr Schüler, the unearthly amount of muck that has been emptied out over my head in recent days has made me more susceptible than usual to the pleasant facts in this world. You are one of these, and for that I thank you. It gave me great pleasure to see that you have not allowed this web of fraud and abuse to deter you; from all that I hear, your performance must have been splendid. In place of lengthy thanks,

I am sending you herewith a provisional print of the Mathis text. But please keep it strictly to yourself, nothing may be said about it in public for the present.

With warmest greetings,

Yours, Paul Hindemith

To Willy Strecker [Berlin-Charlottenburg]

[13 February 1935]

[. . .] Basel was a tremendous success, my conducting talents are developing to such an extent that the National Broadcasting Company has offered me a concert tour next year. I had a long conversation with their continental representative in Basel. He was very keen and reported back home at once. There have been other approaches as well; one from the future secretary of state in the Turkish ministry of education, Cevat Bey (first by letter, then he came here in person), to offer me the directorship of a large Turkish state music school. I didn't turn it down, he sent in his report, and I shall maybe go there soon to take a good look. I wouldn't want to stay there full-time, but for a few months in the year, gladly. The American intended also to enquire about visiting teaching posts in the USA; a few months doing that and possibly a course of lessons in Basel, which has also been offered me — but continuing to live in Germany for the rest of the time, that wouldn't be at all bad. If I am now given notice, I shall have to commit myself to something else quite soon. If not, I should like in any case to give up the school next year and concentrate, apart from a few guest performances, on composing and writing the theory textbook. [. . .]

To Willy Strecker Berlin-Charlottenburg

25 March 1935

[. . .] The fifth scene is finished, it will go off to you tomorrow evening. — Nothing new has happened here, that's to say, I know of nothing. At any rate we can await events in peace. Reading through the score and playing the piano arrangement, I have assured myself that "Mathis" is a respectable piece. It can await its time. [. . .]

To Darius and Madeleine Milhaud Berlin-Charlottenburg

[End of March 1935]

Dear Darius, dear Madeleine, now at last we are back in Berlin — we were in the Black Forest for two months, then for three weeks I lay in bed in Frankfurt — and so here at last is my note of thanks for Darius's score. I have read it, but one really needs to hear a piece if one wants to know exactly how it is. Unfortunately I have only one set of the "Mathis" records and the firm gives me none. Therefore I can't send you any, but as a substitute I enclose herewith the score and (as a rarity) the text, which has not yet been published in any form. Later, when the piano arrangement is published, I'll send it to you. Amuse yourself with the text. It is, I fear, not in your line, you will probably find it boring. ("Mathis" is the painter Matthias Grünewald, whose altar is in Colmar, and the piece is about him.) Next week we are off to Turkey for a month. In May my nice holiday will probably be over and I shall have to return to the school. How are things with you?

Warmest greetings from us both,

Paul the musician

Willy Strecker asked Richard Strauss, in his capacity as president of the Reichsmusikkammer, to examine the work of some of Hindemith's pupils to satisfy himself of Hindemith's musical credentials.

Strauss's opera Die schweigsame Frau, scheduled for production in Dresden on 24 June 1935, brought him into trouble with the Nazis on account of his working with a Jewish librettist, Stefan Zweig.

The absence of Der Hund von Saulheim (The Hound of Saulheim) from any reference books suggests that it was just Hindemith's joking invention.

To Willy Strecker   Berlin-Charlottenburg

31 March 1935

Dear Willy, yesterday evening, just after your call, Stein rang to tell me about the presidential meeting that took place in the afternoon. Strauss reported on the conversation with me and was apparently satisfied, both with me myself and with the schoolwork that I showed him. He had also spoken in the ministry to this effect. So nothing stands in the way of my teaching activities, unless the ministry still has some political doubts. These would in fact be very convenient for me: since until today I have not been given notice, I shall remain unmolested until the next legal date for giving notice, and it is clear that I should prefer to resume teaching later rather than sooner. There is no ban on the playing of my music, Stein said, and if any conductor has the pluck to start, he can rely on the support of the Musikkammer. Despite this, I am in favour of waiting another season. We would no longer gain much by shooting off straightaway—but if we wait calmly, we shall win plus points for ourselves by autumn.

It seems the all-out attack on our dear pet Herzog is now about to start. It all came up for discussion at the meeting; Stein and Havemann took the lid off everything, confirmed by Raschloch. Strauss did not allow himself to be converted all at once; only when he heard that Herzog, with the backing of the Kulturgemeinde, had declared himself in favour of boycotting a performance of "Die schweigsame Frau" even if approved by the very highest authority, did he decide he'd heard enough, and it's said he is now on his way to Goebbels to put a knife into the favourite. I pumped some extra air into the trumpet by giving Stein a written account of my relations with Herzog, for use as required. My hope is now to find myself standing by the coffin of this contemporary on my return. I am even prepared to give the first performance of "Der Hund von Saulheim" in Berlin to mark the occasion.

It appears therefore that things are slowly beginning to move. I am quite glad to be going away for a month, so as to let things evolve on their own. I believe the worst is now behind us. [. . .]

Hindemith was in Turkey in April and May, and on his return to Berlin he prepared for Cevat Bey a plan for setting up a school of music in Ankara. This special report was directed to Goebbels's Propaganda Ministry with the intention of clarifying how Hindemith's activities benefitted Germany's cultural reputation in Turkey.

The new viola concerto was *Der Schwanendreher*, first performed in Amsterdam by Hindemith on 14 November 1935, with Willem Mengelberg conducting. The violin and piano sonata was the Sonata in E.

To Willy Strecker [Berlin-Charlottenburg]
15 June 1935
[. . .] [Postscript dated 17 June 1935] Yesterday evening I had a long talk with Havemann. He sees the situation in the rosiest light and is convinced that everything will be in order by autumn. I gave him my Turkish report, which I had completed in the meantime, together with a special report for the Propi, and he is seeing to it that this lands on the right desk today. I think it should have a good effect. Till then I am all for doing nothing rash. — The score is going well, it will be finished in a few weeks. Then comes the new viola concerto. In the meantime, as a restorative, I have composed half a sonata for violin and piano—easy and very pretty. [. . .]

Carl Ebert, formerly director of the opera house in Berlin-Charlottenburg, was also involved in the organization of the new state-subsidized Conservatory for Music and Drama in Ankara. Alfred Braun was a former radio producer in Berlin; arrested in 1933, he had spent some time in a concentration camp.

Furtwängler ("big Wilhelm"), after an interview with Goebbels in which he expressed regret for having interfered in the government's control of artistic affairs, was allowed to resume his conducting career, though not to occupy his previous appointments in Berlin.

To Gertrud Hindemith Frankfurt
[17 December 1935]
Dear Pushu, so now I have landed back here. In Turin it snowed without stopping for three days, the snow lay around just like in Leningrad. The grey weather,

the endless wide streets, and with it the oppressive warlike atmosphere, etc., etc., it was all reminiscent of Russia. I visited the picture galleries, it was impossible in that weather to do anything else. The rooms are very fine, though most of the pictures are hung so that they dazzle you, and in many cases are hung in unlit corners, so that they were often unidentifiable in the prevailing gloom. All the same, I saw a few really magnificent Van Dycks, Brueghels, also some fine early Italians, fine Rembrandts, and Holbein's Erasmus of Rotterdam. The visit was at any rate worthwhile.

I arrived in Basel late in the evening, and in the hotel I was given the lion room of last winter. I had a long talk with Karl [Carl Ebert] and Gertie about the Turks. As a result he has to some extent revised his original very idealistic plans. He will not be able to go there in January or early February and will probably turn up just when we are there, perhaps with the same train I shall be using from Geneva. Both were the same as ever, though unfortunately he talks politics, thinks that in this respect he alone possesses wisdom, and tries to convert one, in which attempt she emphatically and unpleasantly seconds him. The Brauns (Alfred) were, if anything, better company. He is also employed at the theatre in Basel, and they are finding things tight on his small salary. They live with the child in two rooms in a little old hotel in Kleinbasel and declare that, despite all the difficulties, they are now happier than before, when they were living false and meaningless lives. He is the mystic of old in more concentrated form, sits unceasingly in judgment over himself like a mixture between Strindberg and an anchorite, and longs with every fibre of his being to be back in Germany. His exalted and esteemed patron Karl, blessed by fortune, can scarcely be allowed to see any of this, since, immersed in his hatred, he sustains and supports Braun only if convinced that the poor man would sooner be selling matches in the streets of Winterthur than thinking of the land of the barbarians. We spent an endless evening together, long into the night, Braun relating tales of freemasonry, then we got on to matters harmonical, and there was no end to that. For Braun it was right up his alley, the Eberts, like all theatrical people, were stupid.

Yesterday I made up for lost sleep and in the afternoon left for here, landing at Mother's in the evening. Nothing new here. [. . .] And what is happening where you are? I assume nothing of significance. Big Wilhelm, if he has in fact been permitted to go whining to the yet bigger being, will have achieved nothing beyond a postponement, and that won't hurt in the present circumstances. Write and tell me all the news and come yourself as soon as you possibly can.

Your devoted

Y.

Hindemith had been engaged to play his new viola concerto Der Schwanendreher (literally, "the man turning a swan on the spit") with the BBC Symphony Orchestra conducted by Adrian Boult at the Queen's Hall in London on 22 January 1936. On 20 January, King George V died.

The "Old Hundred," a melody dating back to 1551, is also the basis of the hymn "All people that on earth do dwell."

To Willy Strecker   [Written during a journey from London to Berlin]

23 January 1936

Dear Willy, you must be told at once all the things that have been happening. I don't know whether you had your splendid radio set tuned to London yesterday evening. If so, you will have noticed that the swan could not be roasted owing to a dead king. In the morning of the day before yesterday there was great despair at the BBC. Boult and Clark wanted me to take part in the concert at all costs—it was held in the studio, not in the Queen's Hall. We debated for hours, but no suitable piece could be found, so we decided that I should write some funeral music myself. As I read yesterday in the newspaper, a studio was cleared for me, copyists were slowly brought to the boil, and from 11 to 5 I did some fairly hefty mourning. I turned out a nice piece, in the style of Mathis and Schwanendreher with a Bach chorale at the end ("Vor deinen Thron tret' ich hiermit," very suitable for kings). It is a tune every child in England knows, though I did not find that out till later. Maybe you know it—they call it "The Old Hundred" or something like that. We rehearsed it well all yesterday, and in the evening the orchestra played with great devoutness and feeling. It was very moving. Boult was, by English and his own personal standards, quite beside himself, and kept thanking me. My various pupils are now busy writing articles about the affair, they are very proud that the old man can still do things so well and so quickly. The orchestra's solo violist is soon to give a few repeat performances of the piece.

Shouldn't we perhaps make use of this story? Would you like to circulate it to the German press? It is after all no everyday occurrence when the BBC gets a foreigner to write a piece on the death of their king and sends it out over the complete network. I'm now going to specialize in corpses—maybe there'll be some more opportunities. Should the piece perhaps be published in England with a piano accompaniment? I shall be getting a copy of the score in a few days' time (it is just for a string orchestra, the piece is 8 minutes long). You can have it then and see what can be done with it.

The Schwanendreher will be done later, probably end of August. [. . .] Otherwise I have seen or heard nothing of London this time, having been seated permanently behind viola or notation paper.

A bushy sailor's greeting to all the Strecker clan,

    Yours,

        P.H. Bespoke Tailoring

The Sonata in E for violin and piano was given its first performance in Geneva in February 1936 by Stefan Frenkel and Mme. Orloff.

To Willy Strecker

Istanbul Palace,
Ankara
10 April 1936

[. . .] I am working hard here on the theory book. When the egg is ripe, I want to write another three chapters for it. As it is now, the thing seems to me unclear and unfinished, and I am being held up by a single point, from which I hope to extricate myself soon. The promised piano sonata is also progressing slowly but surely, I shall probably bring it back with me complete. [. . .] I read that the sonata is to be done in B.-Baden. I know neither the violinist nor the pianist and hope it will be (or was?) good. If still pending, a rehearsal under expert guidance (you? Willms? Lübbecke?) would of course be very desirable, my tempi etc. could be used as models. Here there's a lot of work, both pleasant and tiresome. One slowly puts one little brick on top of another, but it will be a long time before they form a usable building. More than half of our time is already gone, and so far there has been hardly a moment for wishing oneself back home. [. . .]

Hindemith's activities in Turkey and his success in London with his *Music of Mourning* had improved his standing with the Nazis, and he was teaching again in the Berlin Hochschule. At the same time, however, that he received the offer of a commission from the Luftwaffe for a musical work, he also learned that official approval had been withdrawn for a production of *Mathis der Maler* in Frankfurt.

The first performance of Hindemith's Piano Sonata No. 1 (*Der Main*) was scheduled to be given by Walter Gieseking in Berlin in the autumn.

To Willy Strecker

[Berlin-Charlottenburg]
29 June 1936

Dear Willy, despite the baking heat I am in such a writing mood that you too shall get a few lines to wind up with. Today I have at last completed the much-mentioned piano sonata. I have taken a great deal of trouble over this piece and hope it will make a good impression. The two movements missing until now should also satisfy our severe Gieseking. Leaving aside the modifications he will make in any case (there's no escaping that with him unless your name is Josef Marx or Castelnuovo), he should be getting his money's worth.

[. . .] I have received a commission from the Luftwaffe. They want to have a representative piece for a highly official orchestral concert in the autumn—I've been thinking of Icarus or some other long-lost air passenger as underlying theme. As welcome as it is important, this seems to me an opportunity not to be missed, and I have said yes to it.

It looks as if Frankfurt cannot be relied upon, and I feel that is nothing to cry about. The slump in musical life is growing so fast that something will soon have to be done about it; one will then be glad not to have taken part in the debacle. [. . .]

Heinz Tietjen was the director of the Berlin State Opera.
Herzog paid a visit to Ludwig Strecker in the early summer and assured him that Rosenberg's Kulturgemeinde would not oppose a production of *Mathis der Maler* in Berlin.

To Willy Strecker   Berlin-Charlottenburg
                                                        8 July 1936
Dear Willy, here is the oft-mentioned sonata and, so you won't think senility is setting in, I'm also enclosing a smaller brother: I did another right away, just for practice. It is the lighter counterpart to the rather weighty first. Altogether composition is going vigorously, I have also written some songs. In addition, the requested piano arrangement of the roasted swan will be finished this week or the beginning of next. Then I mean to interrupt the composing (though that won't be easy, with things in such full flow) to do some more work on the theory book. For today, on account of tiredness, just these few lines, more soon.
    Beat wishes to you all,
        Yours,
            P.H.

In the meantime a few more things have come to my ears. Under the seal of secrecy (which here receives a slight dent) I have learnt that [Stravinsky's] "Le baiser de la fée" is to figure in the State Opera's repertoire next winter, clearly with the full backing of Tietjen. Furthermore, that this time friend Herzog's Kulturgemeinde has at last landed in the soup, since it will be granted no more money, and that is the reason why approaches are now being made to people with better prospects. This is probably the explanation of H's attempt to pump your brother. I would advise caution. It is clear that we have the thicker skulls, and I should consider it a great mistake to sell ourselves now, when we have come through the worst with heads held high. Even if nothing were to happen, each extra day of holding out counts in our favour. Herzog's boss R., cornered by arguments and events, recently condescended to enquire how one can familiarize oneself with something by the infamous cultural bolshie. In consequence he was given the Mathis gramophone records. I don't know how it turned out, but in Herzog's offer to negotiate I see the likelihood of success.
    The Luftwaffe is standing firm on its decision. I want to give them something really good—I am certain that this piece, if reasonably successful, will mean

"Mathis" in the State Opera. The prospects are not quite so gloomy as they look at first sight. [. . .]

I have discovered that the English Music of Mourning had a far greater effect than we knew of at the time. It seems that this was the first blow that started the change of mind about me.

Gieseking will surely be glad to play the second sonata to you.

Yours, P.

To Gertrud Hindemith [Frankfurt]
20 August 1936

No, my dear, it is not all right. Come just as arranged, I urgently need you. If you don't come, I really don't know what to do. The exertions of all this composing have left me feeling rather low, so that Mother is getting worked up and is not at all happy about it. But I just can't apply the brakes; unless I'm held back by force, I just have to go on writing. It's impossible to go out because of the rain, the thought of seeing people is highly distasteful—whoever it might be!? And just to sit around doing nothing—that I can't do with this writing rage spurring me on. So, if you don't come tomorrow, you will later perhaps find another piano sonata lying on the table, but an alarmingly reduced me sitting beside it. And what can I say to your dear old mother, who apparently can't wait to see you? Besides all this, out of sheer boredom I am racking my brains about an opera text, maybe I shall come up with something. Be a good lion and come with the grey-beast. The sonata is now completely finished, written out and markings all done. Come, otherwise I shall present it to the lama Papp. Farewell, dear,

Your Y.

Klais is a village in the Bavarian Alps.

Peter Raabe succeeded Strauss as president of the Reichsmusikkammer in 1935.

Hopes that the atmosphere was easing were dashed in the autumn of 1936 when the Propaganda Ministry admonished the violinist Georg Kulenkampff for playing Hindemith's Sonata in E at a concert in Berlin. At the same time, Gieseking was ordered to remove the piano sonata from his forthcoming concert. The authorities were apparently perturbed by the demonstrative applause the violin sonata received.

The string trio with Hindemith, Kulenkampff, and the cellist Enrico Mainardi was in the end not permitted to perform.

To Ludwig and Willy Strecker Berlin-Charlottenburg
[November 1936]

Dear brothers, herewith, as a sample, the first and second chapters of the book, I hope it will arouse no displeasure. [. . .] It is tough work. The month in Klais, where I worked solidly, was not the end of it, the typing, the polishing, and the preparation of examples are still causing much effort back here.

For that reason, I have not bothered my head about anything at all for the moment, beyond having had a detailed conversation with Stein. The affair has raised a lot of dust. Either things will move in the opposite direction in the near future, which I do not expect, nor (to be honest) really want, or the existing tension will increase even further, which we will note soon through sales of the piano sonatas and at Christmas of the book. I do not intend to show the book to any official bodies in advance, and above all not to Raabe, that most prominent of all the cowards. On the whole, nobody appears to have anything against me personally, the established trio (Kulenkampff, I, and Mainardi) is apparently to be allowed to start in January. I will discuss the Luftwaffe piece as soon as I get to see the colonel. In this case too I should be for not rushing things. I don't on any account want to give the impression of trying to reach my goal sooner by creeping into another hole — not even an air hole. A bit of pride precisely at this point might pay better than haste. [. . .]

Enjoy yourselves with the somewhat unusual reading material.

Warm greetings from the pen-pusher

Paul

At the beginning of 1937, Hindemith paid another short visit to Turkey. Returning to Berlin at the end of February, he made preparations for his first visit to the United States of America.

Ernest R. Voigt was president of Associated Music Publishers (AMP) in New York, a firm that represented several European publishing companies in the United States, including Schotts.

Oliver Strunk was director of the Music Division of the Library of Congress in Washington.

To Ernest R. Voigt   Berlin-Charlottenburg
                                                              1 March 1937

Dear Herr Voigt, Herr Strecker showed me your letter a few days ago. Many thanks for your efforts. I shall arrive on the "Bremen" on 31 March. The Seymour Hotel that you recommend is quite agreeable to me. Please book me a room there for that night. On the following day, I would want to travel to Washington, unless I hear from Dr. Strunk to the contrary. Perhaps you could get in touch with him on this matter as well. I should also be grateful if you could discuss the probable programme and any other relevant details with the League of Composers, so that not everything will be left to the last moment. I am no friend of photographers, microphones, and interviews; if you could succeed in preserving me from all but the truly indispensable and erecting wherever possible a barbed-wire fence around me, you can be assured of my eternal gratitude. We can talk about the private concert in Buffalo when I arrive. The others taking part will in any case be deciding their own contributions to the programme, and for me it will be a matter of the solo sonatas for viola, the one with piano, and beyond that the other pieces of chamber music (playing or conducting). For the orchestral concert, I suggest the "Mathis" Symphony, if I am to conduct only one work. If two, I should like to add the overture to "Neues vom Tage" to it. Or have there been different ideas? Please send me a brief outline of all you have in mind.

Meanwhile warm greetings,

Yours,

Paul Hindemith

Cameron Baird, a friend of Voigt's, was head of the music department at Buffalo University.

Bernhard Heiden was a former pupil of Hindemith's in Berlin.

To Ernest R. Voigt   Berlin-Charlottenburg
                                                          17 March 1937

Dear Herr Voigt, many thanks for your news. I am glad that everything already stands in good order. I shall now not be arriving until 2 April with the "Deutschland." The ship takes two days longer, and that suits me very well, for I have quite a lot of work to do. W. Strecker, who originally planned to come with me, cannot do so after all; my wife is also staying here on account of all the work, and so I am coming alone. I shall be available for rehearsals throughout the time in New York. It would be very nice if you could get in touch with Mr. Strunk, so that we can have all the participants together at one time. I am not sorry that you were unable to arrange more concerts. There will be enough to do as it is. Unfortunately, I have no printed documents at all. I have kept nothing of that kind, except for some very remarkable bad reviews, but you would hardly find any good use for those. There will be time enough after my arrival to settle all other matters. I should just like to ask you to bring some money to the ship for me. Since we are not allowed to take any out of Germany, I shall arrive as poor as the proverbial church mouse and become a burden on your state welfare if you do not provide me with an advance.

I am also writing at once to Mr. Baird in Buffalo. You have of course read his letter in which he suggests performing a piece by a former pupil of mine on the same evening. I feel this is not a good idea; I do not know what the piece is like, or altogether how my pupil has developed. Besides that, I should be reluctant to see my affairs linked to others. I have no means of knowing whether I shall be offending the friendly Mr. Baird by rejecting his proposal. Could you not gently convey to him that we will be doing the Buffalo chamber music recital without a Heiden composition? I should also like to replace his friendly offer of accommodation with a hotel, if it can be done without insulting him. Not out of mistrust, but because, as an old touring musician, I am used to hotels. [. . .]

Before leaving for the United States, Hindemith decided to hand in his notice at the Berlin Hochschule. He wrote to Stein on 25 March 1937, the day of his departure from Hamburg on the liner *Deutschland*, dating his resignation from 30 September 1937.

The larger part of his letters to his wife during his first visit to the United States took the form of a diary giving a straightforward account of his activities, which he sent her in batches. Just now and again, as the opening words under each date indicate, they assume a more personal tone.

Hindemith spent much of his time on board ship writing and revising his book. He arrived in New York on 2 April and was met on the quay by Voigt and his fellow director of Associated Music Publishers, M. E. Tompkins, as well as by his uncle Gustav Hindemith and his son Rudy.

To Gertrud Hindemith   2 April 1937

[. . .] How very funny it is to get to know people to whom one is so closely related. The old fellow is exactly as one imagines an immigrant of the eighties to be: master of everything, at 75 still merry and bright, knocks back his beer like an old trooper. His main job seems to be blacksmith. I would have placed him rather among Mother's relations, he bears little resemblance to the other Hindemiths, if one leaves out of account Ongl Paul's well-known clear and unfailing familiarity with all events of the universe. Occasionally one detects an inflection or a look of Father's, and the family can be seen in his hands. The cousin, however, is entirely un-Hindemithian. He is a photographer, a thin, apparently somewhat delicate man around 43 years of age. [. . .]

Associated Music Publishers, whom Hindemith called AMP or Pub, had their office on West 45th Street, opposite the Seymour Hotel where Hindemith was staying.

3 April

I was up by 5.30 making my room-refuge look more homely. I then put in some hard writing on the analyses chapter and afterwards visited the Musicpub opposite. We fixed everything for the next few days, programmes, travel arrangements, etc. Tompkins, the second Pub, is all one can demand in the nature of a smooth-faced, keep-smiling businessman with a pipe in his mouth. Mr. Voigt, who incidentally speaks German brilliantly, is on the other hand thin and crafty, he knows what's what. [. . .]

In the afternoon I went for a walk in the box of bricks. It may be impressive, but it's certainly not beautiful. Excepting perhaps something like the Radio City, whose narrow main building, over 300 m high, has, taken as a whole, a certain beauty, though the details are less pleasing. Tremendous amount of traffic of course, and everything that overawes the humble citizen. In Fifth Avenue one fantastic shop after another. The good Lord has the lowest houses, his churches stand rather shamefaced between the more imposing buildings. Maybe he is suffering from false modesty, though it might also be that he wants to make plain to the foreigner what the people in his own country can do. These people, incidentally, are a fantastic hotchpotch. Their jaws, including the feminine ones, move continuously from left to right like cows chewing the cud; the gum consumption must be enormous. In the two days I have been here, with no reason to complain about the lack of facial expressions, I have not seen a single pretty face, neither male nor female. [. . .]

Towards evening I had a date with my cousin Rudy and his wife Eunice. He is somewhat Ladwig-ish, a bit reserved, she is Duprat, but 30 years younger. They invited me to a Russian restaurant, where I was once again recognized, but was able with protective cover from my cousin to escape. Afterwards we went to the studio in Carnegie Hall in which they live. She is a singer, seems from what my Pubs say to have been good. Apparently gives singing lessons here. He has a workroom in Downtown, I saw some excellent pictures he had taken. They are both good people, earning an honest living and wearing themselves out in the mad scramble. They were very considerate and said hardly a word about their or my professional activities. They have even bought tickets for the concert here for themselves and my old uncle.

4 April

Today I visited my uncle's house together with my cousin and saw all sorts of things. One first takes the ferry across to Jersey City, where most of the railway stations are. Then by train (exactly as in the films—we at home are obviously outrageously spoiled in these matters) out into the country, which seems to consist of rather poor oaklands and ugly villages. The country roads are full of living cars, dead ones lie scattered all over the place in their thousands. In Port Jervis we were met by the next cousin, Emil, who looks even less like a member of our family, and he drove us about 20 km to Rio. He is a genuine, harmless, and nice farmer's boy with hands like three other family members put together and a leathery brown skin like an old trapper; he too is nearly 40.

The old uncle touched me deeply and filled me with great respect. He has a timber-frame house with some 9–10 rooms, stables, garage, and machine shed, and he and Emil look after it all by themselves. Since the boy is also employed in the neighbouring power station from noon till 3 daily, the whole burden of the business lies on the 73-year-old man. Today he had prepared a meal of roast pork with sauerkraut and mashed potatoes, excellent. He told me all kinds of things and showed me round his property.

He built the house 30 years ago all by himself, gathering the bricks and boards one by one. Later he enlarged it with Emil's help, laid in steam heating, running water, and electric light, for which they also set up their own generator. They make their own agricultural implements too in a fully motorized workshop, also equipped by themselves, he shoots stags, slaughters oxen, pickles, makes jelly, washes, and has—as if all this were not enough—founded an orchestra, and seven people from the neighbourhood come to his house once a week to play in it under his direction (he is the group's pianist). He bought the piano some time ago for 6 dollars and restored it. He tunes it himself of course; it was in perfect condition. Emil plays the violin without crushing it in his great paws, and according to my uncle, they play, besides operatic excerpts of all sorts, the Mendelssohn and Bruch concertos, admittedly not very well, but all the same.

Some hidden family characteristic must be emerging in the old fellow. I even believe that here our intrinsic talent shows through. Anyway, he is the one who, in his total lack of inhibitions, seems the most natural of us all. The constant work in natural surroundings, the necessity of exerting himself to the utmost, has made of him an honest, powerful chap worthy of the greatest admiration. He is a bit smaller than me and now walks with a slight stoop, but he is obviously as strong as an ox and in better health than his sons, of whom Rudy has become melancholy and worn down by the New York rush and Emil suffers from stomach ulcers and has already had some frightful operations. (I did not see the third son, Ferdinand. He is a projectionist in a Port Jervis cinema, and, since performances last all day on Saturdays, he couldn't come over.) The old man in his equanimity accepts everything with the same serenity: his two dead wives, his son's illness—and also the "happiest day of his life," when he has in his home a member of his family from the old country.

In the afternoon we drove around the very pretty countryside, which reminds me of the Uerzeller Hills, and the old fellow called in everywhere. Since he was for a long time a justice of the peace and is now a tax assessor as well as the holder of sundry other municipal posts, everyone knows him, and clearly everybody is glad to see him. We had some drinks in various inns, that is to say, just the old man and I. He made no kind of fuss about me, I was just his nephew from the old country. A few keen wireless listeners knew a bit about me, but such external matters mean nothing to the old man.

Somewhat dizzy, very thoughtful, and all but concussed, I returned with Rudy at about 6 in the evening, made acquaintance with the ear-splitting underground, ate in an Italian restaurant and took to my Seymour bed. [. . .]

7 April

This morning I wrote the very last letter of the theory book. [. . .]

The opening concert of Hindemith's tour was part of the Eighth Washington Festival of Contemporary Music, with which Mrs. Coolidge was connected, and it included the first performance of his Sonata for flute and piano, composed in 1936.

8 April

The day passed in rehearsals. In the morning with [Georges] Barrère and the pianist [Jesús Maria] Sanromá from Boston. He is a Puerto Rican; his playing is first-class. Arrived fully practised and played, apart from a few bars, fully in the spirit of the composer. The two are a wonderful duo; they make the piece more beautiful than it really is. [. . .] To add to that, Barrère is a very nice Frenchman and a quite magnificent musician. [. . .]

Hindemith travelled to Washington by train on 9 April, after rehearsing in Carnegie Hall with a specially assembled orchestra under the conductor Carlos Chavez for a performance of his *Schwanendreher* concerto that was to take place in Washington.

In his opening concert, the Madrigal Singers from the Dessoff Choir (conducted by Paul Boepple), sang four of Hindemith's *Lieder nach alten Texten* (*Five Songs on Old Texts*, written 1923, revised 1936); the tenor Frederick Jagel sang four of his settings of Hölderlin's poems (not hitherto performed in public); Hindemith himself played his Sonata for unaccompanied viola, Opus 25, No. 1; and Sanromá performed the third piano sonata, composed in 1936.

Mrs. Meyer was the wife of Eugene Meyer, publisher of the *Washington Post*.

10 April

Today was a busy one. Even before 9, I was in the Library [of Congress], where I first of all visited my Mr. Strunk. He is a young, pale, nice man who studied in Berlin with Johannes Wolf and Robert Kahn. He also took an entrance examination in composition in the Hochschule 10 years ago, and apparently I was one of the people who failed him. So we immediately discovered the necessary points of contact. The chorus was already rehearsing like mad on the podium, so I moved to a room and practised. Then all the other rehearsers came along as the time for the concert drew slowly nearer.

It began at 11.15. Barrère and Sanromá blew the flute sonata magnificently. They made a very good impression, the large audience responded warmly at once. The songs came next; Jagel sang them well, but it was evident that he had arrived with the night train. I was number three. When I came out the applause was very long, and everybody rose from their seats. I played in the way Charlemagne used to play his solo sonatas: effortlessly and impressively. The success was very great. The chorus, who came on after me, sang superbly.

At 1 there was a festive <u>lunch</u> at Mrs. Meyer's place, Nadia Boulanger received me like a blissful piano teacher at the debut of a pupil, hugging and kissing me before the assembled crew, and I began to fear this might be the usual custom as I was steered towards Mrs. Coolidge. I had to take the place of honour beside Minerva, and I had a long conversation with her. Like all the others, she tried to persuade me to move here permanently, saying that any arrangement that would suit me could be made. What she would like best, she said, would be for me to teach at one of the universities or large music colleges, even if not on a permanent basis. I made polite noises. [. . .]

11 April

[. . .] The rehearsal began at 10 A.M. on a very fine Sunday morning. Chavez came through more or less unscathed; though I played strictly in time, he doesn't find it very easy to follow. Every time a little ritardando or a change of rhythm occurs, one can feel him inwardly sending out an urgent plea to Quexicatuatl for help. After the rehearsal Mrs. Coolidge gave a lunch. She sat booted and spurred at the table like a robber knight in armour and presided. She obviously takes her heavy office very seriously and is tireless in attending concerts, <u>lunchs</u>, and <u>receptions</u>. Even after the present <u>lunch</u> had ended, she sat down again on a little chair by the door, eyes and ears primed, to receive the salutes of the dissolving company. It reminded me very much of Polyphemus's cave, in which all the departing sheep had their bellies examined. This was followed by yet another concert, in which for the sake of decency I had to listen to a quartet by [Roger] Sessions. A marked example of <u>Potchambermusic</u>, terribly boring. After it I retired to my well-earned bed. As final item in the evening concert: I roasted the swan, played very well, and had great success. Chavez steered himself and a too loud orchestra tolerably through the rocks. About half the entire world's violists were present, and afterwards they came along very politely and sang my praises.

What followed after the concert? A reception. This time at the home of Mrs. Morgenthau, whose husband, the state treasurer, has signed his name on all the state bank's dollar notes. There was the usual chatter, the few people who at the previous <u>lunchs</u> and <u>receptions</u> had not yet learnt that I was in this country for the first time used their cunning to worm it out of me now. Finally there was beer with a smaller company at the Strunks', and then this day of glory came to an end.

In Boston, Hindemith played his *Schwanendreher* concerto with the Boston Symphony Orchestra under Arthur Fiedler and his Sonata for unaccompanied viola for an invited audience at the Chamber Music Club. His rehearsals in New York were for two concerts in which he was to play the *Schwanendreher* concerto with the New York Philharmonic Orchestra under Artur Rodzinski.

[New York] 14 April

Dear Lion, I have just returned from Boston. How I did there you will see from the following reports. Washington was a very great success, some very fulminating things were written. Within its smaller framework, Boston was also very good. On my return I found two little letters from you; it has taken ages this time for anything to reach me, and I was so longing for it. The new crayons look really good. I hope news will now come more often. You can't complain about me, can you?

A pity you didn't hear the little songs in W., they sound really good. And the choruses have turned out well. I told dear old lady Coolidge that I would dedicate them to her, which sent her into ecstasies. The concerts here are tomorrow and the day after. The orchestra rehearsed this afternoon without me, tomorrow morning I have a 2½-hour rehearsal to myself. If everything continues as it has begun, toi, teu, täu, I shall be happy. [. . .]

I must certainly come here again next year. In what capacity I don't yet know, probably a mixture of courses and concerts. Despite the comical aspects of its official machinery, music here does have its serious and prospectively very rewarding side. [. . .]

So, my dear, you now have reading material enough from me. Remember your Red Indian Yiyak with Yashni and give my regards to all two- and four-legged creatures.

With fondest lion thoughts and much longing,

Your Y.

15 April

Until today the going has been quite easy, but now the big time starts. Rehearsal in the morning. The famous orchestra is not all that excessively enchanting, compared with the Boston people it falls a long way behind. Neither is the much-praised Rodzinski as good as I expected. He is very slow on the uptake, follows badly, and is also technically not quite of the best. A single rehearsal for a new piece is anyway too little, but all the same, with goodwill and great effort on the part of all, more could have been achieved than here.

I slept in the afternoon and the concert was in the evening. The programme is clumsily arranged, the slender Schwanendreher being played between [Strauss's] "Tod und Verklärung" and [Beethoven's] Fifth Symphony; and besides that, a sparsely scored piece is in any case at a disadvantage in a space as huge as Carnegie Hall. The harpist played a large number of wrong notes; as for the main trombone solo in the first movement, the trombonist blew nothing at all. Rodzinski fished around quite a lot, he will never grasp the tempo in the last movement. In spite of the poor conditions, the reception was fairly good, but I feel not much of the piece was understood. I went out during the symphony and so escaped the rally of concert hyenas which, according to eyewitnesses, assumed gigantic proportions.

After the concert, Nadia Boulanger gave a reception that was as distinguished as it was boring. Here she makes a less reassuring impression than in Berlin. I have the feeling that she is engaged in some kind of musical politics and is on an official, but secret, mission promoting some cause. Stravinsky, who is in New York for rehearsals of his ballet and who sat in the front row at the concert, very decoratively detached, was also there, followed by his satellite [Samuel] Dushkin. He was telling everybody that Der Schwanendreher is an immensely important piece, and I heard in the following days that he was still dropping this sage discovery into various thirsting ears.

I soon disappeared.

16 April

[. . .] Today was a bit better, but also not very good. I had invited the entire Hindemith family to the hotel bar after the concert. My uncle left his lavishly fed cows early in the morning and travelled here with sons Emil and Ferdinand. This additional cousin is even more of a clodhopper than his sturdy brother. They were all terribly proud of their so publicly employable relative; they said hardly anything about the concert itself. They certainly get more pleasure out of playing Die schöne Galathee back home. My uncle in his rural simplicity was the nicest of them all, though clearly he is slightly looked down on by Eunice, wife of the soft and helpless Rudolf. At six the whole family group left to catch the train back into the country. [. . .]

> Hindemith had begun writing his new Sonata for unaccompanied viola before leaving New York; he played it in Chicago on 21 April but was dissatisfied with it, and it was not published during his lifetime.
>
> Hans Lange, Hindemith's concertmaster colleague in the Frankfurt Opera orchestra, emigrated to the United States in 1923.

19 April

[. . .] In the afternoon I went with Tompkins to Grand Central Station to board a train to Chicago. The train is named "Commodore Vanderbilt" and runs fast and smoothly except when starting off: the driver has obviously not yet got the hang of it and treats us to some horrible jolts. The tracks lie along the river Hudson. People call it the American Rhine, but that is foolish, for the landscapes are not at all similar, and besides, the Hudson valley is beautiful enough to stand beside famous originals without fear of comparison. The sunset was splendid. I got down to some fairly hefty composing, for I had decided to play the new sonata in Chicago. This was easy to do in the comfortable sleeping-car compartment. We were travelling, not in the usual American sleeping-cars, in which men and women snore at each other separated only by curtains, we had roomy single cabins which offered every imaginable aid to comfort, from a WC of one's own to a slit in the wall for used razor blades. I went to bed early.

Tompkins told me that the comical station names along the track were of Indian origin, and it was not at all easy to convince him that Syracuse was not one of these. One passes through many famous places of classical antiquity such as Athens, Utica, Rome, etc., and the Europe of later times is also worthily represented by Venice, Toledo, Salamanca, among others. A comparison between Harlem and the Dutch city demonstrates, however, that it is better to stick to the original.

[Chicago] 20 April

We arrived at 8.30 and were met by the secretary of the Art Club, where I shall be playing tomorrow, and by my former desk colleague Hans Lange, who now conducts here as the deputy of [Frederick] Stock, who is ill, and may take over his post entirely. Of Chicago I have seen hardly more than the lakeside and its closest surroundings; I was still writing music. Lange managed quite well, but he is still the small, very limited musician, to whom not even years of playing with the New York Philharmonic and a post as Toscanini's assistant has imparted a broader style. I was forcibly reminded of the exacting Turks. Of all the conductors I have had in America so far, not one would have been kept permanently in Ankara (except perhaps for Fiedler in Boston), whereas here they are either big stars or dressed up as big stars. The orchestra consists mainly of German musicians and is professional, but not first-class. [. . .]

From Chicago, Hindemith travelled to Buffalo by night train on 21–22 April. There he was to conduct the Philharmonic Orchestra in his *Mathis* Symphony and to play the *Schwanendreher* Concerto under the direction of the orchestra's permanent conductor, Franco Autori.

[Buffalo] 22 April

[. . .] Heart and soul of musical affairs is the young vice-director of an iron pipe foundry, Cameron Baird. My musical grandchild, for during the time when business was bad in America he travelled to Berlin to study music; he came to me and I directed him to [Harald] Genzmer, who gave him lessons and later passed him on to Heiden—to the latter's good fortune, for the kindhearted Baird was a great help to the Heidens when they moved to America. Today, too, he got them to come up from Detroit and stay with him.

We lunched together and then went to the rehearsal. I started with "Mathis." It had in fact been performed here last year, but it must have been a comical performance, or they played something quite different; none of them recognized the piece. The orchestra is as stupid as a crowd of puppies, the people forget from one minute to the next and cannot concentrate. The strings, up to the solo violist, are without exception bad, the brass is good. I drilled them terribly hard, but they were very grateful for their unaccustomed enjoyment and praised me to the skies. The rehearsal took place in the club room of a German male choir with plenty of beer on tap. Baird, to refresh the plagued creatures, invited them to a glass during the intermission. A gentleman who obviously did not belong to the orchestra and whose function I could not otherwise divine, made good use of this. He told silly jokes and in his tipsy state tried constantly to engage me in his somewhat hobbling conversation. I was very reserved with him. Next morning I read in the newspaper all the things the "shy German music master" was supposed to have said. The man was a reporter: he did not of course give the reason for my shyness. [. . .]

[New York] 27 April

[. . .] In the afternoon I had to pack and had invited my cousin and his wife to a short farewell drink in the bar. At 6.30 Pub Tompkins provided a meal, after which we all went to the Metropolitan Opera for the Stravinsky.

It began with Apollo, the music of which struck me today as very corpse-like; this must surely have been because the good Igor is a truly mediocre conductor and cunningly avoids any step in the direction of free and spontaneous music making. The dancing could not be compared with Diaghilev's production. The Apollo himself was not thoroughly secure, and none of the others was 100 percent. All the same, the American Ballet is a good company; the present Russian one that gave guest performances in Berlin is reputed to be less good. The choreographer Balanchine has ideas, and his request to me to write a ballet for next winter must be taken seriously.

The "Jeu de Cartes" looked well on stage and was a pronounced success. The music, the score of which I had previously glanced through, confirmed my earlier opinion. It is very clear and simple. Unfortunately, not the simplicity resulting from the final reduction of fine ideas to their clearest expression, but the simplicity of good light music. It is merry, in parts witty, and the score is of course well made. If Igor considers the Schwanendreher important, I fear I can't say the same about his new piece. It pleases; perhaps that is something, but I feel he intended more.

I couldn't stay for "Le baiser de la fée," because I had to board the ship. [. . .]

Hindemith travelled back to Germany on the liner *Europa*. Back in Berlin, he completed the semester at the Hochschule and then went to Turkey for two months.

His compositions for the remainder of 1937 included the orchestral piece *Symphonic Dances*. The ballet on which he was working with Léonide Massine was *Nobilissima Visione*.

To Emma and Fried Lübbecke [Berlin-Charlottenburg]

[31 December 1937]

Dear Emma, dear Fried, you have remembered us lavishly. We are very touched and sing you our thanks in chorus, to the extent that is possible. The book on the Turks will be our reading material on our next voyage, the red musicians (handle with care, time bomb in the mandoline!) will decorate the wall in the last months we shall be permitted to enjoy our home here.

We have had a good rest after all our hectic travels, and now I am back to some hefty composing. Just as well, for I have to complete an extensive ballet score before I leave for America (beginning of February). The intervals I fill up with a new sport: I play the cello (!!) alongside the enjoyable exercises on bassoon and clarinet, initiated some time ago. Gertrud exchanged our old double bass, which in the end did nothing but stand around in corners like a tiresome relative, for a handsome cello, a welcome Christmas present that was as surprising as it was cheap.

Outdoors it seems not yet to have decided whether the bells or the fireworks should keep the upper hand. Meanwhile we sit expectantly with a bottle before us and are confident the final victory will go to the explosions. We are fireworking only in spirit, and we send you a few powerful and effective rockets with our good wishes for 38.

Your Paul

The head of the music school in Ankara was Dr. Ernst Prätorius; Eduard Zuckmayer, brother of the dramatist Carl Zuckmayer, was one of the German teachers appointed at Hindemith's suggestion.

Muhsin Ertugrul, generally regarded as the founder of modern theatre in Turkey, was at this time artistic director of the Istanbul Municipal Theatre.

Hindemith did not return to Turkey again.

To Cevat Bey at the Ministry of Education in Ankara

Berlin-Charlottenburg

3 January 1938

Dear Herr Cevat,

[. . .] I had a long letter from Dr. Prätorius in which he gave me a precise account of the present situation. From this I see that what I predicted to Ebert would be the result of his unwise behaviour towards the musical directorship and what I also warned you about before leaving Ankara—that the next revolution could be expected to come before long from Necil—have come to pass. You did indeed tell me, after you yourself had spoken to Necil, that this was quite impossible, but I have come to know my music-making friends so well in the meantime that I know exactly what to expect from them. I cannot judge from here how far they have gone this time and what intimidating effect they have had; however, I believe I can fairly safely foretell that the next assault will be at the beginning of March, and I believe it will be in the form of a combined attack: Necil will come forward as speaker for his seconders, Nurullah and Halil. I am not in favour of forceful methods, but here there is only one way if you, and therefore we, are to achieve the peace so vitally needed for our work: to make an example by sending the long overdue Halil to the provinces. There are legal grounds enough. The present arrangement in the school is so well ordered and the plans for next year's extension so promising that it would be a pity to see it all destroyed by the shortsighted squabbling of a few ignoramuses. The greatest danger in my opinion is that Prätorius will one day lose heart and take advantage of the favour in which he is held by the Reichsmusikkammer to jump at some brilliant post back here. What would then happen in Ankara I have no idea— I at any rate could hardly summon up courage to start again from the beginning against the whole morass of resistance, stupidity, and bad will. It is therefore absolutely vital to keep him in a good mood, and the other German musicians like- wise. The demand for musicians is so great here and salaries have risen to such a level that it is becoming increasingly difficult to find good people willing to serve abroad.

As regards Necil himself, it seems his complaints against me are that my orga- nization plans are bad and everything I am doing is done just to satisfy my own ego. The worthiness of the plans can be judged only after they have taken effect. This can already be seen in the orchestra, which suggests the plans are not all that wretched. And the reason we have achieved little in the school so far lies, apart from the unhappy accommodation, teaching, and other conditions, mainly in the misman- agement of past years, for which our leading complainant himself bears a fair pro- portion of the blame. I should certainly not have thought he would choose to attack us in the very area in which he himself failed one hundred percent in the teaching plans, leaving us to suffer the consequences of his directorial activities for another three years at least. Regretfully I must deny our friend Necil any expertise in vocal and instrumental training. The little bit of cello playing he has of necessity acquired does not entitle him to judge these matters anymore than the four years in which, as director, he did nothing for the school. He would have had plenty of opportunity to put his wisdom at the disposal of his pupils, so why did he not do so? He can safely leave it to me to judge which instruments the pupils should study and how much time they should spend with them; I have been long enough in my profes- sion to understand these things better than a man who has poked his nose into

European schools only very briefly and is today at about the same level of musical education as one of my many not yet fully developed pupils. The recorder appears recently to have assumed an important role in the heads of our knowledgeable protesters. On that subject I can say that here in Germany I was one of the first to promote the revival of this ancient instrument, and I had already played old and written new music for recorders before these youngsters had ever heard the instrument's name. So, if Necil wants to propagate the recorder, he had better first sit down and learn to play it, so that he will at least know what he is propagating. To what extent the recorder will be useful for teaching purposes in Turkey (the preference for this instrument lies not solely in its easy playability—in our case it is connected with a host of historical and cultural associations; that can be seen in the fact that the instrument has gained no acceptance in Italy and France, for example) will of course be gone into next year, once we are settled in the new house along with the institute, and, with the fresh intake of students, will no longer be confined to working on the reconditioning of ancient ruins. So do not let yourself be talked into anything by people, Europeans included, who know nothing about these things. The only one of our musicians who has had practical experience of recorder playing and who has not just gained a "good idea" of it in the role of a more or less interested onlooker, is Zuckmayer, and I began discussing the question of recorder teaching with him long before our clever Dicks got the idea of using the recorder as a weapon against us.

The fact that Necil accuses me of egoism convinces me that his campaign against me and my plans stems not from deceit, but from pure stupidity. I could without a doubt have found more comfortable ways of satisfying any egoistic urges I may have than by providing him with an opera subject, for example, or in general labouring not exactly rewardingly with such underhand firework dealers as him and his comrades. My only egoism is to spend as much time as possible within my own four walls composing. Even Necil will have to admit that there is little chance of that in Ankara.

It would not be necessary to expend so many words on the undertakings of a still very immature musician if it were not for my fear that he might take advantage of your lack of knowledge in musical matters and succeed in making a breach in one corner of the solid wall of your trust in me. If, while I am not in Ankara, you rely on Prätorius and, in the case of specialized subjects, on the individual specialists associated with him, you will be better advised than by your young men in the grip of passion and hopes of personal advantage.

The time for making weighty decisions regarding developments and the various ways of dealing with them will come when I am back in Ankara. All the same, it would be a good thing if, by energetic intervention, you could restore the peace without which there can be no progress in our work.

While in Istanbul on my return from Ankara, I saw a performance of Lear and a Turkish comedy in Muhsin Ertugrul's theatre. It was not of course the Burgtheater or the State Theatre in Berlin, but the zeal and goodwill of all participants, together with acting that, for all its awkwardness, clearly did not lack talent, were so impressive that I found myself confirmed in the opinion I formed at the very earliest stages of establishing a theatre in Ankara: that anyone thinking of presenting plays without this man is guilty of the worst possible foolishness. On the following day, I came on him preparing a letter to the ministry expressing his intention of giving up his work at the school in Ankara. As the inevitable outcome of such a step, I foresaw subversive activity on the part of Muhsin's supporters, a progressive widening of the gap between Turkish and European views on art, and finally the collapse of the structure we have so laboriously built. I persuaded him not to send his letter, but to put his views in person to the ministry and to the prime minister. I told him that in all justifiable demands he would find in me a helper whose sole concern was for progress in the development of Turkish art. He held back at first, then poured out his heart to me and complained of many things, most of them similar to those from which we ourselves suffered sorely in our joint work with the theatre school. When he declared that, in Braun and Kuchenbuch, Ebert had brought to Ankara the worst people it was possible to find, I told him that I could not pass judgment on Kuchenbuch, since I knew nothing of his study subject. I reserved my opinion on Braun, saying that, like all previous newcomers, he must first be given time to settle down. After that, one could see what he is capable of. We were entirely of one mind that it is fatal for any study centre if every few months some "big shot" comes along to whip up the students and the school spirit, then for the rest of the time they have to work with reserve teachers, so to speak. Prätorius has now confirmed what I saw for myself during the few days I observed Braun in the school: that he has adapted himself excellently to the prevailing circumstances and performs his task very well. In addition, he is easy to work with, and even in tricky problems of joint work between the conservatory and drama school there are no signs of friction, anymore than there are between me and the German musicians with whom I work. It seems to me that he is just the man for our school. Without wishing to interfere in the affairs of the drama school, I should see it as the best solution if you were to keep Braun there on a permanent basis and entrust the direction of the drama school to him. Then it will be up to him to come to an understanding with Muhsin, and I am convinced that he will achieve this with ease, whereas Ebert, because of his character and his previous clumsiness, will never succeed. [. . .]

The theory teachers allowed for in the new budget cannot be got by the means you suggested. The man in Istanbul (I have forgotten his name) is, according to Necil, completely unsuitable and, since here Necil's own interests are not involved, I have no reason to doubt his judgment. The other man of whom I spoke — Azizes

Mann—is not yet ready for it. A foreign teacher will therefore have to come for the conservatory, and yet another for the institute, though this one can also be used for other purposes. It now all depends on whether you write to me early enough, giving me permission to look around. In the first place, such people are difficult to find, and in the second, I shall be going off to America again in a month's time, so the man must be found before then, since he will of course have to sit down at once to learn Turkish. I feel you somewhat overestimate the dangers of a theory teacher who does not speak Turkish very well. By now I have become fairly familiar with the attitude of the Turks towards their own language; I am also aware that our dear friends will concentrate with bliss on this point when their attacks on the newcomer's artistic activities prove to be in vain, but I also have experience enough of the willingness of Turkish students to make themselves understood with those who do not yet speak very well. Prätorius and Zuckmayer, Schaffrath as well, have demonstrated that with application and persistence one can manage very well to communicate without making too many mistakes, and a theory lesson is after all not a lecture on the most intimate subtleties of Turkish life and Turkish customs. If I receive news in time, a couple of theory teachers speaking good Turkish will be able to start work in the autumn. [. . .]

    Your already very Turkified

    Paul Hindemith

Hindemith's letters to his wife during his second visit to the United States were cast in the same diary form he had used during his first visit. He arrived in New York with the liner *Deutschland* on 18 February 1938 to undertake a short tour of both playing and conducting engagements.

    In his first concert on 23 February, at Bryn Mawr College near Philadelphia, Hindemith was joined by the pianist Lydia Hoffmann-Behrendt, who had taught in Berlin before she emigrated to the United States in 1934. This concert consisted of works by Hindemith for viola and piano, alone and together.

    On the following day, he travelled to Boston for a concert conducted by Serge Koussevitzky. This performance included the Concert Music for string orchestra and brass instruments, Opus 50, written for the fiftieth anniversary of the Boston Symphony Orchestra in 1931, and the Kammermusik No. 5 for viola and orchestra, written in 1927.

To Gertrud Hindemith   [Boston] 24 February

    [. . .] The piece [the Concert Music] pleased me as a composition very much. I was pleasantly surprised, for I scarcely remembered it. It is serious, but at the same time very fresh, sounds clear throughout and not at all ugly. After it we rehearsed the old viola concerto—I very much on show, since the nonparticipating members of the orchestra, and in particular the entire viola contingent, were sitting in front of me with piano scores and solo parts watching my fingers. I had been expecting that and had practised hard on the preceding days, so I was in good form. However, that didn't prevent me, after the good score of the Concert Music for string orchestra and brass instruments, from finding this piece overly ornate and overloaded in spite of the small number of instruments. On top of that, I found it hard to summon up the energy, after the 90 times I had previously had to play it, to cope with the many difficulties of the solo part. Still, with a bit of effort I managed it. It is much too difficult, for the orchestra too, though the people here played it flawlessly—they really are, as I told you last year, the best orchestra in the world. [. . .]

25 February

Today was a real day of battles. I had arranged with Sanromá to rehearse in the morning. We rehearsed the viola d'amore sonata and the old viola sonata with piano very thoroughly. He is such an outstanding musician and as a pianist so splendid technically that it is pure joy to play with him. We have arranged to play together often next year. Following the rehearsal I just had time to change and to eat my lunch before the concert began.

The "Concert Music" went excellently, as I had expected after yesterday's rehearsal. Good success with the audience. I was also in good shape and gave an impressive performance. Nadia Boulanger was there at the beginning, greeted me with the usual embraces, but had to leave after the first piece, since she had something to do in Providence. She was very enthusiastic. [. . .]

After the concert I did some more rehearsing with Sanromá, and then once again there was just time to return to the hotel, change and have dinner. One of the violists had promised to pick me up in his car and drive me to Cambridge, where the next concert had been arranged at Harvard University. He came rather too late, for there had been a sudden snowfall and progress could hardly be made through the streets. So we came on the hall patiently waiting. Still, what use would it have been to me if I'd been punctual? Mr. Piston was pacing up and down in gloomy despair, shaking his head and muttering repeatedly: "No Hindemith and no piano." There was indeed no piano there. I was seized by such a fit of laughter that I had to sit down on the steps for quite a while. It was never discovered exactly why no grand piano had been delivered, apparently no one was to blame. I persuaded the distraught man at least to telephone the piano firm to ask whether one was on its way, and in the meantime I intended to make a start with the solo viola sonata. When I then made the curious and surprising request for a desk to be brought on to the stage, panic broke out all round: there was no desk available far and wide. Eventually amid laughter and curses I sent out a scout, who returned after a while with a snow-covered desk from somewhere in the vicinity. I then played my sonata. Meanwhile it had been established that there was no prospect of a piano arriving.

Piston wanted to send the whole pack home, but I said on no account, and after a lot of palaver I discovered there was another hall to which we could emigrate, though it was only moderately heated. So the numerous members of the audience marched through snow and slush and we continued our concert in reduced circumstances, though with an overplus of pianos (2). We both played finely. To console us for our previous pianoless state, we were told it was no surprise to anyone here, since already once before a pianist had found himself confronted with a grand piano that lacked both legs and pedals. Afterwards I had a drink with a few musicians in the bar of my hotel, then took myself off to bed to rest my limbs after the day's eventful programme.

27 February

I journeyed with Sanromá to Newhaven—3½ hours—where today's concert was to take place. A young man I knew in Berlin, [Klaus] Liepmann, met us. Yale is a big group of buildings in imported Tudor-English style, and wherever one goes, one has the sure feeling that the people have no idea what to do with the money at their disposal. On the musical front anyway very little seems so far to have happened, and so youngster Liepmann, who formerly in no case figured among the highly prized top flight of European musical culture, is here a big name already, since he has founded a student orchestra, which he conducts for better or worse and mainly worse. I heard a rehearsal in which the pack of apprentices struggled very nobly with a few of my pieces for string orchestra and the Music of Mourning. They played just as school orchestras back home play, and they obviously enjoyed themselves. They started the concert in the evening with these pieces, and [Hugo] Kortschak, who is a violin teacher here, played the necessary solos tidily and modestly. Then Sanromá and I ascended the platform less modestly and let fly with vigour. I first with the old solo viola sonata, then he coaxed the third sonata out of the piano in a way that made it sound like something, and to end with we reeled off the piano-viola sonata. The audience went mad—much to their astonishment, for some of them we met at a small reception after the concert said of themselves that they were notorious everywhere for their cool reserve. [. . .]

Hindemith spent the next two days in New York before setting off for Chicago in the Twentieth Century Limited express train.

1 March

[. . .] One enters its hallowed interior via a carpeted platform, views with astonishment the saloon car, reading car, bar and observation car, the writing saloon, and the hairdresser's shop, but one soon gets the hang of it, all the more so since the sleeping compartments have the by now quite familiar look—but then one is a bit surprised that the traveller is not also offered Roman-Irish steam baths, cinema, swimming bath, bowling alley, rifle range, and other corporeal and spiritual <u>refresh-ments</u>. The restaurant car was first-rate. I consumed the lavish <u>Chief's Suggestion</u> and then sank down in an armchair in the one <u>parlourcar</u> that had no radio and stretched myself out almost as long as an original inhabitant. A proper traveller would now be switching on the entire range of apparatuses in this capital train and making all the white, yellow, brown, and black-skinned attendants hop. I was tired, however, and did not treat myself to the services of either radio set, typewriter, dictaphone, secre-tary, or nurse but retired to my comfortable bed, where shortly before going to sleep I was able to establish that the distinguished driver of so terribly aristocratic a train also belongs to the widespread family of jerkers, jolters, and butters.

2 March

At nine in the morning, the aforementioned limited twentieth century arrived in Chicago. For a while before that, however, one passes through parts of the city so hideous that one wonders how living creatures can vegetate there. The never-ending drizzle, armed with the entire American array of cars, lights, advertisements, life, and traffic, fought a hard battle for the visitor's favourable opinion, but all in vain: the impression of an abysmal, ignominious disgrace could not be dispelled. In New York the hideousness is to some extent softened by a tinge of magnificence, but here in its rawness it is quite simply hideous. Not even the magnificently designed Michigan Avenue (despite that grotesquely patched-up group of houses), nor the car drive along the splendid lakeside can make up for it. One could imagine that to the inhabitants of this terrible city hinterland it must seem like salvation to be slaughtered in an Armour or Swift factory and converted into <u>corned beef</u>. But for that they would certainly not be chosen, for who could expect so miserable a pasturage to result in anything even halfway eatable?

I went straight to the rehearsals and spent the whole morning rehearsing the Symphonic Dances. The orchestra—not nearly as good as the Bostonians—worked hard and gradually became enthusiastic, egged on by my energetic conducting wiles. I had lunch with Lange and then walked to the still very elegant Drake Hotel, which differed from the previous year only through the absence of those young ducks swimming so importantly in the <u>lobby</u>. [. . .]

3 March

Rehearsals occupied the whole morning. I began again with the "Dances," which went very nicely from the start. Then we rehearsed "Der Schwanendreher" thor-oughly; the orchestra still remembered it quite well from last year, and Lange did his stuff respectably too. To end with, after Mozart's E-flat Major Symphony, they rehearsed that ancient old Kammermusik [No. 1] of mine with the siren. One wonders why people made such a fuss about this piece at the time. It is not at all badly written, and there is nothing, apart from a few harmonic and melodic teething troubles, to upset innocent souls. It is not exactly refined, and the extravagant use of percussion etc. was certainly a concession to the prevailing (lack of) taste at that time. But, good Lord, one only needs to look at all the crap that is being produced today in this chemically pure cultural atmosphere of ours, to realize how thousand times worse in regard to technique, invention, musicality, and even character it all is, compared with this not very important piece. And someone who is bothered by a siren would find much wider scope for his indignation in wind machines and bleating sheep. People here are not so malicious. In the evening the piece was a great success (rightly so, for the performance was very good)—in spite of, or because of, the elderly female population from which concert audiences are recruited here as in all other American cities (in which connection it is open to doubt whether it is permissible to bring together two such differing conceptions as recruits and dolled-up crones). They probably felt themselves transported back to youthful times of unfulfilled desires: when the siren shrieked one could literally hear the rusted bones rattling. I played like an old violist who had gone through many fires unscathed, and the dances also went very well. Huge applause. Afterwards there was a short and meaningless meeting with old Stock, the conductor here, in whose shadow the tender and insufficiently manured plant Lange is making next to no progress towards a modest place in the sun. [. . .]

11 March

Detroit appears to be one of the most charming of cities: anything more expressionless and insignificant can hardly ever have been seen, and one is used to many things over here. My erstwhile pupil Heiden came to the hotel, and we went for a short walk in fine weather. Since we were passing his house, we went inside. I wanted to say howdy to his wife and see his new black spaniel named "Steinway." Cola was in bed with some long-drawn-out female complaint. The little 3-month-old dog, a handsome creature, couldn't contain himself for delight and left puddles everywhere. A saxophonist came and played, with Bernhard at the piano, the latter's new sonata. It was an amazingly good piece, the best piece of work so far from any of my pupils. Very nicely inventive, technically tidy and, apart from 3 blunders of form, flawlessly written. A bit overloaded still, but it is just a matter of time before the ballast is thrown overboard. When I think how pushed around and twisted the boy once was, and what hard work it was to straighten him out with kindness, strictness, anger, and patience, I feel really proud to have drawn something truly upstanding and serviceable out of such damaged material. [. . .]

A leading member of the AMP staff with whom Hindemith became particularly friendly during this trip was Karl Bauer, who had emigrated from Mannheim in

Germany. The play on his name in the following letter was based on Franz von Suppé's well-known operetta *Dichter und Bauer* (Poet and Peasant).

1 April

Travel preparations. I went <u>down town</u> with Voigt to pay my taxes at the tax office and to fetch my <u>sailing permit</u>. At noon I had a short farewell lunch with my relatives and then repaired to the Pubs [Publishers] to prepare a couple of April-fool jokes. With Indian ink I drew an exact likeness of the "B.Schott Söhne" letterhead, and then, over Willy Strecker's forged signature, informed Bauer that from now on all copies of "Dichter und Bauer" published by Schott would be marketed under the title "Dichter und Karl Bauer" in recognition of his services to the publishing house and in particular to the composer P. H.; agreement had already been reached with Suppé's heirs, and they would like now to have his consent. Of course, the fooling was obvious and, after a few minutes of astonishment, Bauer saw what was going on and who was behind it.

The second, even more obvious joke had very different results. I arranged for a letter from Hamburg (with a forged postage stamp) to arrive for Tompkins with the afternoon mail. Tompkins is in charge of the department in the Pubs that supplies hotels and restaurants with music over telephone lines; it goes under the name of "Muzak." A firm called "Transmus" informed him that their representative Faulhaber had sent them a glowing report on "Muzak," and the establishment of a branch in Germany to relay it via trans-Atlantic cable was being proposed. The Reich government was prepared to cooperate and the cable company was also in agreement. I thought Tompkins would a moment later emerge laughing. Not a bit of it. I had invited Tompkins, Bauer, and Strunk with their wives to dinner at the Seymour in the evening, and, since again there was no mention of the letter, I asked Bauer whether nothing had been said about it in the office. He had heard nothing, so, fearing some silly complication might arise, I began to uncover the jokes: Bauer had to give an account of his letter, and Tompkins almost killed himself laughing at this April fool. When I then asked him whether he had not also received a letter, he could think of none. Only when I mentioned Hamburg did he slowly begin to realize. And now it turned out that, on that very afternoon, "Muzak" had held a conference with their directors, financiers, and lawyers, in which an English project had been discussed. While they were still basking in the sure prospect of opening up international connections, my Transmus proposal arrived and gave added strength to their grandiose plans. They began at once to discuss how the German affair could be arranged, and it was only the earlier arrival of closing time that prevented a detailed programme being cabled at once to Transmus A.G., formerly Dumbeutel and Sohn (address: Hamburg, Im Loch 175). As a result of these revelations, our dinner went off very merrily, and Tompkins as Muzak-Transmus Combine had to put up with a great deal of chaff. Finally, to satisfy the curiosity of my guests, I fetched my viola d'amour from my room and played them a few lines.

Hindemith travelled back to Europe on the liner *Hamburg* on 2 April. He went to Zurich to attend the first performance of his opera *Mathis der Maler*, which was given in the City Theatre there on 28 May 1938.

The ballet on which he was working with Léonide Massine in Monte Carlo was *Nobilissima Visione* (American title: *Saint Francis*).

The "enlarged Boepple choruses" comprised the four pieces sung by Boepple's Madrigal Singers in Washington in 1937 plus the song "True Love," completed in 1938; the whole collection was eventually published by AMP under the title *Five Songs on Old Texts*.

The book of exercises for the "Unterweisung": Part I of *Unterweisung im Tonsatz* (*The Craft of Musical Composition*) was published in German by the Schott Verlag in 1937 with the subtitle *Theoretischer Teil* (*Theoretical Part*). Hindemith was about to start work on Part II, which was eventually published with the subtitle *Übungsbuch für den zwei-stimmigen Satz* (*Exercises in Two-Part Writing*).

To Ernest R. Voigt   Savoy Hotel, Zurich
                                                    7 June 1938

Beloved Pub, here at last is the long promised letter. Don't be cross with me for keeping you waiting so long, you can imagine how much new work tied me down immediately on my return. I spent only a week in Berlin but composed a clarinet quartet and three cello pieces during that time, then stayed a few days (also composing) at home in Frankfurt, then came here to supervise the first orchestra rehearsals of my opera. After that came 2 weeks in Monte Carlo—intensive work with the Russian ballet (they have actually all joined together and now form a Russian-Polish-French-English-American conglomerate of some 120 dancers and 15 directors). The performance of my ballet will not be until the middle of July in London, when I shall conduct it. We set quite a lot on its feet in Monte Carlo—or, if you prefer, we set their feet on the ballet—and it promises to be gorgeous.

We followed that with a bus drive through the French Alps in pouring rain and landed up here at the height of rehearsals. The first performance was on 28 May. People came from all over the world, tremendous interest and brilliant success, which was almost more pronounced even at the second performance yesterday. The piece seems not at all bad, and all begetters and midwives masculini generis, from composer and publishers to the entire theatre personnel, were highly delighted and satisfied. [. . .] If I go on to tell you that last week we made a lovely walking tour through the Swiss Jura, in the course of which I got thoroughly sunburnt, and that tomorrow we are going 2000 metres up for a 4-week holiday in the Valais, you will be brought more or less up to date on my personal fortunes.

In the meantime there has been, within the framework of a seemingly disastrous music festival in Düsseldorf, an exhibition of "degenerate music," in which an entire booth was devoted to me. Evidently, however, the whole thing was such a fiasco that not even German newspapers were permitted to report on it. After enduring a week of protests and a reduction in size caused by the withdrawal of composers who, being in possession of the party badge, could not be called degenerate and others who were washed white again by the intervention of foreign embassies, etc., the auspicious institute finally closed its doors.

Now to our business affairs. [. . .] For next year I expect to have the following new pieces for concert use: a concert suite from "Nobilissima Visione," a viola sonata with piano, a violin or cello concerto (that will get its turn in the autumn) and, beside these, the aforementioned novelties of course, a sonata for bassoon and piano, the enlarged Boepple choruses, a handful of songs, and possibly scenes from Mathis. In the coming weeks I hope to begin the book of exercises for the "Unterweisung." [. . .]

And how are you? I have been a bit worried about you, and I wish that you too would now take 4 weeks off and regain your strength in the mountains. [. . .] Greetings to the entire Pub, from the massive Bauer down to little Miss Jenkins. And for you a particularly warm greeting, from my wife too.

Yours,

Paul H.

Supplement for the prospective purchasers of Transmus.

In the oceanic museum in Monte Carlo there are deep-sea fishes which carry a long cord with an electric lighting organ attached. Why not fill the ocean depths with "Muzak" programmes, without which life is surely somewhat monotonous in those damp regions? The antennae of the aforementioned fishes could surely be adapted easily enough for transmission purposes; any technical difficulties there might be could at any rate be overcome. Admittedly, all we at present know about the musical receptivity of the denizens of the deep can only be based on divers wearing the latest pressure-resistant deep-sea diving suits. As far as all other living creatures down below are concerned, it can doubtless be assumed that, for purposes of musical training, they have at their disposal pianos and other musical instruments from sunken vessels. There may well be a distinct imbalance, however, between the numbers of available instruments and such fishes as are interested in music. It is suggested that every effort should therefore be made to bring "Muzak" concert programmes to these poor deprived creatures, in which connection careful consideration must be given to adapting the choice of pieces to the nature of the audience. For pieces such as "My parrot eats no hard-boiled eggs" only minimal comprehension is likely, owing to unfamiliarity with either parrots or hard-boiled eggs, while with others, for example "This will make the flounders flounder," it is perhaps necessary to pay regard to possible hurt feelings on the part of the species thus addressed, that is to say, deep-sea "Muzak" consumers. Should, despite these drawbacks, the "Muzak" directorship be minded to turn their attention to this new and immeasurable field of activity, I should be happy to approach "Transmus," indisputably the first and only concern dealing with oceanic transmissions, and enter into negotiations with Herr Dumbeutel. I await more detailed instructions.

On behalf of the tele-headed fishes most closely involved,

P.H.

Nobilissima Visione, Hindemith's ballet on the subject of St. Francis of Assisi, was first performed by the Ballet Russe de Monte Carlo at the Drury Lane Theatre, London, on 21 July 1938, with the composer conducting. The rival company, the Ballet Russe du Col. de Basil, was performing at the Covent Garden Opera at the same time.

To Ernest R. Voigt   [On a journey from London to Berlin]
                                                    24 July 1938

Dear friend, I received your letter in the loveliest of summer holiday resorts, high up in the mountains, with the Matterhorn outside the window and Alpine meadows covered in flowers. I didn't reply to it at once, because I wanted first to see how the events in London turned out. In the meantime the ballet has been launched, and I am now on my way home.

The Monte Carlo Ballet, which is completing its season in spite of competition from the other Russian touring ballet (Basil's), is now very good in terms of dancing, and it is having very great success with its new pieces. "Nobilissima Visione" (that is my ballet) is not of course an eye-catcher in the old style and is not exactly full of sparkling wit, but all the same it makes a fine impression, with all the trappings of success that a composer greedy for recognition could wish. Even the earthshaking [Sol] Hurok was so impressed that he pressed me to his smart businessman's heart and is insisting on my conducting the piece myself in New York and surrounding villages.

And so we come to the reply to your cable. The ballet company begins its tour in October in New York and wants to start straightaway with my piece. Hurok is therefore ordering me to come to America around this time. This seems to me unnecessary and to put a heavy strain on the ballet's budget without increasing the takings to any great degree on account of my name. In any case it could only be a flying visit of 14 days or so, since I shouldn't have anything "regular" to do until much later, and I neither will nor can spend the whole time sitting around in New York. I have explained all this to the people in London with wagging forefinger, but in the end Hurok must know whether he wants to pay for it, and if in his enthusiasm he sticks to his decision, I may possibly turn up over there very shortly. But this has nothing to do with our plans. The only question is whether the gaps in my itinerary can be set against the gaps in the ballet programme in such a way that one or two conducting engagements could be fitted in without any trouble. I have not discussed this with the people over here, because I don't want to make a nuisance of myself and because it seems the route of their tour is not yet fully fixed. I feel it might be best for you to ask Hurok about it after his re-enthronement in New York (probably in September)—or, if I really am to come over in October, to leave it open till then.

So, as our plan stands at the moment, it seems that my concert arrangements will be from the beginning of February to the end of March, that is to say, they will take up about the same amount of time as the previous tour. The original plans did, I know, point in a rather different direction, but I should be glad if it could now all be arranged within these time limits. In April "Mathis" is being given a concert performance in London, and the Zurich Opera will give a guest performance of it in Amsterdam, and in both cases I have been asked to attend. And I should much like to have some time for my own work before the tour begins, all the more since, if things go right, I shall be leaving Berlin and hoping to land up in Switzerland. (Say nothing to anybody about this, I want it to go through as unobtrusively as possible). Since responses to your offers are not arriving in any great numbers, it seems to me that it should be possible to keep within these dates. I feel a bit sorry for all the work you are putting in on my behalf, but, first, I know that the demand for my wares over there will never reach the level of sweet popular songs or Gordon's Gin; and second, I shouldn't at all enjoy being exploited by a hundred-percent trafficker in human flesh and marketed <u>attractively branded and labelled</u>. So, if you are not sick of all the trouble, I would ask you to continue along the same lines as before, always with the understanding that you will stop work as soon as you wish to be quit of it. [. . .]

I shall not be going to Turkey in the autumn. So far I have heard nothing from there, which may be due either to their customary sloth, the summer heat, or a music budget lower than expected. If an enquiry comes, I shall have to turn it down, partly because of my house removal, partly on account of Hurok's plans, and finally because I should like to find out for once how it feels to be allowed to spend a few months composing without interruption.

It is a shame that Mr. Tompkins let the Transmus project slip through his fingers; how lovely it would have been if the ballet performance in London could have been delivered to the entire range of Muzak outlets—even at the risk of the tele-head transmitting station's not yet being in service, since in the nature of things negotiations cannot be conducted in this remote and watery district as smoothly as in 25 West 45th. But a new and even greater opportunity will surely crop up in time for next April! [. . .]

Hindemith had now resolved to leave Germany and settle in Switzerland. After a visit to Zurich for further performances of Mathis der Maler he went with his wife to Venice to attend the music festival at which he was to conduct his music for the ballet Nobilissima Visione. After a leisurely tour through Italy, they returned to Switzerland to take possession of their new home, an Alpine villa at Blusch near Sierre in the canton of the Valais.

To Willy Strecker   [Sonvico, Lugano]
                                                  20 September 1938

Dear Willy, today is a somewhat quiet morning for the first time, so you will get a report on the past 2 weeks right away. When I left after speaking to you on the telephone, I did not quite reach my destination: at the Baden station in Basel I was sent back again, because an aliens' police stamp in my passport, which until now had not been necessary and which I had consequently completely overlooked, had expired a few days earlier (such things can actually happen to old and canny travellers!). So there I sat in Freiburg, frustratingly held up still further by the non-working Saturday afternoon and Sunday, and waited together with Chief Inspector Kopp for word from the Berlin police. It arrived on Monday and I could set off again, this time with success, but it left a slightly bitter aftertaste, for my newly gleaming aliens' stamp was not even noticed. [. . .]

On Tuesday Gertrud arrived, on Wednesday I was in Zurich. Mathis is coming up again on 5 November. I spent a whole morning with the theatre's holy men, discussing the reshaping of the sixth scene; it seems that they grasped the idea and intend to start again from scratch. I shall be able to deal with it in good time. On the following day we unloaded our main luggage in our new quarters and then went off to Venice.

Despite the overcrowding it was as splendid as ever. The music festival was a bit of a muddle, and the preceding concerts made no kind of impression, either for or against, on the visitors. [. . .] Molinari conducted the Rome orchestra in a magnificently played retrospective concert of the past few decades: Busoni, Respighi, Ravel, and Stravinsky—his Sacre played with a lightness, perfection, and loyalty to the score that the work has probably never experienced before. Yet the evening was somewhat curious; one sat there rather like the participants in that legendary meal at which an English archaeologist served his guests rice pudding made of five-thousand-year-old Egyptian grain. Of course the composers have not yet reached this ash-grey age, nor the works acquired the patina of charming mummies, yet one sat there, not very deeply moved and on the whole surprised that such extravagant efforts should be made just in order to shout the composer's more than usually divergent private opinions overemphatically in one's ears. It is utterly ridiculous to dismiss it all with the term cultural bolshevism; it is even superfluous, for I am certain that in a few years' time nobody will in any case find the way through to these things, since they lead in a direction into which they can be followed only if one is familiar to some extent with the musicological and other conditions prevailing at the time of composition and the personal peculiarities of the composer himself. For my piece I had rehearsals enough, and the orchestra played willingly, patiently, and well. That evening it was the last work in a generous dish of tutti frutti: Lualdi, Honegger, Walton, Marinuzzi. Honegger (a small nocturne) got a very good reception, whereas by far the most respectable piece—Walton's viola concerto, conducted by him and violed not quite adequately by Mr. Riddle—made little impression on the Italians; such things are just not in their line. The two Italian lollipops, which I expected to run off with all the plaudits, did nothing of the kind; that was left to the "Visione." The piece sounds splendid in its concert arrangement. It can be left just as it is, though I must ask you to have the printing errors listed on the enclosed piece of paper removed from the parts; they should then be free of all errors. The ballet will be performed at the next Maggio musicale in Florence. A contract has already been signed with Massine, and I shall conduct it.

After Venice we extensively enjoyed Padua, where, after the already familiar Giotto, Mantegna was for us a very big discovery. In Ferrara we saw an Italian world hardly known to us before now, and we then moved on to Ravenna, which we once again explored thoroughly. On Sunday morning to Forli with a rather disappointing Melozzo exhibition, in which there were about as many Melozzos as there are Schott sons in the publishing house of Schott, and in the evening we landed back in Switzerland. We shall be staying here another week, until we can move into our house on Wednesday. We are hoping to find some remote spot in which I hope to finish the preparatory work on the second theory book.

And that's it. I enclose the only two reviews on Venice that were to be found. Also an article by [Alfred] Einstein about the theory book that appeared in "Mass und Wert" (a Mann-Lion-etc. periodical). It is not of any importance, all the less so since he hasn't read it properly, mixes everything up, and doesn't get the point. However, he means well; and I am almost proud when these learned intellectuals find it possible to apply phrases like "splendid word," "well expressed," and "happy formulations" to an amateur scribbler like me.

Farewell for now, and warmest greetings to you and the entire holy family.

21.9.

I waited for today's mail, but there was nothing in it worth mentioning. In the *Frankfurter Zeitung* I read a detailed review of the Venice festival, in which the "Visione" was not mentioned at all. By current standards that is hardly surprising—it just proves to me that the decision I have now made was entirely right. A change in the obstinate insistence on a completely idiotic system can hardly be expected in the near future. There are only two things worth aiming for: good music and a clean conscience, and both of these are now being taken care of. Looked at from this point of view, all our previous efforts were a waste of time—and when I see yet another shit-pants being taken seriously, as happened last year, when it is of no interest to anybody what he says, good or bad, about a work—or even if he ignores it entirely—then retrospectively one feels a lump of regret in one's throat, particularly when one sees these insignificant figures dwindling in their final nakedness to almost less than nothing against a background of musical people in general. [. . .]

Urgent request once again: Tell nobody where we are. We shall have no peace otherwise. We are meeting all kinds of people here and are also saying nothing to anybody.

To Ernest R. Voigt   Sierre (Valais)

Poste restante

10 November 1938

Dear friend, many thanks for your long letter and the New York newspapers. It seems that the ballet was a good success, even if I find it a bit uncanny that everybody should be blowing a euphonious trumpet of unqualified praise. I am very glad that I was not there, for it would really have been the height of extravagance to have come over just for four performances and to wag the stick on a few occasions. Hurok the flesh dealer knew of course that, as far as time was concerned, I could have come, for we chatted long enough about it in London. The reason is rather that he does not enjoy having anything much to do with me, because to him I seem a bit sinister on account of my undisguised contempt for dealers in human flesh, yet on the other hand he cannot deny that his ballet horses run better when doped with my "Visione" than with any other kind of boosting pill up their a——s. Well, I am glad it went as well as possible.

The plans for the concerts in February and March are exactly as I envisaged them. You really have no need to apologize for having achieved so little. It is quite enough—I know only too well how much work such things require, and naturally it is not possible to achieve for somewhat demanding modern music as much as for a well-trained musical lion. It is fully enough for me, I am satisfied and beg you also to be a little pleased by and proud of the results of your exertions. But write to me soon about any programme wishes you may have, so that I can deal with them in good time. Meanwhile I'll look into the shipping prospects and then write again shortly. If Hurok or Massine wish to use me here and there during any gaps in my tour I am of course willing.

The revival of "Mathis" has now taken place in Zurich. Thanks to some fresh castings and with the aid of one completely restaged scene, it was much better than in spring; the success was again extraordinarily great. I enclose a press clipping, from which you will get some idea of how it went. I was there for only a few days, I find life in the "great world" no longer very congenial since I have become fully rusticated up here.

You grieve for me and my fate—nothing could be less deserved: if I were pious, I would go down on my knees daily for having landed up here. It is the loveliest spot on earth: 1400 metres up, meadows and woods glowing now in the full range of colours, a little village of 15 to 20 houses, cowbells, fruit trees, a big vegetable garden, a fine little country villa with room for both of us and his lordship the dog. A piano is here, some of our music, books and instruments from Berlin. We have bright sunshine all day long, a view down the loveliest of all river valleys, the Rhone valley, opposite us the highest Alpine peaks in gleaming white, behind us the southern chain of the Bernese Alps. One works in the house, saws and chops wood, builds and repairs, cultivates the garden, picks fruit and berries, walks for hours and within a single day is on top of the nearest high summits. And composing goes as well as anywhere. So envy me rather! If not driven by force from these surroundings, I shall be here for a long time to come. Willy Strecker stayed with us recently for 3 days, which we spent walking, talking, and drinking. He was entranced.

This time I have no information regarding new Transmus campaigns. The demand for music, particularly from overseas, is extremely small up here. Best wait till everything is snowed up, then perhaps new possibilities will emerge.

Meanwhile I send you my best wishes. In spite of all the beauties here I feel something like a slight yearning for you and your little cubbyhole. Well, I shall soon be sitting at your writing desk again and maybe decorating your telephone table with another little four-footer. [. . .]

Fondest wishes,

Your P.H.

Hindemith left Europe for his third visit to the United States on 28 January 1939, travelling on the Dutch liner *Volendam*.

Old Shatterhand is a character in the popular novels about American Indians written by the German author Karl May.

Der Stürmer was a vulgar Jew-baiting weekly periodical published in Nuremberg by the Nazi gauleiter Julius Streicher.

To Gertrud Hindemith [On board the liner Volendam]
28 January 1939

Beloved lion, it was sad to see my good Wapuff, otherwise so bold in the face of all situations, left standing there so dejectedly on the platform. I only hope that the life and bustle of the world city Basel cheered him up a little and that the Shrovetide play also helped. The train journey was quiet, overheated, and completely undisturbed, except for an old Dutch couple who, however, made themselves scarce in Strassburg.

After Longuyon there was something that called itself Voiture Buffet, but apart from that was ugly, not very clean, and only moderately tasty. I made use of it and then more or less dozed away the slow journey to Lille. There the world's most nose-in-the-air porteur accompanied me to the Royal Hotel, which was closed except for the night porter and a waiter stacking chairs. Only with some difficulty did I manage to obtain a half-bottle of Perrier, and it was just as difficult to convince the simpleminded night porter that he should wake me at a quarter to six. The hotel had all the attributes of a Royal, electric door locks, instructions to the guests under glass-topped tables, buzzer telephone, and all other ingenious refinements. For the rest it was hideously shabby, dirty, and it smelt of wee-wee. However, I was tired enough not to let anything worry me. My eyes took in only the clock on the wall opposite the bed, and then I fell fast asleep, though not before setting my new alarm clock as an extra precaution. I woke around 1:25 and realized that, relative to all the church clocks in Lille, my alarm was 20 minutes fast. I was not prepared to let it cheat me out of those 20 minutes but was also too lazy to adjust it, so I simply turned the alarm off and went back to sleep, trusting faithfully to the waking talents of the night porter. He wock not. I awoke at 10 minutes to 7, the train was due to leave at 7.03.

Seldom have I got dressed as swiftly as this morning. Of course there was no chance of catching that train, but there was still time to make use of the French I have stored up in the past few months in bawling out the night porter, then to pore over the timetable with his daytime colleague. The next train would not arrive in Boulogne until around noon. At last, in an obscure corner, we found an omnibus that would leave Lille at 7.15. I roused all present to their feet with curses, then set off at the double through the dark and hideous city in pursuit of the houseboy with my luggage. All the dustbins were filled with yesterday's (Friday's) fish bones, which black cats were gnawing. Never in my life have I seen so many fish bones and so many black cats in so short a time.

I boarded the omnibus just as it was about to drive off. A very stern driver was at the wheel. It riled him when passengers had their own ideas about coming in or out of the door or when they didn't give him the exact fare. He scolded all of them, me only slightly, however, on account of my little bit of luggage, squinting at it standing there in the middle of his lousy bus. It stood beside a man some seven feet tall dressed in a leather cowboy outfit, somewhat the worse for wear, but hung with large medals and other trophies. At his side was a leather-covered walking stick six feet long and so thick that Philiberte could just about have got his arms around it. And on the floor he had yet another, a kind of red pole with a broken bronze eagle, a mirror, and a bicycle bell attached to it. He sat, silent and unmoving, like a pensioned-off Old Shatterhand, beside a young married couple, the male member of whom, named Nono, was not feeling well. Afterwards I saw that the <u>Wildwester</u> had two lovingly shaped wooden legs painted a bright scarlet. He was a living sideshow, exhibiting himself for money, and he was travelling to St. Omer, where he had a rich field for his activities in the shape of many fairground stalls and open-air markets for wardrobes, sewing machines, and piglets.

It was somewhat strange to be driving through the district I stumbled around on foot 21 years ago. Everywhere signposts to the villages I had known, partly as dugouts, partly as billets where children came begging, and partly as coffee-serving housewives who had stayed behind. In Armentières we even drove past the houses which in those days I had freed of their stocks of gutters and gutter pipes (these had then to be smuggled over to the upper command posts during the night and sold to them). After a journey that passed through some prettier hilly country only towards the end, we arrived in Boulogne just before 11.

Since the ship was due to sail at 11.30 and I still had to fetch my trunk from the city railway station (I had already almost resigned myself to the prospect that it too might have conformed to the general disorder and gone on strike somewhere along the way—but there it was!) and also to visit the shipping office, I quickly seized the next best taxi and urged the nice elderly man at the wheel in great haste towards the station. It was like a Buster Keaton film: the station was just round the corner, the shipping office exactly one street further on and only half a minute away from the pier from which the steam tender would take me out to the ship. The ship arrived an hour late anyway. So at last I had time to catch up on my missed breakfast, which was in fact even <u>offered</u> me by the Holland-America Line.

The little boat was very cold and pitched and tossed rather violently on its way to its larger colleague further out. Arriving there, we found the entire side besieged by the plentiful troops of passengers, making it look like a propaganda page from the "Stürmer." The ship is packed to bursting, loaded with inhabitants one wouldn't really wish to make a habit of. The only two clearly non-Hebrew passengers sat at my lunch table, the still empty chair was the first officer's. He couldn't of course occupy it at noon today, since he had to get his steamer under way again. The waiters are very nervy, serve some guests three times with soup, others with none at all, forget drinks, throw cheese into the laps of the poor seafarers, and quarrel among themselves in half-lowered voices. The ship itself is not bad, though the cabins are all pretty cramped; it may be that the luxury cabins up in the loft are roomier, in line with their dearer prices. But the little boat has sailed nicely and quietly so far. It seems to be very well balanced (allowing for the smooth sea). After the meal I busied myself with unpacking and having a thorough shave, and now I have just moved out of the lounge, where the afternoon tea band has just moved in, and am in the smoking room, through which a gentleman is wandering, asking all his relaxing contemporaries whether they are Herr David. The question, though receiving no affirmative answer, is certainly understandable.

So, my dearest Hasha, these have been the main events up to mail collection time for Southampton. Now you won't be hearing from me for quite a while; but, so that you won't have to wait any longer than necessary, I'll write to you immediately after I arrive on the other side. Do not forget the poor world traveller, think kindly of him, and consider yourself hugged and stroked with many Yashny. A paw for Alfi and a greeting to Adele.

Your Y.

Hindemith arrived in New York on 7 February 1939. Apart from a concert with Lydia Hoffmann-Behrendt in Cleveland on 10 February, he remained there at the Hotel Seymour until leaving for Chicago and California on 16 February.

Rudolf Heinisch, a painter, was a lifelong friend from the early Frankfurt years.

To Gertrud Hindemith   New York

13 February 1939

My most beloved Hasha, I landed back here this morning, was busy till a short time ago with all kinds of people and discussions, and now the Pub (Voigt) has just left after bringing me your two letters. One's heart gets heavier and heavier reading all these reports of the splendours of Blusch, Cretelle, and the valley of clouds. A Wapuff drowsing in the sun—and I wandering around between sleeping cars and hotels! Still, one week has now passed, and I shall manage somehow to keep my homesickness at bay for the rest of them. [. . .] On Wednesday evening (8.II) I went to the Blue Ribbon with Rudy and his wife Eunice for some Sauerbraten, which did me good after the food on board ship, already described in detail. Rudy has moved up from <u>Downtown</u> and now has his studio in 45th, two houses away from the Pub shop, where business appears to be going a bit better. [. . .]

On Sunday I arrived in Port Jervis at 6.30 in the morning and was met by cousin Emil. I had kept this day, on which, because of the complete closing-down of all human habitations, there was nothing else to do, for a visit to my uncle. And I certainly did not regret it. The old man is a gem. Ecstatic that I had come. His health is now much better than before, since he has been having massage treatment. I spent a real Sunday in the country with him, inspected everything, and was told everything. My considerable knowledge of farming matters enabled me to express the proper appreciation. It is indeed admirable what this old fellow manages to do, all alone with his Emil. They own a huge piece of land, which they work with a tractor and the various appliances that go with it. They also have a truck and a big Chevrolet. There are three cows, and it is nice to know they have no intention of putting the oldest one down; they have had her for over 20 years but will grant her her share of hay to the end of the good creature's life. Seldom have I made two people so happy as when I sat down and made music with them. The old boy has got himself a Steinway piano, and, with his thick Hindemith skull and in shirt-sleeves, he pounds it loudly and lustily. He can get his 76-year-old fingers round anything, admittedly plays wrong notes here and there, but never gets seriously lost and manages even the most perilous situations without turning a hair. The lad is just the same. With his Heinisch-like figure he sits with his fiddle (holding it in his paws like an orangutan with a bread roll) and plays the wildest things without batting an eyelid. In this way we executed a fantastic French duet for two violins and some trio arrangements of symphonic and operatic excerpts. After that I played a few over-tures in piano duet form with the old boy, and neither breakneck speeds nor tech-nical difficulties could get him down. In the evening we came up with a few things more—a Haydn trio, Schubert marches, <u>and so on</u>, and both were ecstatic. The old man saluted me with tears in his eyes and said it was a <u>great honour</u>, and for his son it was a <u>fairy tale</u>.

In the afternoon we drove around the country in the car, everything was iced over—an entirely different form of freezing from any I have seen before: what had thawed during the day had now frozen over again on top, smooth as a mirror, and the entire land gave the impression of being covered with a gleaming mirror of milky glass. In the evening, very tired, I fell into bed early and slept without a break till 7. We had breakfast and then they both took me into Port Jervis, where I caught a bus back here. It is a drive of 2½–3 hours through pretty country, past the remark-able villages of Mahwah and Hohokus, not to speak of the Hackensack river. All along the roads there are <u>inns</u> and lodging houses, all looking very jolly. There is also a snake farm, which is signposted miles in advance: <u>Hold a snake, take a snap-shot</u>—that ought perhaps to be one of the first places to which the Wapuff will be taken on his first appearance here. [. . .]

I arrived back here around midday and am now slowly getting myself ready for the grand trip across to the other side. But I am now feeling so tired that I find it dif-ficult to write. So I'll finish. [. . .]

14.II

I have just seen that the mailboat doesn't leave till tomorrow, so I can add a few things to the scribble made in great tiredness. Not that anything has happened since yesterday evening. [. . .] Over the Christmas holidays Koussevitzky did the Sym-phonic Dances in Boston no less than six times with great success, also once here, and on account of the success he repeated them last Saturday. I couldn't hear them, since I was in Cleveland, but I'm sure he performs them well. Mathis, Dances, and Nobilissima Visione are running all over the place. The ballet does really seem to have been a great success. But I have heard nothing from Massine here either. It is possible our paths will cross in California. In San Francisco I shall be conducting the String Orchestra and Brass Instruments music, and in Los Angeles the ballet suite, and both times I shall be roasting the swan. I have talked often to Voigt about the plan for summer courses. He is sticking obstinately to the idea, but I fear, after experiencing Blusch, neither 10 horses nor their equivalent will drag me back here in summer. So I am considering whether I ought not to start something of the kind in Montana [Switzerland] for 6 weeks in July and August. However, I am completely undecided and just cannot make up my mind. Think it over carefully yourself. If you are willing, I'll do it, if not, I'll let it slide. [. . .]

Turkey, I feel, we can consign to the bonfire. It seems to be becoming more hopeless daily. And why should I waste so much energy wading through that swamp? Thanks to the currency arrangements and my activities here, we are over our difficulties for the time being, so we do not need the Turkish money. True, it was often pleasant there, and even oftener interesting and instructive, and I would not have wanted to miss those days spent in Stamboul, Ephesus, etc. with my good lion. But it cost us dear enough.

Are you stroking the donkey diligently? I am very homesick for our musical sessions. Last night I woke up, because I had been practising the Mozart bassoon concerto in a dream and one passage would just not go properly!

So, my brave lion, the "President Harding" now has enough to carry to the good Pirwag; a thousand kisses, much much love and best wishes for his musical and other activities.

Your Y.

To Gertrud Hindemith   New York
                                                        16 February 1939

My dearest, Wapuff at the Hallentather pianino—that is a truly impressive painting; the only odd thing about it is that he is holding the left pedal down continuously. But it is understandable that a sensitive soul does not <u>transmit</u> the strength of its feeling with full three-stringed power to the world but keeps the greater part of its powerful acoustic experience to itself. Quite right! Your accounts of sunny weather and the ultraviolet balcony make my mouth and all else water, it is truly monstrous having to read such reports when it is raining in streams in a horribly stuffy atmosphere as yesterday or is icy cold as today. I am now off to pleasanter regions however—in two hours from now the train leaves for the west. Tomorrow evening I shall still be in Chicago, and from Saturday morning on it's one thing after another till Monday evening. Here nothing has happened since my last letter. I was thoroughly lazy and did hardly anything worth mentioning. However, quite a lot of things have been fixed up. One evening I had a session with Balanchine, who wants to make a ballet of the Symphonic Dances. If all goes according to plan, I'll work out a story for him and add to and subtract from the score—and it will all be well paid. I intend to think about the story during the journey and have got several things from the city library here to take with me—what it is to be the curious colleague will learn only after the nut has been cracked. After a quick glance through the Kepler novel I had already seen it is as you say, but have no fear, he will look very different when once I really get down to him. I already have several ideas and shall one day discover the point from which to start his world moving. [. . .]

Other novelties include a new pair of gabardine trousers I have bought to replace the flannel ones. They are extensively mechanized (for instance, they boast a zip fastener instead of buttons) and promise to look very well on me. The flannel trousers were looking very shabby and, besides that, had acquired (obviously on the ship) a grease stain the size of a five mark piece that was very difficult to hide. Now I have only to look around for a checkered cowboy jacket and then I shall be more or less complete. I won't send you any money, since you will be getting enough now. I intend to let it mount up here till I have collected together a substantial ship's cargo. [. . .]

The German cabaret comedian Werner Finck had been banned from the stage for making jokes that displeased the Nazis.

A conference to discuss the differences between Arabs and Jews in Palestine was taking place in London.

The French conductor Pierre Monteux was musical director of the San Francisco Symphony Orchestra.

To Gertrud Hindemith [San Francisco]
26 February 1939

Beloved leonine creature, the readable "Echo" reached me yesterday. I already knew about the Finck affair, it was the first thing a reporter told me on my arrival in New York. I still get a slight retrospective shudder every time I hear such reports; not so much on account of the measures of a boneheaded government or even of their pitiable victims—they ought gradually to have come to see that there is no room for jokes of any kind—but I think to myself how terrible it would be if one had likewise sunk down to this castrated level of helpless apathy and all too subtly concealed resistance. We must be thankful that we have freed ourselves from all that and hope that we can continue to enjoy our freedom. The day before yesterday a woman came to the artists' room, a Frau Pohl, who kept the boardinghouse in Vienna where I slept after leaving that performance of Cardillac before the end. Her visit was in fact utterly pointless, but she did tell me that, on the first day of the Austrian conquest, Tex was taken to Dachau and is still there today. She knew nothing of Anni and the children. Despite all these things and despite one's rage over them, Palestine will remain in the air and not come to anything. We shall manage very well without including it in the list of our experiences. It will rather be this region, I believe, that will grow in importance as a working area, and what would really please me would be a few months each year of work over here to earn us the following year in Blusch. Then as far as I am concerned Cevats can continue to fall from power—in any case one can never depend on the moods of these dictator-happy tin-pot republics. [. . .]

A few days ago I had lunch with Monteux. He is a nice, inoffensive fellow and an excellent conductor. She, on the other hand, very fat, now grey, got up for the evening in a gown with flower facings and gold dust in her hair, is an earthquake that sets the pointers of lesser seismographs hopping madly around. He has the orchestra here in good trim. We rehearsed well and in great detail and in consequence the Schwanendreher went well and without incident both times, especially yesterday evening. I also conducted, the work being the Boston strings and brass thing. It went without a hitch and earned great applause. The orchestra put themselves to a lot of trouble and played excellently. From the very first I felt at home with these men, and they with me too. So we got along fine, and our work together was really pleasant. They had played the ballet shortly before, and everybody came up to tell me how beautiful it is and how much they enjoyed playing it. There are a lot of Germans in the orchestra, also Bohemians, Austrians, and Russians. Yesterday a cellist who had studied in the Frankfurt Conservatorium and had now and again helped out with the Rebner quartet, took me around the city to the Golden Gate, through parks and observation hills, to the fishing district and through Chinatown. The city is beautiful and its situation quite beyond compare. On top of that, the mild Dalmatian climate and the conspicuous niceness of the people — thanks to these my stay here is very pleasant. [. . .]

The film production at the Disney studios at the time of Hindemith's visit was *Fantasia*.

The Zurich Opera gave a guest performance of *Mathis der Maler* in Amsterdam on 9 March 1939. The "rival undertaking" in London was a concert performance of this opera in English in the Queen's Hall on 15 March; Dennis Noble sang the title role, and the conductor was Clarence Raybould.

To Willy Strecker

New York

12 March 1939

Dear Willy, at last I can get down to writing to you. In all this time there was too much work to do and, added to that, the eternal distraction of repeated travel. I am now here for a few days and in peace at least until tomorrow morning. The Russian

Ballet will then be arriving here, and if you are familiar with the monopolizing nature of Massine and his satellites, you can imagine what will then happen to my peace.

So far work has gone smoothly. [. . .] There were two concerts in San Francisco with Monteux, I both played and conducted. Then I spent a day in Hollywood and took a pretty close look at the strange goings-on in the studios. The only thing of interest was Disney's Micky Mouse factory. They are at the moment trying to make a serious film with Stokowski's "baton wielding" as the main content and his tasteful musical knowledge as oracle and supreme opinion. One could sob loudly and tear out one's few remaining hairs to see such a good idea, which could become a great work of art, falling into the hands of such a musical charlatan. [. . .]

A few weeks ago Balanchine, after having set a company on its dancing feet for next season with the help of a number of financial people, was planning a danced version of the "Symphonic Dances," of which he had already had a piano score made at great cost. On my journey to California I prepared a very nice draft about the Children's Crusade, but on my return I learned that the whole thing has gone up in smoke, since there had been insufficient engagements. When the other Russians heard I was writing something for Balanchine, they lost their heads completely and kept ringing me up from all over the place, lamenting and complaining, just as if I had no other business but to write for them. They are very happy with their Visione and seem really to have been a great success wherever they went. They are in a terrible hurry for a new ballet, so I made them a detailed plan for a comic piece about pirates and a girls' boarding school. Massine thought it wonderful, but he has his mind set on the idea I discussed with him earlier (the land of Cockaigne in the style of Brueghel), so I shall now have to wait to be told which to start on. Tomorrow they'll be doing the St. Francis again.

The book, on which I have made no progress throughout these weeks on account of the glut of work, has been considerably revised and will be sent off in its final version before I leave here. I feel it has become a practical proposition, and your keen-eyed augurs will have several days of work to do examining it through their microscopes. I wish them joy. [. . .] The additions to the theoretical part I shall probably do on the ship going home. I shall hardly find time earlier, for I still have to compose the viola sonata for the concert here. [. . .]

I have received an ecstatic, almost tearful telegram from Amsterdam. Were you there perhaps? They wire that the performance was good and successful. The rival undertaking in London will evidently be launched the day after tomorrow. I hope they'll get some idea of what it's about.

On the way home I shall be playing twice in Paris, and in mid-May I am to conduct the Russian Ballet in Florence. I wish I were already at the stage of boarding the ship, my work here done. Well, the time will come. [. . .] Warmest regards to everybody, and do not forget the poor orphaned traveller for whom the stone deserts of Arizona and the salt plains of Utah are gradually becoming his daily bread.

Your P.

Nicholas Nabokov, a Russian-American composer and cousin of the author Vladimir Nabokov, was chairman of the music department at Wells College, Aurora. Hindemith consistently spelled his name Nabokoff.

Hindemith and Sanromá performed the Sonata for viola and piano at the New York Town Hall on 23 April 1939, but according to the Schott catalogue they had given the first performance at Harvard University on 19 April.

Gaîté parisienne was a ballet with music by Offenbach and Rosenthal. Hindemith's impatience with Massine's vacillations was aggravated by the choreographer's current marital troubles, to which Hindemith was an unwilling witness, and also by his plan to stage the "Bacchanale" from Wagner's *Tannhäuser* with décor by Salvador Dali. Sergei Denham was general manager of the Monte Carlo ballet company.

To Gertrud Hindemith   [New York]
                                                        14 March 1939

[. . .] Early on Monday morning Massine rang—he could not of course wait. In the meantime the Balanchine affair had gone up in smoke following the withdrawal of the financial people. Massine was pleased about that, but the comic ballet about pirates that I gave him in Chicago doesn't attract them. So there I sat, with two usable ballet stories on my hands. He did want his Brueghel, however, so we rummaged around in the German bookshop till we found books with the necessary documents. Since then I have been tinkering yet again with a new theme and am well on the way to finding something good. The ballet opened here yesterday evening. I didn't want to go to the performance, but at the rehearsal they all behaved as if success and their own happiness hung on my appearance, so I went and, after the warm reception of the really good performance, made a few obeisances. Afterwards I sat by myself in the Blue Ribbon with a glass of Mosel and sweated over the new ballet story. I was really astonished how beautiful the Visione is and how clean the music sounds. The choreography is also really lovely, apart from a few silly things, and they all danced with the proper dedication and obvious confidence. [. . .]

What you say about the summer courses is only too right. So away with the idea. That is all the easier since today an interminable and enthusiastic letter came from Nabokov in which his college suggests establishing summer courses especially for me. I want to examine all the proposals closely first and also wait till I've seen how things go in Hollywood next week. Then I will talk it all over in detail with Nabokov when I'm next here at the beginning of April. The proposal is a good one and, in combination with a few concerts or a film commitment, would be worthy of serious consideration for next year.

The book, of which only the preface remains to be done, has gone off to Schotts after I put in a lot more work on it and improved it. Now I must get down to finishing the viola sonata, which is to receive its first performance here on 23 April. [. . .]

I now have half my banishment behind me. Soon I shall once more be able to rest on Wapuff's sympathetic breast! [. . .]

To Gertrud Hindemith   Chicago
                                                                  18 March 1939
Beloved Pushu [. . .] I had an interview with Massine. [. . .] I gave him a clear outline of the present and future prospects of his ballet company, telling him that because of his artistic uncertainty he is abusing the work and application of his people, that this year he has been living on the success of two pieces (Nobilissima and Gaîté), and in order to continue to exist here he needs at least four good novelties, of which two must be great successes. That among his plans there was not a single one that promised success, and all of them, with one single exception, were artistically open to objection. That already he had got all musicians ranked against him with his danced symphonies, and that he is on the best way to going down in the history of ballet as a good choreographer, but an artistic blemish. That, handled as it had been handled until now, the ballet company would survive hardly longer than the next season. That he should restrict himself to choreography and leave the solution of productive artistic problems to other people. That he should divest himself of the ring of barmy celebrities and old wives who influence him in everything he does. And finally, that I refuse to enter into a permanent close relationship with a company whose artistic direction is so uncertain of itself and so lacking in taste. At best I would work with them in an occasional capacity.

He was much impressed, implored me to do a new ballet for next year, and also to take on the post of artistic adviser myself. After all my experiences, that was just about the last straw!! But he is a poor fellow despite all his talent, for in order to keep things going reasonably well he has to lick the boots of all his rich sponsors—yet at the same time he is an incorrigible egoist who thinks he must do everything himself, even when he sees a thousand times that artistic problems cannot be solved between a couple of rehearsals in the middle of a hundred other appointments. [. . .]

Afterwards I was with Denham and Rubinstein in the office, and I told them the whole story over again. They were astonished to be faced with such a clear and unvarnished reckoning and became quite weak at the knees. In the end we made an agreement for the new ballet on the same basis as the previous one, only with safeguards against name changes and suchlike things. It was impossible to get more money out of them (Kurt had told me earlier than even the $2,000 would have caused them great concern). They were even naive enough to demand that any possible gramophone or film rights arising out of the music should be assigned to them. Seldom has the house heard such scornful laughter as mine! Since then I have again gone on the search for a ballet text and, with the help of the Brueghel pictures, have hammered out something in the nature of a Flemish peasant Persephone on which I now intend to work on the journey west. Promises to be very fine. [. . .]

> In both concerts in Los Angeles Hindemith conducted the Nobilissima Visione suite and was soloist in the Schwanendreher Concerto (conducted by Otto Klemperer).
> The Nazis had issued a decree that all artists unemployed or not fully employed be directed to "more useful tasks."

To Gertrud Hindemith   [Los Angeles]

27 March 1939

My dearest Pushu, it is a true solace in this region of phantoms, delusions, and demons to receive a letter from a genuine living creature, especially when the first snowdrop from the garden and the Cretelle daisies are enclosed with it. "Longing for home" is hardly the expression any longer for all the things that make this city increasingly unenjoyable, in spite of its heavenly surroundings. The final outcome of my experiences is: if at all possible, not to have to come here, not even in effigie. [. . .]

In this giant city one can hardly talk of a musical life apart from the movies. There is not even a proper music school. Klemperer conducts the orchestra, but that stands alone like the famous tree in the Odenwald. There is nothing in the background like a musically educated community or even interested or supporting organizations, unless one likes to see the usual crowd of fat old women, Board of Trustees, or something in that light. It always makes me feel slightly sick when (as I have repeatedly seen happen) some meatball in full rig places herself in front of the orchestra and negotiates with them over duties, salaries, and artistic matters. A mere conductor has no right to interfere! There is in fact, for training these future patroness-cows, a Junior Women's Association of not yet overripe ladies, whose job it is to pay this year's deficit of $150,000 partly out of their own handbags and partly by cadging it elsewhere. On Friday morning I had to arrange a half-hour of the usual question-and-answer chatter with this body. To some extent this was not quite so abyssmally stupid as most times, since obviously beneath the furs of all imaginable two-footers and four-footers, beneath the dried prunes, the mousetraps, the breakfast crescent rolls, dumplings and lumps of liquorice (and all the other things they wear, together with coloured feathers 80 cm long, as hats) and beneath the millimeter-thick lipstick, the carmine-shading-to-blue fingernails, the fever-red rouged cheeks and the eyebrows waxed together like the points of Mikosch's moustache, there are a few pretty figures to be seen. Lert, who after all had a name as a long-serving conductor at the Berlin State Opera, if not as a first-class one, conducts something like a semi-amateur orchestra in Pasadena, Schönberg is giving lessons in harmony to beginners at the university (serves him right), and in similar ways all the one-time bigwigs now paddle around rather like the musical director in the well-known town of Kyritz an der Knatter, with the only difference that this Knatter, when compared with the <u>Los Angeles river</u> in matters of artistic fecundity, transcends the Castalian spring about as much as the river Main transcends the Königsbrünnche spring.

I played flawlessly in the two concerts. We rehearsed very thoroughly, adding on nearly 8 hours for both pieces, and the orchestra was then correspondingly light and transparent. The Nobilissima suite (in which, on account of the big body of strings in the concert halls, I doubled the wind instruments and injected a few more trombones and a tuba) went well and, like the roasted swan, enjoyed a success as never before.

After the concerts, Berlin turned up in full force, the image of what it was 15 years ago, and it went on up to yesterday!! Let us joyfully cross ourselves thrice and loudly sing halleluja that we have nothing more to do with it!!! [. . .]

The artistic measures in Germany are completely in line with all the Reich's undertakings, which seem now to be exclusively governed by paranoia, sadism, and a shortage of raw materials. I always feel like that mouse, recklessly dancing outside the doors of the trap and even entering it—then by sheer luck happening to be outside as the doors snap to! [. . .]

Mashmu, dear one, now I'm hungry.

To Gertrud Hindemith   [New York]
6 April 1939

My best-beloved grass-lion, when after four nights of sleeping cars I arrived back here early the day before yesterday, I was overjoyed to find both your letters, the parcel of books was also here. Many thanks, at least I now have something for the free moments (really they are hardly more than that) remaining before my departure. [. . .]

It is to be hoped that the powder keg in Europe will not have exploded before then. It all looks very murky, and I await the future with not exactly the rosiest of feelings. If it comes to a wholesale crash (and it sometimes seems that is bound to happen), then our beloved Valais might also be engulfed, and there would be no other way for us than to move on again. And the only path open would lead us here. Well, for the moment the danger is evidently not acute, and I am staying calm. All the same, I intend to take some security measures in the next few days and try to ensure that, in the event of urgent danger, we can steam off here at once without having too many difficulties with the consulate. Don't worry about it anyway. It is well known that no sparrow shall fall to the ground without being taken care of, so it will also be all right for the lion. It is (yet again!) very good luck that I have made these few trips to America—and particularly this last one, which I so much looked down on, has been in every way more important and more successful than the previous ones. I am certain that, on account of all the credit I have built up, I shall have no difficulty getting in here if things get too hot. [. . .]

My dear Hashar, I don't need to go into everything in your letters and parcels, it would take too much time, and you know anyway how much joy everything coming from you gives me. So for today farewell, and remember as I do that I shall soon have you with me again, and how much I long for that.

Goodnight, belovedest,

Your Y.

Hindemith left New York on 26 April 1939. Back in Switzerland, he started on a flood of composition. In addition to the works named, he wrote a violin concerto and a number of songs, both choral and solo.

Earlier that year Hindemith told Willy Strecker in a letter of "a great coup which I hope to bring off next spring: an opera about the German astronomer Johannes Kepler (1571–1630) to be called Die Harmonie der Welt [The Harmony of the Universe]."

The book the Schott Verlag was preparing to publish, undeterred by the outbreak of the Second World War on 1 September 1939, was the Übungsbuch für den zweistimmigen Satz (English title: Exercises in Two-Part Writing), Part II of Unterweisung im Tonsatz.

To Willy Strecker [Blusch]

25 September 1939

[. . .] I note that I am well on the way to producing some very respectable things. The violin sonata lies complete in the drawer, the final movement is a triple fugue that will make a connoisseur's heart jump for joy. Besides that I have done 6 little choral songs to French words by Rilke, and I am just now completing a clarinet sonata. All these things I regard more or less as preliminary studies for Kepler, with whom I am once again seriously occupied. I hope soon to be able to report some definite results. I see it in my mind's eye as something very large and very weighty. The piece will have six scenes. It begins in Prague with the death of the astronomer Tycho Brahe (1601), then comes a very dramatic scene in the imperial palace with the mad emperor Rudolf II. Third scene very quiet and lyrical: Kepler with his much younger second wife before their marriage (1613) in Linz. Then another big theatrical scene in Württemberg, where Kepler's mother is tried as a witch. Fifth scene in Sagan with Wallenstein, and sixth 1630 in Regensburg, where Kepler dies—a mixture of ordinary private life, great world events (Imperial Diet,

30 Years War) and cosmic things (astronomical allegory). I only hope I can bring it all together as I now have it in my head. I shall need time and a continued period of peace—let's hope I shall be granted it. [. . .]

It is amazing that you are bringing the book out in spite of all the difficulties, but I am very glad, for I promise myself that it will make a considerable impression in spite of these not exactly encouraging times.

[. . .] Here everything remains unchanged just as you know it. Our moderately active life fluctuates between musical instruments and garden products—all the same, our horizons lie far enough away—and not only on account of the giant peaks opposite. Alfi has had another fight with Medor and came out so badly damaged that for two days we despaired of his recovery. Today, however, he is getting about without bandages and, whenever he hears his enemy barking, he growls, which gives us the best grounds for hope. Incidentally, for you as mushroom expert the news that I have prepared a really excellent mushroom extract for use in soup, etc., and that we yesterday pickled our first mushrooms in vinegar. [. . .]

The piano arrangement of the violin concerto was made by H. G. Schnell. Willem Mengelberg invited Hindemith to conduct the Amsterdam Concertgebouw Orchestra at the first performance.

To Willy Strecker [Blusch]

18 October 1939

Dear Willy, your packets have all arrived. First the two Kepler books. They are just what I was waiting for, and I am finding in them all the personal things that are characteristic of the man and so important in portraying him. The text is progressing slowly but surely. All the same, I want first to finish the contractually promised Massine text, even though there is a danger that the people will be prevented by present events from making use of it; but this should be settled in the foreseeable future, and I don't anticipate needing all that much time for the music either. One cannot in any case work continuously on Kepler, and indeed it takes a lot of time just to familiarize oneself thoroughly with the historical details, not to mention the man's own writings, which are not at all easy to read—all in all I still have a lot to do.

The other very delightful packet arrived the day before yesterday, containing the new book and the piano score of the violin concerto. The book makes a truly fine impression, and, when one glances through it like some unbiased reader, one has the feeling there must be something well worth knowing inside it. I believe it will surely find its public, perhaps even more quickly in these dreary times, and so, from the standpoint of the publisher too, it is probably good that it should be published now. I had many doubts that it would prove possible, so I'm now all the more delighted. I of course look on it with enamoured eyes, but that really does not prevent me from seeing the actual fact of publication in the proper light. I have the feeling that, for you personally, this little work was not just a routine publishing item, it is as if an unusual amount of goodwill and good wishes on the part of the publishers were printed alongside it (perhaps in connection with the evil signs attending its birth), and for this I give you my special thanks. You must also thank all your people very warmly for having so devotedly applied themselves to this complicated and in some respects somewhat unaccustomed work. In view of its difficulty it is a particular pleasure to see how wonderfully clear it all appears. Let us therefore send this well-turned-out book on its way with our blessing and hope that you and all the other publishing departments will get as much pleasure and satisfaction from it as I did at very first sight.

The violin concerto is also not to be sniffed at. The piano arrangement is quite outstanding and very playable, even for nonexpert pianists. Schnell has done a masterly job. This piece is respectable and can be introduced everywhere with a clear conscience. [. . .] I have heard nothing so far from Amsterdam, neither a refusal nor a change of plan. I am writing to them again today. If the situation becomes more favourable in the next few weeks, I can of course travel via Germany at the end of November and carry out my engagement. In the opposite (and I feel much more probable) case I should prefer him to wait until I can come in person. [. . .] Apart from the Boston performance, I wish in any case to reserve the piece for myself—with different violinists. [. . .]

Here everything goes on as always. Autumn is in with a vengeance. We had three weeks of uninterrupted rain; it looks hardly reassuring for the grape-gathering, to which we have been invited. The garden still keeps us busy. There have been plums in masses, which in the shape of jam and abundant gift baskets have gone the way of all plums. The pears have been very good, and now come some very promising-looking apples. Cabbages, winter salads of all kinds, broad beans, etc., etc. . . . there's still plenty of work and pleasure. For the rest, we have moved the piano and all connected with it into a single room for the sake of the heating (apart from those upstairs, which are nice and warm to work in), and there, beneath two new homemade lamps and with the aid of our self-tuned Hallenbarter, we devote ourselves to our beloved house music. [. . .]

Keep as well as you can despite all the surrounding atmospheric and intellectual gloom. [. . .]

Serge Koussevitzky invited Hindemith to teach a composition class at the Berkshire Music Center in Tanglewood, near Stockbridge, Massachusetts, in the summer of 1940.

The second volume of his Unterweisung im Tonsatz was published by AMP in 1941;

Otto Ortmann translated it into English. The translator entrusted with the first volume, Remi Gassmann, was replaced by Arthur Mendel, and AMP published his translation in 1942 under the title *The Craft of Musical Composition*.

To Ernest R. Voigt   Sierre (Valais)

8 November 1939

Dear friend, it is a long time since I last heard from you, and so I assume things continue to go well with you. For the moment I can report that the same is true of us. Among all these seething world events we find ourselves sitting like a miracle in one of the few still quiet spots in Europe, to which the sounds of war penetrate only faintly, though quite discordantly enough. No one can say how long it will last, but nevertheless we trust in our good star, which led us here in time and will also, we hope, continue not to let us down.

Your recent cable referred presumably to Koussevitzky's enquiry, for otherwise I should surely have heard more from you. The enquiry has meanwhile arrived. As you probably know, it concerns next year's six-week summer class (10 July to 20 August). I have of course accepted. A contract is said to have been sent off in the meantime. On this account Nabokov's plan will of course be superseded; I shall be writing to him to that effect in the next few days. I have already begun to consider how to arrange the work for this class. Six weeks are a very short time, only just about enough to arouse in listeners hungry for knowledge a desire for more intensive work. I am therefore wondering whether it would be possible immediately afterwards to add an additional four weeks for interested students, preferably in the same place, but as a private venture of my own. What do you think? As soon as I hear that you find this idea feasible, I shall of course consult with Dr. Koussevitzky. Now the foundations have been laid, you can of course attach any further engagements on offer to it, either before or after. You already know the nature of the various possibilities. The work in Berkshire (and a possible class to follow) will be greatly helped by the recent publication of my book of exercises, which Mainz had no doubt already sent you. Is Herr Ortmann now in fact working on it? It would be fine if the English version could be ready for use next summer. I have heard nothing more from Gassmann, you presumably also not. Perhaps he is using the war confusions as a further excuse for putting it off. I feel we shouldn't waste much more time on him. [. . .] If the second volume appears in English, that will be quite sufficient for all practical purposes. The purely practical work is not dependent on the theories set out in the first volume, and thus the theoretical part can safely be left for publication later, with a more trustworthy translator working on it. [. . .]

The first performance of the violin concerto will be given in Amsterdam at the end of this month—under my direction, if I manage to get there. I cannot of course travel through France on my German passport, and I have no wish to go via my beloved fatherland. So that leaves only a roundabout journey by ship with the possible risk of mines or internment. [Added in margin: No longer available either.] Besides, the journey takes 10 days. Good, isn't it? It is really not very easy these days to worm one's way through all the dangerous, sensational, irritating, tiresome and so utterly unnecessary happenings that crop up almost daily. I shall be happy when I am allowed to board the ship to America unhindered! [. . .]

> Your not exactly bellicose
> Paul Hindemith

To Willy Strecker [Blusch]

29 November 1939

[. . .] Tomorrow I shall be sending you two sonatas, the one for clarinet and the one for trumpet. It didn't happen earlier because we were playing them ourselves and could not part with them. I assume you will be drumming up the attention of the whole pack of experts, particularly for the trumpet sonata; it is maybe the best thing I have succeeded in doing in recent times, and that is quite a good sign, since I do not regard any of my newest productions as of little value. The violin sonata I have just sent off to Bern, where it is being copied for a soon-due performance. You'll get that too as soon as it comes back. On Saturday I shall be going through the harp sonata in detail with an Italian lady harpist, who is passing through this district especially for the purpose. The horn sonata will then, depending on the work programme of the Viennese copyist, lie ready for delivery. Perhaps before then there might also be a few more new things. [. . .]

Another cable has arrived from America. Voigt is offering a further course at a university. It is touching that he takes so much trouble over me, but this offer (which is clearly intended as a kind of lifeline) is not quite the right thing. The pay is not good enough, and besides, it would start in February, and that seems to me, in spite of everything, too early. Something better will surely turn up to follow on the Boston affair. All the same, this offer shows one can still reckon on further work over there. [. . .]

For three days we had the most splendid skiing weather, now we are back with thaw and slush. We have bottled the sauerkraut and the chicories sit in their forcing box, so they will produce nice white stalks in time for Christmas. The whole family sends greetings to you and the whole <u>maison</u>. Alfi gives a paw, and his playmate and bed companion, the little kitten, sends a miaow greeting. Fare ye all very well!

> Your Paul

In view of Hindemith's commitment to the summer school at Tanglewood, Voigt and Nabokov took steps to adapt and even widen (through the inclusion of Cornell University) their plans to persuade him to leave Europe for America.

To Nicholas Nabokov   [Sierre]

4 December 1939

Dear friend, your and Mr. Voigt's enquiries were unexpected. Since I have so far received only the telegrams, and any kind of detailed written explanation is still lacking, I find the whole thing somewhat unclear. So what I am writing now is dictated by this lack of clarity and will perhaps be overtaken by a letter arriving today, tomorrow, or at some time or other. [. . .]

I suspect that your offer regarding Wells and Cornell is born of a certain concern for my fate. I thank you for being so concerned, though so far there has been no cause for any great concern. But I do of course realize that over there, far from the field of fire, Europe's problems are taken far more seriously than here, and that above all the feeling of nervousness is far stronger there than here, in close proximity to all the horrors. Of course we are not entirely unworried about the future; in the conditions of political brigandry prevailing today no one knows what tomorrow will bring, and it is always possible that by next spring the shambles will have become general—though I myself do not believe that. So far I have been left completely in peace, not presumably on grounds of excessive considerateness, but because in Germany men in my age group have not yet been called up—not even people in the higher military ranks, among whom my corporal's rank (I was far short of being a general!) can hardly be reckoned. Things will probably remain like this over winter, since an intensification of war activities seems unlikely in the cold season, and this war seems at the moment to be distinguished by too short battle-fronts and a surplus of soldiers. But come what may, it is comforting to know that there is a way out! [. . .]

You say that for six weeks between February and June I am to teach in Cornell and Aurora. That can surely only mean that the six weeks would come together in one convenient spot within these chosen months, for 1000 dollars would be rather low payment for a commitment to stay put from February until June. [. . .] You further say that I should be functioning as <u>Musical Instructor</u>. I have at the moment only a vague idea what that would mean. [. . .] Six weeks are of course not time enough for regular tuition, and the <u>lecture</u> system, maybe quite suitable for scientific subjects, is of little use for musical composition, on account of its practical—and thus in no way scientific—nature. Well, you will be clear enough in your own mind what form the thing should take. You have worked long enough on this subject, and you know from my blue book roughly what my working methods and views are, so you will be able to bring what I have to offer in line with the existing or projected facilities.

Looking at it from the standpoint of my present circumstances here, I would say as follows:

I am prepared to accept in the event that, as assumed above, it involves a six-week job without other commitments. In that case I would request that the date of this study course be set as late as possible, so that I should not have too long a gap between the end of the course and the Koussevitzky affair (from mid-July). Mr. Voigt tells me there are also prospects of other things, concerts, etc. These he would be able to fit in before this commitment. That would enable me to leave here at the last possible moment, which would suit me very well on account of work and also several concerts over here. A formal adherence to the first of February as the starting date might, in case of emergency, be an advantage. As things stand, the financial situation would be that with your and the Boston offer I could just get by without any substantial extra earnings. In normal times it would be senseless to do such a thing, but the prospect of perhaps escaping a great danger thereby would make it seem ridiculous to refuse. Besides, it is not impossible that one or two other things will come along once these two matters have been fixed. I should come alone to start with, then send for my wife once business has improved financially, or in the event of the war continuing beyond next autumn. You would need to send the American consulate in Geneva a request, as formal as possible, to provide me with a visa despite my German passport. Without some urgent official pressure, the consul would on no account condescend to do so—he already caused me considerable difficulties the last time. That is really all of any moment I have to say just now. I am eager to have further news from you and to hear what you think about it all. For now let me thank you warmly once again, and give my regards and thanks to your directorate and to everyone at Cornell connected with this project as well. I hope that what I am able to contribute will be of use. [. . .]

Fried Lübbecke was working on a book about Matthäus Merian, the sixteenth-century Swiss engraver who settled in Frankfurt and produced views of various towns.

To Emma and Fried Lübbecke   [Blusch]

6 December 1939

Dear Emma, dear Fried, it always takes a while before you get an answer. In the meantime Gertrud has consoled you with a letter and the little album. There was a lot of work here, since the little springs of composition were flowing fast, and the clearing work in the garden also took a lot of time. Otherwise nothing of any significance has happened. We are snowed in once again, and so the activities of all occupants have shifted entirely indoors. Among other things, the lady of the house belabours the beloved Hallenbarter both lovingly and untiringly, the head of the house stands upstairs at his window staring out over the white countryside, Alfi sleeps in each corner of the house in turn when not being ruffled and otherwise maltreated by his playmate and bed companion, the little kitten.

Your parcel of books was just right for such a household. Pictures of Swiss costumes are something like patriotic appendages in our rural life here, now that we are pretty well stuck down as honorary Swiss citizens, and the herb book has given me many new and useful ideas for the little herbal plantation I have already made for the winter and for the more extensive herbal bed I have planned for next year. I shall be wandering through the meadows next year with redoubled attention! There are times when one could wish to walk over them with the character and taste buds of a cow—just as it would often seem better to be a cow than a human being in the ever-increasing obtuseness of present times. But no—not as long as one can still make music. Gertrud wrote to you about my conveyor-belt production. It has slowed down in the last few days; after the trumpet sonata there was only one for trombone, which I have begun, but am now stuck in the middle. [. . .]

American teaching and concert plans are gradually taking shape for next year, and, as things become clearer, these seem likely to be fairly comprehensive. Cables and letters are passing to and fro in quick succession. If, as we hope, these plans are realized, I (or perhaps both of us) will miss the growing season in our garden. That is a pity, but it will perhaps be an advantage to witness world events, which are in any case highly unpleasant, from a more remote standpoint.

We are looking forward to the Merian book. It will surely be as pleasing and as useful as the book about Frankfurt; in this field, in which people like ourselves are not as much at home as we are in music, it is always good to learn how to observe familiar things more closely and recognize their relevance to human beings and events. I can imagine, Fried, that the theme is much "up your alley." Will you soon have finished the book? You are right: one could become very melancholy if one were to take a closer look at a cross section of our own times. The longitudinal section of past times may also show that things were not much better then, but the transfiguring twilight in which the deeds and figures are wrapped is a bit kinder than the stabbing Jupiter light in which today's events unfortunately appear to us. If one can busy oneself lovingly with the things of the past and in addition create things that will one day belong themselves to those periods of the past most worthy of admiration and continued attention, then the present disturbances surrounding us can assume gigantic proportions, they can smash mountains to pieces, but they cannot damage the tiny seeds. [. . .]

To Ernest R. Voigt   Sierre
                                                                                          11 December 1939
Dear ERV, your <u>avion</u> letter of the 1st of this month has just arrived, many thanks. Meanwhile my letter will have reached you, so you will already have learnt something of my opinions. [. . .]

Now, above all, regarding Hurok. I am very glad that you are not negotiating with him all too urgently. First of all, as far as he is concerned, I am not an object with which he can make any big deals. Maybe with a lot of publicity and big beat-ings of the drum he could fix up a tour that would look good, but that would work only once and no more. The people would be terribly disappointed with the goods on show, for what I have to offer is by no stretch of the imagination an easily digestible utility article, and with such highbrow things business can be done only when their dead creators have statues standing in as many big cities as possible — it will, I hope, be quite a while before that happens. You know only too well how I feel towards trumped-up affairs like these: now more than ever I should consider it damaging to the things I have been sent here to do. There could of course be some sort of agreement, whereby I should accept engagements from him (with your approval), but the right to choose must be mine, for I am first and foremost a composer and a teacher, and only after that a reasonably well trained parade horse. If you can rope him in along these lines I shan't object. [. . .]

I assume you are a little astonished at the lack of urgency with which I am treating this whole affair. It is on no account a lack of appreciation for what is being offered that lies behind my coolness; on the contrary, I am highly delighted to be given the chance to come over there in good time. It is just that here, as I said recently, one is less nervous (despite all past experiences, the best villas are still sit-uated directly below the summit of Vesuvius). Of course one cannot know every-thing that might happen, but to me it seems certain that nothing of any significance is to be expected this winter. That is why I am reluctant to give up all the things that keep me here — our new home that has grown very close to our hearts, the rela-tionship with Schotts, and current concert and other commitments — except in an emergency, and only at the last possible moment, and then, if there is any chance, only temporarily. It is not enjoyable, as you can imagine, to rearrange one's whole life twice in two years, quite apart from the fact that it is very difficult, when one is to all intents and purposes outside, to get back in again! But this is crossing bridges before we come to them, time and events will be more powerful than any of our plans and considerations. I feel at any rate that both sides would be best served by a visa made out for 1 February with an entitlement to put off the date of travel, if necessary, by six to eight weeks. What I am also anxious to avoid is the odium of being seen over there as a political refugee, which in my opinion cannot be regarded as by any means a good recommendation. [. . .]

Weltharmonik was the title of a German translation of Kepler's De harmonia mundi. Hans Böttcher was a musicologist in Berlin and a friend of Hindemith's.
    Willy Strecker's son Hugo, who was working at the London branch of Schotts, was a British subject.

To Willy Strecker   [Sierre]

9 January 1940

Dear Willy, Christmas and New Year passed off according to schedule, with the giving and receiving of presents, visits, and theatrical performances. In addition, there was our landlady's big wedding, at which I played on my viola, also the making of theatre decorations for the village, wine bottling in Sion, and other important occasions of that sort. My work was a bit neglected, I have done nothing beyond the Massine text, which is now more or less on its feet. The violin sonata was sent off to you and is doubtless now being worked on. It looks as if Kepler will start growing again only when I'm in Pub territory; the books I need will surely be available there in the event of your sources not bringing them to light. Dr. Böttcher has sent me as a gift the Weltharmonik, which has just been published in translation and on which I had until now cast only a Platonic eye on account of the high price; this is a valuable aid that makes life much easier, for the Latin original is really much too involved and time-consuming for dilettantes like me, and the two translations of extracts that I possess give only an inadequate picture. I want (for financial reasons as well) to have the ballet fully finished, so that I can get down to the opera in real earnest. [. . .]

Our house music is flourishing. I have borrowed a fiddle in Sion and since then, in addition to the horn and bassoon that are frequented as extensively as ever, I have been devouring the violin repertoire, until I am now performing the craziest of violin concertos from Bach to Paganini almost better than in the blossom time of my youth—we never do less than 8–10 per evening. A shame that this practical music making, which is so useful in every way, will soon have to be interrupted.

Hugo has written in a very happy and contented mood. He is in good health and "the first shock (including the emotional) has been overcome, and there have been so many new and valuable things to learn and digest, both at work and from an ever-increasing circle of friends, that, without reading too many newspapers, there are times when one can forget the war completely." Business, he says, was almost at a standstill during the first months, but happily it has now begun to recover. He even offers to use his influence in organizing a concert for me, but I'm not sure whether he is joking or in earnest.

So, that is all for today. [. . .] Brother Ludwig is to get an extra paragraph for himself.

Affectionately,

Your   Paul

Dear and esteemed brother Ludwig, you are truly kind and noble to remember us with so warm a letter, when we have not written to you at all for a whole year. But you do of course know that, though I always write "Dear Willy," it does not indicate a preference for your little brother; all business and friendly news is meant just as much for you too. We thought of you at Christmas and talked a lot about you. In past years this was always the time we all came together in your house. How it has all changed, in the world's fortunes as well as in our personal fortunes! Some of your now so very grown-up children must certainly have been with you, so you will have had a glittering and joyful celebration despite the dreary times. To me it seems increasingly that celebrations are becoming rarer, and the joy that glitters comes only when it is felt inside oneself and not expected from lighted candles on Christmas trees. We here enjoyed our fruitful solitariness, which in one year has rewarded us with more than twelve years in Berlin. We should be glad to see you here one day for a stay. But when will that be?

Let us hope for better times and wish each other as much good fortune as we can conjure out of our little human spheres of influence!

As ever,

Your   Paul & Gertrud

Paul Sacher was the director of the Basler Kammerorchester, a chamber orchestra in Basel with which Hindemith had frequently played. After the war, Hindemith wrote his symphony *Die Harmonie der Welt* to mark the orchestra's twenty-fifth anniversary in 1952.

Werner Kägi was a violinist.

To Paul Sacher   Hotel Schweizerhof, Bern

27 January 1940

Dear Herr Sacher, you should have received this letter a few days ago; but nothing was finally decided until yesterday, and that is the reason why I am writing so relatively late. You will no doubt have heard from Kägi that I shall no longer be here in March. I have to go off to America next week in order to take up some teaching posts I have been offered there. You can imagine that in the present circumstances such offers can neither be refused nor postponed. I must therefore ask you to release me from my engagement for your March concert. I do not like taking this step, for it is always annoying to be forced to withdraw a promise, and I had been particularly looking forward to this concert. I hope that you will understand my position. The present course of events has become so muddled that I suppose it is not to be wondered at when changes and surprises occur in the lives of individuals too.

Of course I don't know whether you will be obliged by my withdrawal to change the whole programme. Should you wish to dispense with the swan that was to have been roasted, you will perhaps find among Schott's publications other things of mine that could be used if necessary (4 Marienleben songs with orchestra, Nobilissima suite, violin concerto . . .); if the viola piece remains, however, you will perhaps find in Kägi a good exponent of the solo part, unless you want or are committed to another soloist. For safety's sake at any rate I played the piece through with him yesterday evening.

I should like very much to hear now and again about you and your work with the K.O. [Kammerorchester], and hope as well to see you and all other friends and acquaintances again in the not too distant future.

When will that be, I wonder?

Affectionately your

Paul Hindemith

To Willy Strecker   [Blusch]

30 January 1940

[. . .] I am leaving on Sunday. It is true that these days we cannot know everything that is happening, but by all appearances your fears would seem to be unfounded. I believe that the information I have received is somewhat more reliable than yours, and on no account would I rashly place myself in any difficult situation. You can therefore be reassured on that score. In my opinion you could easily have come here. At any rate the visa from here would not have been difficult to obtain.

The offers I have received look very promising—in the meantime they have increased to 4, and I think there are still more to come. That is very much in line with my wishes, for it was vitally necessary that something of this kind should come along in the course of the next few months. [. . .]

In the by no means easy negotiations of recent times, the attitude throughout the entire range of offices and departments has been one of unsurpassable friendliness. Things that would normally have required weeks, months, and in a few cases years to settle were sorted out within days and hours. Altogether we have been treated lovingly in literally every respect since the very first day of our arrival here, and I think it will stay that way both here and elsewhere. Voigt and the others taking part in the project must also be given good marks. Let's therefore face coming events confidently.

Farewell, and warmest greetings to all,

Your   Paul

"Hardened spirit" (*Verhärtetes Gemüt*) is a reference to people who deny the goodness of God in Gellert's poem "Die Güte Gottes."

To Hugo Strecker   Blusch

2 February 1940

Dear Hugo, a thousand heartfelt thanks for all the trouble you have gone to in the interests of my safety. I cabled you at the time because I was being told on all sides that the journey would not be without its dangers, and because the Pubs also wrote to me in this vein. Closer enquiries did, it is true, help to lessen these fears, but all the same one does not set out quite so confidently and unconcernedly as in peacetime. The written testimonials you have sent will at any rate be an extremely valuable aid, and I shall board the ship in a very much easier frame of mind. The consul in Geneva was altogether very friendly, but he does not have the authority to issue a permit of any kind, and he returned the letters to me for use with his recommendation. With these all will go smoothly.

I am very touched that Sir Adrian Boult should have written such a genuinely warm and convincing testimonial for me. In the past years I have experienced things at home that have made me despair profoundly of my fellow countrymen. Except for your father and a few other loyal friends, literally nothing remains there. Here, on the other hand, we have from the very beginning experienced much kindness from people whom we did not know at all and to whom we brought neither advantages nor disadvantages. And now, at a time when hatred and evil appear to be ruling the world, one has been shown on more than one occasion where friends are on whom one can count. And, because of that, one's progress towards the "hardened spirit" of the church hymn will at any rate not be quite as swift as earlier experiences would lead one to expect. So that you with your friendly help and Sir Adrian with his letter were, beside the concrete fact of helping to smooth my way, something like a consoling ray of light. For that I thank you very much and should like to ask you for the time being to let the kind letter writer know what pleasure and support he has given me. I shall tell him the same again when I write him a detailed letter from over there. [. . .] Warmest greetings, also from my wife, who is remaining here for now,

Your

Paul Hindemith

Hindemith left from Genoa, Italy, on the Italian liner *Rex* on 6 February 1940 and arrived in New York on 16 February.

His Swiss friend, Georges Haenni, was founder-director of the Conservatoire in Sion.

To Gertrud Hindemith   On board the liner *Rex*

12 February 1940

Best dear one, two telegrams (one from Naples, the other from Gibraltar) and a letter should have reached you by now, so that you have no need to worry. It has all gone well. There was a stop in Gibraltar around 7 in the morning — the stay was supposed to last an hour. The previous afternoon I had again felt some slight doubts as the men in the purser's office here on board took my passport but showed no interest at all in my fine letters from Adrian, etc. So on waking I wondered whether, as a precautionary measure, it might not be best to pack my bags, so that in case of a sudden evacuation one would not be deprived of all one's belongings—and an hour is after all a very short stay. In the end I didn't pack. Well—at 12 noon we still lay opposite the great rock, with Algeciras on the other side. Around 8 I had with great glee seen a small English police boat leaving the ship; so it was all over, I thought—the load on my mind tumbled into the water with an audible splash. Now in a high state of relief, I could study my surroundings; really very interesting, this rock that commands the sea as Haenni commands the Valais; and the many ships, all of which the Germans believe they sank long ago. At last, around 9, the cabin steward, who had been looking for me for some time, found me: the <u>British authorities</u> wishes to see me. The devil alone knows who had gone off in that little police boat. So down I went to a room full of captains, lists, and ashtrays. A friendly, elderly English sea captain invited me to sit down, but I didn't quite trust his friendliness when I saw a piece of paper with the names of the only four German passengers on board lying in front of him. The ages of each were written beside the names; since a 30-year-old mother was no more liable for military service than her two sons of 2 and 3, my 45 looked very ominous indeed, particularly with the thick blue ring with which it was embellished. The friendly man asked how long I had been living abroad. He then said that things were not exactly looking good in Germany, to which I replied that I knew nothing about that, since I had not been there for two years. And then I offered to show him my fine testimonials. But he didn't wish to see them either but just said, "<u>Right so, Mr. Hindemith, good-bye and good luck</u>." (I hope he'll soon be an admiral.) We took leave of one another with a cordial handshake; and with that the last remains of the load on my mind vanished. The examination of the tourist and third-class passengers took until after 12 noon, and then we continued on our journey. The only additional contribution I made to this happily concluded episode was to place a Swiss five-franc note in the chapel <u>offerings</u> box, thinking in this way to be acting in the spirit of the alas so distant lion.

14.2.40

The voyage ends tomorrow morning, and I must say that I am gradually beginning to look forward to having my feet on firm land once again. The voyage that had been so fine up to Gibraltar unfortunately did not continue so pleasantly. Friday was not too bad. The wind was indeed strong, but one could at least go on deck without being blown away. During Saturday, however, a proper storm arose and persisted until yesterday (Tuesday) morning. The worst was in the night from Monday to Tuesday, when the ship adopted the ill manners of a badly balanced rocking horse. It hopped, rose and fell haphazardly and without warning, rolled and pitched in all directions, and made a nerve-wracking noise with all its creaking, scraping, panting, tearing, and shaking. Evidently I am now fairly immune to seasickness, at least as regards its visible effects. Unfortunately, however, there remains one effect against which one is evidently quite powerless: an absolute loss of energy and utter inability to do anything, however trivial, or carry a single thought in one's head. On Saturday evening I attended the obligatory captain's predinner cocktail party, and after that did not put in an appearance anywhere for some time. From Sunday to Monday afternoon I simply stayed in bed—not because I felt ill, but because I had not the willpower to get out of bed and dress myself. But then on Monday I felt so filthy and stinking that I did in fact go outside—but then, to make up for it, lazed in bed again yesterday till 5 in the afternoon.

Today everything is back to normal, the sea is behaving itself and the wind is no longer unduly strong. Clearly in such an apathetic state of mind there could be no question of Brueghelling. On the first day I discovered a few more nice details, and maybe this afternoon I shall manage to work out a new plan: the Carnival and Lent picture as starting point and pivot, and the main idea more the parable of the blind, in which Griet in conjunction with an itinerant preacher will be the leader whose stupidity and blindness puts the villagers on the wrong track. Let's hope . . .!

In the cinema every afternoon. There were two English films that were good, otherwise American and French ones whose wretchedness defies description. If this is really the level at which the intellectual activity of nations functions today, one might almost come to the conclusion that a large part of humanity deserves to be wiped out by war. Italian cinematic art was restricted to a glorification of their homeland, either through a representation of Respighi's ridiculous Fontane di Roma with a great deal of water, a close-up of sea horses being born through a hole in the stomach of one of their parents (I believe with sea horses it is the papa), or to end with a history of aviation (who was it? Always of course the Italians, except for Lilienthal and the Wright brothers), in which Leonardo da Vinci distinguished himself with a bass voice deeper than any cellar, but otherwise was positioned in front of the camera or so skilfully whisked past it that one saw nothing beyond his loose coat. Completely in defiance of history he actually flew his plane. — The company on board is a ragtag-and-bobtail collection that offers little incitement to closer inspection. A few obscure film celebrities and a Dutch dancer who trains each morning in the Spanish style in the bar with the help of gramophone and castanets. He was to have given a performance last night wheather permitting, but it didn't permit. The only one to whom I have spoken a few times is an elderly Chinese man who sits at the little table behind mine and lives on soup and eggs (no bad ones!). As far as one can gather from his poor French, he is something in the nature of a musical expert employed by the government in China, and he has apparently established several conservatories. Besides that he has, like all conscientious Asian theorists in music, invented a musical notation system "on the basis of J. S. Bach's theories" (possible that Bach did once send these theories to China, so that they were lost to the rest of the world). Last night paper hats and little blowers were laid out, but it didn't produce a proper party atmosphere. Only a couple of Japanese sat brightly capped, blowing their horns orgiastically now and again between courses of the gala dinner. The dancing in the bar afterwards was very lively; I sat for a while opposite the Chinee; the music was so loud, however, that I didn't take in what he was saying. It apparently concerned the former cultural minister Becker, but I shall never know what was behind it all. At one stage he asked me whether there were any well-known German composers still alive; I didn't know that either.

So, my dear, there you have in essence the unessential. I would rather be sitting beside you at the Hallenbarter, fiddling, hornblowing, or bassooning. Let's hope it will soon come back to that! With all this water around, one can really become melancholy, and for a gentleman all on his own a ten-day ocean voyage is anything but a pleasure. How nice it is, after all, to sit in the morning in one's studio, knowing all the good creatures are nearby. With the help of my dear Pushu it was a splendid and a happy time up there. At the moment the achievements of <u>God's own country</u> tempt me not in the least. Could I come on any good way of returning with the prospect of a relatively secure living, I would turn the ship round now. Still, so far everything has gone well, perhaps this ship is also steaming towards a happy future. Pushu will soon come to join me, and from that day on everything will look much friendlier. Farewell then for now, my old and trusted companion in life and art; be kind to your absent traveller and think as lovingly of him as he of you. Greetings to the whole village, stroke the four-legged fellows, and look out on the peaks and the valley for me as well with double love.

     Your

     Y.

Cameron Baird in Buffalo had joined with Voigt and Nabokov to provide Hindemith with sufficient teaching work to finance his move to the United States. Baird's ambition was to establish with Hindemith a large school of music at Buffalo University, though all he was able to offer at this time was a series of short courses, both on the campus and in the town. There were two courses on campus each Wednesday and five for professional musicians and teachers in the town (one of these for teachers from Niagara Falls). The course described by Hindemith as the most interesting was an advanced composition class of qualified students, and it included the organists Robert Noehren and Herbert Fromm, who became friends.

El Greco's portrait of the bespectacled Grand Inquisitor Don Fernando Nino de Guevara is in the Metropolitan Museum, New York.

Hindemith's work at Wells College for Women in Aurora, which had been arranged by Nabokov, consisted of six lectures given each Tuesday evening from 19 March to 30 April.

The British actor Maurice Evans, together with the stage director Margaret Webster, formed a company to present Shakespeare's plays in the United States; his full-length Hamlet dated from 1938.

To Gertrud Hindemith   Hotel Lenox, Buffalo

23 February 1940

My dearest little creature, I now have at last some work behind me, so I can report to you in more detail. New York passed undisturbed, since nobody knew of my presence there. On Saturday evening I went to the cinema to see the big Disney success: another Snow White–like affair, this time Pinocchio, the story of a boy puppet who becomes a real boy. There are many nice things in it, nothing unbearably sugary apart from a sweet, pale blue and gold angel; but since there is no striving towards any kind of greatness, and the whole huge outlay is expended merely on indeed very pretty and at times very comical frivolities, one is left very dissatisfied. There are a couple of very fine rogues, consisting of a fox with a green coat and his companion, a very shabby lion or pumalike creature. And then the owner of the marionette theatre, a concentrated super-Wapuff. But all just grotesque, and lacking any further development of that striving towards something higher which, after several passages in <u>Snowhite</u>, I did expect to see.

I set off at 8 on Sunday morning—a stretch of country that I did not know. It leads through the Ithaca region, which I wanted to take the opportunity of seeing at least superficially (it seems to be very pretty). I had written to Nabokov asking whether he would care to come to the train in Ithaca around 4—however, he cabled during the journey, declining; and that was just as well, for despite the timetable the engine driver decided otherwise and made a shortcut just before Ithaca.

I arrived here at 7 in the evening, to be met by Cameron Baird on crutches (he had dislocated a foot tobogganing) and quite a large retinue. After a short conversation, I sent them all away, went to my hotel quarters here, and got settled in. The hotel is a repository for old ladies; it lies in the middle of my places of work, and opposite there are even trees with sparrows, admittedly somewhat sooty, flying around. It is in a quiet position, no more than 50 cars drive past in 10 minutes— 200 paces further on there are 50 in one minute. I am living on the 7th floor; on the 8th, the highest, completely in defiance of national tradition, there is an unassuming, nondescript, but—like all else here—very clean dining room (breakfast 0.45, lunch 0.60). I have a pretty living room with the regulation chairs, lamps, and small table, and a little bedroom with the likewise obligatory good bed, and bath attached. This costs $70 a month.

Early on Monday I was at the university, far out of town, about 6–8 kilometres along Main Street. <u>Chancellor</u> and <u>Dean</u> received me in a really very friendly way and we got everything fixed. The <u>Chancellor</u> is a very nice elderly gentleman who looks somewhat more friendly than the bespectacled Greco inquisitor. From this angle everything looks quite encouraging. They all regard me as a big shot, help where they can, but otherwise leave me completely in peace so that I can do as I like. The interest is quite strong; at any rate such that so far I have 19 lessons each week. The musical situation in the university is only moderate; there is a Mr. Van Lies here who apparently dispenses the bare minimum. The students, it seems, are what that would lead one to expect. Those who have selected me—about 15 boys and girls—are pretty awful. I have the feeling that most of them are coming simply out of curiosity and otherwise have such a vague idea of music that they can't even read it. This lot will come along for the first time next Tuesday, and I hope they will all act terribly stupidly; then I can say they are useless and should not bother their heads about music.

The remaining groups are much better. They are more or less all music teachers from the city who want to widen their knowledge, among them some really intelligent ones, with whom it will be a pleasure to work. Those who have little or no previous knowledge will be dealt with on Wednesday evenings in a class of about 30, though what I am supposed to tell them over a period of three months I have at the moment not the slightest idea. Yesterday and this morning I had two other groups of 5, both of good standard, though with little background knowledge. The most interesting club is a group of 6 organists, composers, etc., who will be meeting for the first time next week and, what is more, just round the corner in the 1st Presbyterian Church. Since the university is so far away and most of the people have occupations here <u>downtown</u>, all the classes, except for the university courses I am hoping to shed, take place in various nearby studios, which makes things much easier. How things will develop from there I can't yet say. A further addition will probably be an interpretation class, in which the Baird family and other Buffalonians in the form of variously constituted string quartets will have new things drilled into them—that could be quite good fun.

Tomorrow morning I am off to Aurora to get things fixed up there. With that added on, it will altogether be a pretty hairy load of work, all the more so since the rail connections are such that there is only one good train a day, and otherwise one is left kicking one's heels for 6–8 hours just on account of a few miles. I am not yet feeling completely at home (hardly possible, I suppose, after just 6 days), but I am hoping to become acclimatized before very long and will then be able to tell you my thoughts on the next step. I am not yet clear whether Buffalo will become a permanency. It is certainly not the worst, but that there could be something better is equally certain. There have not of course been any further offers yet, since hardly anyone knows I am here — and anyway it will surely be better to wait till after this term, when my successes, which seem quite probable following the tests I have so far made, will speak for themselves. Then one can start looking ahead.

For the moment I'm sitting here with no money. The $60 I brought with me have shrunk to 10, and those will go on the rail fare tomorrow. The Pubs undertook to send me 50, but obviously they've forgotten. I wrote to them yesterday about it, so they ought to send me something by tomorrow morning. I didn't want to start off here with a loan, though Baird has offered me money. Next week will be the first, and then I suppose the university must pay me. There has so far been only very vague talk about the school plans. At any rate it seems to me that there is not much money available for them.

On Tuesday afternoon I went to see the full-length Hamlet, played by the Evans company, about which I wrote you last year from Boston. The performance was very good, at exactly the right level between good box-office theatre and intellectual excess. Evans as Hamlet very simple, incisive, and convincing. The play in English is really quite magnificent, and it is absurd to omit a single word — even those words that are not always printed, about <u>maid's legs</u> with Hamlet between, were delivered. At times I felt a real sense of awe, and I asked myself whether it is at all encouraging to go to see such giant figures and feel the conviction creeping up that in comparison one perhaps has nothing at all to say.

I still have no answer from Massine, though possibly it has just not arrived yet. I have heard that the ballet company will be dancing here in the middle of March, so I shall see him then. I have now at last got the text together. I am still polishing it and adding the inscriptions, then I shall send it to my severe critic Pirwap. I think this time he will be satisfied with it.

Voigt cabled yesterday that Koussevitzky would like me to be at his New York concert (tomorrow), in which he is doing the Mathis Symphony. I have cabled a refusal. First, what with? And second, why?

Yesterday Chancellor Capen gave a big buffet lunch and I had to go. The entire university (that is to say, the teaching staff) was squashed, loudly chatting, into a single room, and a bit of cold chicken dressed with a bit of galantine wriggled its way through the crowd, followed by the inevitable <u>coffee</u>. I got to know about 100 people and forgot them just as quickly. A few nice ones among them, elderly professors, mostly very English; and this term's visiting French professor from Lille was also quite useful. Apart from these, I was inescapably hemmed in by elderly music-loving owls, one of whom spoke so many words without stopping that the very thought of her still takes my breath away. Never mind, it was all well meant, and public holidays such as this (it was Washington's birthday) carry certain obligations.

Except for one evening at Baird's, when all the lesson candidates had to report and be allocated, and which in consequence lasted rather long, I have disappeared to bed around 9 each evening and am always out of it by 6. I have not yet been into town, just a few times around the nearest blocks. — Buffalo has introduced itself in a horrible condition. Rain, snow, unparalleled slush, sheet ice — it has been God-awful. Today the sun shone for the first time, so it didn't all look quite so dismal.

So, old chap, with many words and little content I've now told you how things look and how I'm doing. On the whole I am feeling a bit stupid today (that may be due to the change in the weather), so that my report has come out rather dry. But that means nothing, the next in a few days' time will be a bit more cheerful. I miss my Wapuff, though I don't think he would be all too happy here. Certainly it's a huge city, but apparently very provincial. A bit further out there are sure to be some pleasant places, however, and with the appropriate horns and bassoons we shall be able to pass the time enjoyably again. We shall know more before very long, won't we?

For today you will find enclosed very many and very warm kisses, many envious greetings and much Yashny. [. . .]

Your old   P.

Last night a phone call came: <u>Here is Mrs. XYZ speaking. Mr. Hindemith, a friend of ours from Boston has just arrived. He says that you are the greatest living composer, and so I wanted to ask you, whether you would like to come tonight into my house. . . .</u> Was I unable? And how!

To Gertrud Hindemith   Buffalo
                                                                        27 February 1940
Dearest Pushu, I hear a ship is leaving at the end of this week, so you shall today receive the continuation of my long letter of last Friday. I was feeling rather grumpy when I wrote that, for, owing to the neverending organizing, I could hardly find time for any proper work, and besides that this caricature of a town, consisting, apart from a very few pleasanter streets, only of kilometres of Siberian timber-frame houses without a trace of charm, is hardly enlivening, particularly when covered in slush, sheet ice and snow — and the snow is black into the bargain. New people are continuing to apply for the classes, so the original figure of 5 for the smaller ones has risen to 8–9, and the general course, which is starting tomorrow, will have an audience of 40–50 instead of the expected 20. By tomorrow, Wednesday evening, I shall have gone through the whole series for the first time, so I shall be in a better position to see how it is all going and how the work must be distributed over the period up to mid-May.

On Saturday afternoon I went by train to Syracuse, from where I was taken by car to Aurora. I stayed there over Sunday, and that was something more like a plea-surable experience after the buffalo-town. Nabokov, despite a boil on his nose, was delighted to have me there. He is a good chap, a bit Russian and slovenly, and his entire household gives the same impression. His wife obviously has no feeling for such things, she is still rather collegegirl-ish and continues to study English literature in Ithaca. He meanwhile stays at home cooking. There were a few very clever and nice people from the teaching staff there with whom one could pass a few hours in decent conversation. An elderly Austrian painter, who has been there a few months as drawing instructor, a professor from the Viennese academy whom I had met once before in Mährisch-Ostreu, very congenial and in particular a gifted typographer, contributed much to the Europeanization of the atmosphere, especially since his wife yesterday fabricated an excellent chicken paprika—a great relief after two weeks of snakes' grub.

For the 6 lectures in Aurora I have thought up a very nice format. They wanted to sing some new little piece for women's chorus in May, so I suggested composing it together with the girls on the blackboard. The lectures there start on 12 March, one every Tuesday. I shall shove off from here at 10 in the morning to Ithaca, a 3-hour train journey. The lecture there [at Cornell University] is at 4 in the afternoon (also covering 6 Tuesdays)—more general, rather in the style of the general course here—and afterwards an Aurora car will fetch me and drive me there, where the lecture is in the evening. At 8 on Wednesday morning, there is a train to Ithaca which, wonder to relate, has a connection to Bafflou [Buffalo in German phonetic spelling], so that I shall be back here by midday to shave my other customers. Thus the entire Aurora-Ithaca affair can be done easily in one day—though I have promised Ithaca to go there occasionally on Mondays, so that questions in which the people are specially interested can be discussed in more detail (I am completely free on Mondays).

I landed back here last night, and it was snowing and looking not a bit better than three days ago. This week something may perhaps be said about the school plans. But, however that may turn out, I have no very great confidence in this region. Not that I can complain—on the contrary, I encounter fairy-tale friendliness wherever I go. But everything is so very odd.

A telegram arrived recently from Yale University; I should disregard their letter, they would be writing something else. Next day the letter arrived, offering me $100 for 2 lectures on successive days. That is not much, the journey alone with sleeping car would cost 45–50 return. But yesterday Voigt wrote me that the music dean of Yale, old D. S. Smith whom, together with his dry symphony, I got to know in Boston last year, had called him. He wished to have me for a series of lectures (similar to Cornell and Aurora) and to pay $500 for them. That sounds rather more reasonable, and a connection with Yale, the second most famous university in the country (the first—Cambridge [Harvard]—is already occupied by Nadia [Boulanger] and Igor [Stravinsky]), is of course of more value than the best Buffalo can offer, with all its goodwill. In addition to that, the music department has recently received a foundation worth millions. Of course, nothing like this can be done before the Cornell-Aurora affair comes to an end, unless I am prepared to sacrifice a large part of the profit. So it could only be a question of next term. But this is counting chickens before they are hatched—I must at least wait and see whether a direct enquiry will be made and what it will be. [. . .]

I am at last emerging slowly from my Blusch-like lethargy of the past weeks. I feel movement again in the production of ideas; I have already discovered all kinds of things for the lessons, and feel sure the composing will begin again in a few days' time. They write from New York that hardly any of my notes are still in stock, that there is a constant demand, yet nothing from Schott is being allowed through. I have now written asking for estimates of what 100 photocopies of a piano sonata and other more saleable things might cost. Voigt thought it would not be more than 80–90 dollars. I would be prepared to pay that and have a few of the pieces done at my own expense; I'll surely get it back. Something or other of mine must be made available, particularly when I shall now be here for some time, in order that interest—for the moment at least—is kept alive. [. . .]

Dear old fellow, the contrast is a wretched one: Blusch and Buffalo; and even a prettier region, such as one finds around the Cayuga Lake in Aurora or Ithaca (a bit like the Eichesfeld round Leinefelde) hardly chases somewhat melancholy feelings away. But we shouldn't pity ourselves, rather swallow without too many grimaces the bitter pills of separation for months on end, Buffalonian existence, and for the moment still uncertain future prospects—how many would pay millions for the pills we find so distasteful! So let us remain of good cheer. But just now I can't allow myself to think back in earnest.

I shall be writing to all the Valaisians sometime at the end of this week, also to Mother and to Willy, letters you will have to forward, for it is being said that mail to Germany would now be stopped entirely. [. . .]

So, my dearest Hasha, that is enough for today. I love you very much and in my thoughts am at home and with you in the garden, in the surrounding countryside and last not least at the Hallenbarter. Don't forget your old Buffalo Bill. I am hoping to hear from you soon, the first little letter must slowly be creeping in this direction. Greetings to all in Blusch, and stroke the little animals.

  Many kisses
  Your Y.

To Gertrud Hindemith   Buffalo
                      7 March 1940
Dearest Hasha, your typewritten letter (No. 2) came yesterday. [. . .] It was bliss to hear once again the old lion's familiar voice. All the same, receiving such dear little letters is not particularly consoling, for the homesickness that comes creeping

out of them soon assumes the dimensions of a fully grown whale. If after your arrival in this blessed country you also feel as I do, we'll produce a delicious duet. I fear I shall never accustom myself to it entirely. [. . .] The whole thing did not strike me as quite so senseless in previous years, but that was probably because I never stayed very long in any one place, neither was I faced with such long commitments. And then the stay in Blusch was of course no proper preparation for life over here. Before very long, however, Pushu will be coming, and everything will then have a friendlier look—or perhaps it might even become my job to dispel the old fellow's blues. Work does of course give the whole venture some kind of meaning, if not a very convincing one. I do it as well as I can, it is good practice for me and also to some extent a test of strength. [. . .]

I walked to the university the day before yesterday to get a bit of exercise, 1 hour and 40 minutes in mud and slush. It wasn't very nice, but at least it was airy. Nothing has been said about school plans, and I don't think anything will come of it. I'm glad of that, for, were I forced to become director of this school, I can already visualize the classroom in which, after a few years' activity here, I should hang myself. I have been nowhere and have seen no one beyond the people attending my courses. When could I, anyway?! But wait, on Monday evening I did go to a rehearsal for a concert that my organists' group put on the day before yesterday. Unimportant and devoid of all interest, including the compositions of my "pupil" (in this same course) Fromm. It is to be hoped he will learn something in the next few weeks; I think he will (and so does he).

Dear Hasha, farewell, think of your Yijak. Keep on learning Latin and make music in your thoughts with your automatized and somewhat grey colleague (but don't worry, in all respects things are going well with me, and I am also quite cheerful—but I must be allowed to open my heart to my lion!). Yashny for all dear animals. Greeting to all neighbours. Kisses
    Your   Y.

Hindemith was engaged by Yale University for three consecutive Saturdays and Mondays between 30 March and 15 April 1940 to give master classes in theory and composition and to deliver two public lectures. He travelled there each time from Buffalo, beginning on 30 March. The dean of the School of Music at that time was David Stanley Smith; the assistant dean, Richard Donovan, became dean in the following academic year.

To Gertrud Hindemith   [Buffalo]
                                                        31 March 1940
    [. . .] I arrived back from Yale dog-tired at 12:30 last night, now it is just after 7, so you will see the news service for Wapuff functions day and night. Yale was in

every way a truly heartening fact. In their urge to learn and to do they have landed me with so much work (yesterday alone 7 hours!) that I shall have a great deal to do to satisfy them all along the line. Mr. Donovan, teacher of composition and 2nd dean, met me at the station, and from the very first moment made a very sympathetic impression. Somewhat crafty perhaps, but highly cultured and, as it became evident in the course of the day, extremely well versed in his subject, if utterly conservative.

For me things began at 10. About 10 of Dean D. S. Smith's students, male and female, had been assembled, and he and Donovan were also present. The boys and girls then played their compositions, and I was supposed to criticize them. That is not exactly a very pleasant situation to be in, and I told them so: when one criticizes, one makes an enemy of the teacher, when one stays silent or diplomatically skates round the issue, the pupil disapproves. Well, I soon found the right method, once I had spotted the weak point in the teaching. In my usual way I brought up problems that the old man in his dried-up frozenness could never have dealt with and which were so far removed from his method that he couldn't even feel offended when I unrolled whole principles in this manner. I drew up complete harmonic plans in the twinkling of an eye, changed the appearance of complete pages, and showed them a mass of new things. Result: general satisfaction, even from the old man, who was highly delighted to find I was almost stricter than he himself: he had always said pupils should not think they could write whatever they pleased for me!

Lunch with a few other students as a guest in their house. In the afternoon things got very lively. A troop of about 40 advanced theory students, most of the music teachers too. I was not quite sure what to do with them. They wanted to hear about harmony, and so for two hours I raced at high speed through the territory it had taken me years to become familiar with. It was very interesting. The students asked questions and joined in with a will. Some theory teachers came out with violent protests against my assertions, and I had to exert myself to the utmost to overcome them. It was one of the most interesting debates I have ever had on these questions. The atmosphere at the end of the two hours was one of animated enthusiasm—one boy in his enthusiasm had even pocketed my blue book. Following that came another 1½-hr debate over teaching problems with around 6 students and Donovan, who then got into very hot water himself, for the students attacked him violently on the basis of the facts they had just heard. I was left sitting somewhere in the middle and had to smooth things down. Here too every one of the problems was dealt with in a very temperamental fashion, but with great intelligence and good manners.

And that's not all! Donovan had invited the entire music faculty to dinner, and afterwards I had to talk yet again about theory. Spurred on by the afternoon's sport, I had then to explain in minute detail what I would put in place of scholastic harmony and counterpoint, and I did that with the aid of the other blue book I still

had. All these novelties aroused great excitement here too, and, when I left the bat-
tlefield around 10, I had the feeling of having after a hard day's work left these
people with something to occupy their minds. The old <u>dean</u> drove me to the station
and was again very nice—but he is the least significant of the whole group. I shall
be going there again tomorrow morning.

Here I found another letter from my esteemed Wapuff awaiting me. [. . .] The
German music periodicals are really not worth looking at, so you need not send me
any more. Once you are here, you will see how far behind us all that is—not just
50 years, it has never existed and cannot be allowed ever to exist again!

Despite your expectations, Buffalo has not grown any nicer as the weeks go by,
but since I am now there for only three days I no longer notice it so much. [. . .] For
the first few weeks it was unbearable. I am not usually all that nervy, but there are
times when one can really be driven mad by restlessness and tension. In certain
weather conditions the air here is so full of electricity that every piece of metal one
touches—door handles, light switches, scissors, radiators—crackles, and on really
bad days gives off sparks. This year it was particularly bad. But it has stopped now.

Are you gradually making your shipping plans? If you get the Rex, take an outer
cabin with window, otherwise you will arrive here in gloomy spirits. [. . .]

Chicago has written asking for an orchestral work for their jubilee next season.
They will pay $700—I think I shall do it.

Enough, my old friend; a fond Sunday-Yashny and kisses for all the lions. Consider yourself dearly loved by your theoretical colleague!

Breakfast now, I'm hungry! Greetings to all,

    Your   Y.

During his second weekend visit to Yale, Hindemith accepted Donovan's invitation
to join the faculty in September 1940 as a visiting professor, teaching five or six
hours a week, at a salary of $4,000. His present engagements at Yale and other
establishments were gradually drawing to an end and, with only Tanglewood still
outstanding, he was able to turn his attention back to his composition work.

The third volume of *Unterweisung im Tonsatz* was intended to deal with three-part
writing.

Due to difficulties caused by the war, the Strecker brothers transferred the
responsibility of publishing Hindemith's works, both old and new, to Schott's
branch in London in cooperation with AMP, and Hugo Strecker was delegated to
look after his interests.

To Gertrud Hindemith   [Buffalo]

                                                              7 April 1940

[. . .] 6 Pushu letters arrived all together. Since then I feel good and shall be
boarding my sleeping car afterwards in good cheer. [. . .] If Buffalo alone existed,

I should be reading your reports in gloomy spirits. But now that Yale, greeted joyfully by you too (rightly!), is beckoning, I look on the future with significantly more joy. We can have a very pleasant life there, live out of town in a nice little house, and the lion can satisfy his thirst for knowledge to his heart's content.

That you are not intending to come till 5 June is not so nice—do come a ship earlier! [. . .] When you arrive (God, how long it still seems before Wapuff will walk down the gangway with Alfi!!), we shall first spend a few days in New York, so that you can admire this paradise in due form. Next we shall move on as quickly as possible to the Berkshires and find a nice place to rent. Then we shall at once buy the lion a car—a secondhand one for 400–500 dollars, for one can't manage here without one. I am in fact now fully prepared to stay here a long time—the thought is quite pleasing with Yale in the background—and to keep Switzerland in mind for visits in summer or autumn. This God-forsaken Europe has no longer anything to offer us in the way of opportunities, while here one can still work unhindered and with success. By the time the lion arrives, I shall have a clear profit of around 1,600 dollars in my pocket; with that one can get along for quite a while, and there will be some more to come from the Berkshires.

The violin concerto is being done next week in Boston. I'm supposed to go, but don't yet know whether I shall. [. . .]

To Willy Strecker   [Buffalo]
                                                                        26 April 1940

Dear Willy, Gertrud has sent me your letters, and I have received all the sonatas still outstanding from Voigt, many thanks. I was pleased on both counts. Altogether I am slowly beginning once more to enjoy life and things in general. In the past few weeks I simply had no time for them. [. . .] Now I have a bit more room to breathe, Yale and Cornell are done with, and in three to four weeks' time I shall be striking my tents here too. During the summer there is the music festival and summer school (6 weeks), and from autumn I shall be permanently in Yale with part-time activity here. So all is going well.

Kouss. has performed the Mathis Symphony seven times with great success. The violin concerto was last Friday—excellently played, huge success! [. . .] I have broken off relations with Massine on grounds of artistic differences, though I shall still deliver the Brueghel score according to contract. This summer I shall have to start on the third volume of my book, it is urgently needed for my lessons. The second is splendidly proving its worth—there are some mistakes in it, and a few of the rules need to be complemented, but otherwise it is really useful, and all learners are getting the greatest pleasure from it.

I have had a long letter from Hugo regarding the transfer of the rights and possible reprints there. He makes some very good and farseeing proposals that will allow everything to be maintained here on a permanent basis without in principle making any changes in our mutual relationship—about which I am very glad.

I hope you are right with your optimism. I do not altogether share it, but why, like Nora, should we not believe in miracles? (Though I remember that there the miracle turned out badly!)

I'll finish for today. In future you will be getting news of me rather more frequently, since from now on life will be a bit more comfortable, and I can be thoroughly pleased with all my decisions up till now. Greetings to you both and to the whole firm, or as much of it as is still on hand!

Let me hear from you.

Affectionately,

Your   Paul

In connection with his appointment at Yale Hindemith was awarded the university's Howland Memorial Prize, given to "the citizen of any country in recognition of achievements of marked distinction in the fields of literature, the arts or the science of government."

Attached to the first page of this letter was a clipping from the New York Times reading as follows: "Washington, D.C., May 28—The liner Washington, which was to have sailed from New York on Saturday for Genoa, will leave two days earlier, on Thursday, in order to make extra calls at Bordeaux and Lisbon and pick up Americans who wish to return to the United States. This is being done at the instance of the state department. At last reports there were 301 Americans at Bordeaux and 70 at Lisbon awaiting passage home. There are several hundred at Genoa, it is reported."

To Ernest R. Voigt   Buffalo

29 May 1940

Esteemed friend, now we are in the soup! The Italian ships have dropped out altogether; all the same, I did have faint hopes of the Manhattan, which sails from Genoa on Saturday, but yesterday I received a telegram from my wife that this ship was already overflowing with Americans fleeing home. The only possible way of procuring the last berth would have been to go to Genoa on the off chance and see if the improbable could be turned into the possible. But she didn't risk it, since, if it were to prove in vain, she would have had to return to Switzerland—and for that she would under no circumstances be given a visa. In the meantime our baggage sits in Genoa, waiting for her.

The situation would be utterly desperate if I had not been given a faint final glimmer of hope in the form of the enclosed announcement in this morning's newspaper. Experience proves that even on a fully booked ship a place can still be found if one goes about it the right way. Can you put your hand on anyone who could persuade the captain of the Washington to take my wife along? Since the ship leaves New York tomorrow (Thursday), it is of course too late to talk to the man personally, otherwise I should probably have hastened there myself to explain the situation to him—though I think more influential voices would need to be heard than my moans and groans. Perhaps by devious routes you can come on voices of this kind to communicate by telegraphic means wishes or commands that . . . Perhaps my forthcoming Yale appointment and the Howland Prize will be of some help (then it would at least be good for something!); and you need not worry about the expense, of course, I will do everything to get even the most expensive legal course cracking, and oil underground wheels as well, if necessary.

My only naval connection is the enclosed, obviously already somewhat weather-beaten old sea dog Captain Ruygrok, and I don't even know him and have not yet replied to his completely superfluous letter—incidentally, he has not sent his Lev's excellent compositions (for which I have so far not been sorry)—his memory compartment is probably already stuffed full of seaweed. But all the same: the Washington captain is perhaps his very best friend, and perhaps he once rocked the naval secretary on his knee, or some other such coincidence of that kind. In that case (if it leads to any possible opening) I would even praise Lev's compositions and write the old kobold a letter at least as long and foolish as his to me. So, unless you know of anything better, this old crock may perhaps help.

In normal circumstances I should not be coming to New York next week, I still have my last lessons to give tomorrow and on Friday. But of course I shall put in an appearance at once, if there is anything I can do, there are planes enough! [. . .] So I await orders of some kind. As soon as I hear anything, I shall cable my wife; possibly also suggest that she get a testimonial from the Zurich consul—although I don't think he can or will.

I shall be glad when this nightmare is lifted from my shoulders!!! Perhaps something will come along after all to make up for these recent lost days. Seldom in your life will you have seen a banquet to match the one I shall hold if, despite all the difficulties, she does still manage to arrive safely!

In haste, on the uttermost edge of hope!

P.H.

To Ernest R. Voigt [Buffalo]
6 June 1940

In haste!

[. . .] Yale has tried everything via Washington, but received negative replies. Meanwhile the "Washington" is not going to Genoa at all. There are no other opportunities at the moment—it may be that the Rex will sail again next week according to schedule. It may also be that my wife is already somewhere on her way, for I've had no news of any kind for 2 weeks, despite cabled enquiries. [. . .]

Hasty greetings,

P.H.

At the summer school in Tanglewood, Hindemith was one of two composers engaged to teach composition, the other being Aaron Copland. Hindemith took rooms in Lenox, Massachusetts, for the duration of the music festival.

The "emigrant boy" among his pupils there was Lukas Foss.

The new sonatas played during the festival were those written for various wind instruments and piano in 1938–39.

The first performance of the third organ sonata was given by E. Power Biggs at Tanglewood on 31 July 1940.

Otto Ortmann was translating the second volume of *Unterweisung im Tonsatz* into English.

Betty Mergler was a singer friend in Frankfurt.

To Gertrud Hindemith   Lenox, Mass.

14 July 1940

Most beloved Pushulein, distant and devoutly longed-for good companion, three letters from you arrived together today to my delighted surprise, two (of 12 and 19 June) that must have travelled on some mysterious ship, and a Clipper letter that took only 12 days to get here. A sign therefore that a postal connection still exists. After your two previous letters at the end of May (it does look as if everything has arrived) reached me recently in New York before I moved here, I was told on all sides that no more mail was going to Switzerland, and that was still the position a few days ago. Now it seems that a route through France has been opened, so I can breathe a bit more freely. Telegrams are really rather too monosyllabic—but all the same, I shall keep to the habit I formed before the abortive crossing of sending you a telegram every 8–10 days. In addition to that, a little letter will now travel with each Clipper, so as to make the pain of this awful separation at least a little more bearable.

I hope you are trying all you can to get to Lisbon, though now there are dismal warnings of unrest there too. However that may be, I think you might make the attempt, even seek the help of the German Embassy—there was a Herr v. Nostiz there who telephoned last autumn. Once I know you can reach Lisbon, I can put the pressure on here. Till then nothing at all can be done. I can arrange a Clipper seat and everything else; here and in Yale there are good and helpful people who will do all they possibly can bonae voluntatis to bring the lions over. It was through Yale that I got things moving for the "Washington" that sailed from Lisbon three or four weeks ago, though only with the result that the big bug in charge of such matters here, Secretary of State Hull, sent a 30-word telegram to the effect that things could be done only for American citizens. People who arrived on the "Manhattan" said you could certainly have got a berth there, though the ship was filled to overflowing. One really should not be told after the event what might have been done before it—but despite all this we are still, in the eyes of many, in an enviable position. Admittedly in Buffalo I often asked myself why, in view of the steadily worsening situation, the old lion showed no signs of haste—I was terribly nervy and spent several sleepless nights tossing around in my hotel bed. I had not the slightest idea, after my journey here and all the information the consul in Zurich already had, that a further bit of paper would have to be sent from here for you, otherwise I should have had it on its way in good time. The fact that, following your telegram that anyway arrived late, the paper was not to be found in Buffalo and the otherwise really quite capable mooncalf Voigt made a further mess of things, was too bad— but I tried everything that could be tried, and the good Yalers could tell you a tale about all my moans and cries for help. Well, the little letter from your dear lion's paws has shown that you are being patient and calm, and that comforts me a little. I am hoping that the longed-for telegram with news of a travel opportunity will come soon. But try to extend your visa in good time, in case (contrary to expectations) nothing comes along soon; I am sure the consul in Zurich can apply to Washington for that. If not, I must know in good time, so I can get things moving here—not all that easy during the summer holidays, but I'll manage!

Alas, it was all so nicely planned! Here a little house beside the lake had been reserved for us, one of the Boston players had been instructed very early to look for something on my behalf. In Yale too agents were already looking around for a nice home for us, and I was slowly beginning to inspect cars! If one reaps rewards for all one has to go through, we should soon, in spite of everything, be in a position to enjoy these splendours! Let's hope so.

Today is a peaceful Saturday evening; there is nothing going on in the school, thank God, so I can tell you things in the order they happened undisturbed.

My little notebook tells me I last wrote to you on 27 April, so you will be up to date on all events up till then. In the following week Aurora came to an end, but the Buffalo lessons continued. Buffalo began to look really beautiful in May, at least the district in which I was living. In winter I had hardly been aware of the giant trees, then suddenly the whole town was full of wonderful avenues, lawns, and tulip beds. I returned to Aurora once again, partly to give a lecture on theory to such teachers as were interested, partly to attend a farewell party given by the music department. For the chorus composed with the college girls during lectures I wrote an orchestral accompaniment, and the whole thing was then successfully performed da capo on May-day 10 days later, to the delight of all (I was not there). In Buffalo, meanwhile, work was piling up, since the majority of my students were reckoning on credits, which were, however, conditional on having attended 15 double lessons. Since I had started almost a month late and did not wish to put the poor worms at a disadvantage, I made up the missing time for them and also gave my Niagara Falls people (who were the farthest behind) lessons in their home town. The farewell parties of the individual classes were meanwhile assuming overdimensional proportions; there was no end to the hospitality. Baird organized an affair in his country house in my honour, with a lot of people, food, drink, and music—I played the double bass in his little orchestra.

Then there was a lot of discussion regarding my return in the autumn; there was no money and they were seeking ways of raising it. I was not all that wild about taking the Buffalo work on again, for it's better, if one can, to avoid spending two nights each week in a sleeping car. All the same, I wanted to do what I could for the sake of the students, some of whom are distinctly talented and very keen. Later, when the war became violent and the Buffalonians more fearful than the rest of their compatriots, the whole thing finally went up in smoke. The lessons came to an end on 24 May, though I gave an extra lesson just for two classes.

I hadn't written anything for a long time, apart from the Aurora-Wells chorus and a piano fugue on the blackboard in one of the Buffalo classes. I then gradually started making plans and wrote an organ sonata to mark Pushu's arrival. It is based on three of the old songs in the theory book, and one of my pupils played it straight off and with great enthusiasm. We also made gramophone recordings of it, so that old Wapuff could be greeted by it in New York. But it was all in vain, for the beloved lion did not come.

On the day the Italians declared war, I was lying in a corner like a lame earthworm, and I should have been in utter despair if the nice pupil mentioned above (Noehren) and his wife had not come along to comfort me. During this difficult time, these two and another, a German—Fromm from Bingen—proved to be good people, doing all they could within their modest means to help me over my distress. To end with, there were a few chamber music sessions in which I played the fiddle, to everyone's surprise. Then I began slowly to prepare for my move, paid my bills, bought suitcases, sent money to Pushu, and similar things of that sort. Buffalo was over, I had put in some good work there, and it appeared that every one of the participants was of the same opinion. I left on 12 June—first, to visit Nabokov once more in Aurora, which, now cleared of its school population, looked very lovely and springlike on the lakeside.

On the following day, I landed up in New York, where I stayed two days, seeing my translator Ortmann. On Sunday I was with Donovan in New Haven (Yale) and left all my winter clobber (put in mothballs by his wife), the two instruments, and the books I don't need here in his house. Then came a few more days in New York, partly busy (with Ortmann), and partly boring, on the 22nd I came here. It is lovely here, the countryside is gentle, like northern Switzerland, there are dense woods everywhere, mountains trace a softly flowing line all along the horizon, and there is also a lake. The little town is named Lenox, the school and the music festival grounds are half-an-hour's walk away in Tanglewood, a former manor house splendidly situated in a large and pleasant park. I am staying with Mr. Driscoll, a Congregational Church preacher, have two nice, very quiet rooms with trees outside the windows, but make hardly any use of the family. My meals are at Mrs. Hageman's; I found them too costly in the hotel. I arrived here 2 weeks before classes start and so had time and leisure to explore the countryside undisturbed. I went for many walks and saw so many pretty spots in the woods, and particularly in a nearby national park, that for the first time I felt something like love for this country. Besides this I did some vigorous writing and almost completed a cello concerto— I hope to be able to finish the score next week.

The school started a week ago. The whole thing is a mixture of Donaueschingen, Ankara, and the Hochschule, and I am profiting greatly from all my experiences in those places. Here I am of course a very "famous" teacher, and the pupils have already spread rumours of the many unexpected things I make them do. The company is unfortunately not outstanding, except for one small and very good emigrant boy from Germany. During the first lessons there was some resistance, partly because of the unaccustomed work I was demanding, partly in consequence of the absolute lack of attention I paid to the existing scores of my patients. With suitable treatment, however, even the most obstinate began to soften, and yesterday, after I had ground them down by the well-tried method of a three-hour exercise in strict counterpoint on the blackboard, they are now all extraordinarily well behaved, modest, and grateful. The main class—7 so-called composers—is dealt with 4 times a week in 4 morning lessons, each of 4 hours; then there are two other classes, each with 3 lessons a week; and finally on 2 evenings I give two more entertaining courses in the so-called academy (the section of the institute that caters more to amateurs). In these I make the participants (around 100 each) "compose" a mixed chorus and a fugue. It is quite amusing, and everyone <u>enjoys</u> it. My boys were quite appalled when they suddenly found themselves forced to sing what they had written, and even more so when required to take lessons in playing an instrument. The most surprised was my colleague Copland, who wants to do things very differently with his 6 composers and to perform their stuff for them, and who talks always of mature composers, instead of considering them, as I do, utter tyros and obliging them to submit to the appropriate treatment. Koussevitzky is completely on my side and happily agreed to my proposal that members of the teaching staff be forbidden to accept for performance anything written by the composition pupils. Put like this, it all sounds a bit comical, but it is absolutely necessary if one wants to get rid of all that more than monstrous sloppiness and ignorance prevailing in this country in matters of composition and music theory. There is still a great deal to do in the next 5 weeks.

Next week I shall be conducting my Concert Music for String Orchestra and Brass Instruments in one of the internal institute concerts; the academy choir is studying the choruses from Das Unaufhörliche; in 5 other places within the school pieces of mine are also in the programme, and before long Sanromá will be playing all the new sonatas with their respective wind instrument players. This afternoon the trumpeter played his piece for me. It is many times finer and very powerful, and I ardently longed for my dear colleague to have been here—he would have thoroughly enjoyed it! August will be terrible—there will be three concerts each week with Koussevitzky and his orchestra (which is of course here and giving classes in the school), then thousands of cars will arrive and peace and quiet will be gone—but that will pass too. The Mathis Symphony will be played in the penultimate concert on the 17th. Perhaps by then you will already be here, or at least on your way!!!

During all this time I have been well, apart from the complete lassitude brought on by events; despite all changes in the weather, rail journeys, and work, I never once caught cold. Yale has inflicted on me some kind of medal for services to art, and it will be ceremonially conferred next term. In addition, the American Academy of Arts and Sciences has made me an honorary member, in return for which I have copied out the new organ sonata and presented it to them. This piece will be brought out by the Pubs in New York—I have already had the proofs. The book of exercises is also in print and will appear in 6–8 weeks. I am planning to publish a very short and concentrated cheap version of it for pupils. However, I don't feel like writing it myself, and I have told Voigt to commission it from Ortmann. I have heard nothing more from the Russians. They are in South America. I will see how the money situation goes. If I need money and find no other source, I shall write the ballet for them. Otherwise only under pressure (which they evidently do not intend to apply, they appear rather to be glad not to have to honour their contract), for I want nothing more to do with Massine, who has gone completely to pot. My fortune consists at the moment of 1,800 dollars in a New Haven bank, to that 1,400 will be added from here, and later there will be 700 from Chicago, and the Yale salary. There will also be a few other things; there has been talk, for instance, of radio and gramophone recordings of the Nobilissima suite or the violin concerto for 800 dollars. So the position is not exactly bad. I am coming increasingly to the conclusion that Willy is making a big mistake in reckoning on my joyful return home once this present mess comes to an end. The prospects here are good, I am slowly growing used to land and people, and find that neither are worse than anywhere else, on the contrary, they offer great advantages. And when the good old fellow is at last here, we shall be in paradise, and I really cannot see what would induce me to give it up.

As the man of yesterday,

"Having well and soundly slept,

Early to the stable went,"

he found the weather so fine and enticing that he was ready to don his double-sided blue-and-beige silk sports jacket, specially made for such a purpose, with the idea of setting out on a walking tour. But he abandoned this thought in order to continue conversing with his dear solitary lion instead.

If this letter flies across the ocean at the same speed as yours to me, it will arrive just in time for your birthday. It will be the first we have not celebrated together! Last year, in our nice little house in Blusch, Pushu was so sweet and so good on his anniversary, and altogether he has developed into a good model animal in his diverse capacities of house, art, and companion lion! Two days later we drove to Brügge—and in the meantime the world turned upside down! The two birthdays before that we were in Berlin, the first with Heinisch's lion pictures and Betty Mergler's horseshoe, the second a kind of repetition. If things turn out as we wish (haha, who knows what surprises still lie in store for us?) we shall celebrate the next in a nice little house in New Haven or a summer cottage on the Maine coast or somewhere else. Or do you prefer the Rocky Mountains? Or Canada? Or California?

Your description of all the events in Blusch are touching, all the more so since I am already looking back on the little village as something that has vanished forever. It was painful at first, particularly when a leafless Buffalo was showing itself from its most hideous side. But in this place I think much more about how you will like it here, and whether you too will slowly come to discover much that is fine behind all that seems comical and unfamiliar. Further west it would certainly be hard, but here in New England one can easily feel at home. And Yale will certainly please you too, with its fine university and its many opportunities for a Wapuff thirsting for knowledge. And, in addition, boundless forests, lake, New York within reach . . . it could be the ideal spot for us both! Can you find it on your atlas? Lenox will not be shown of course, but if with one claw you trace a line from New Haven due northwards to the Canadian border, you'll find the place about a third of the way along and a bit to the left. To here from New York is a rail journey of almost 5 hours. But should you arrive unexpectedly soon, you'll find me waiting at the ship.

Let us once again talk more precisely about travel matters. Evidently (according to your letters and telegrams) an air service is being set up between Switzerland and Spain. It is to be hoped that this will start soon and you can get a ticket for it. What I have been thinking is this: now the war in France is evidently over, you might perhaps get permission for a rail journey through France. Whether ships are still sailing here from Lisbon I was unable to find out, but it seems some are back in business. I'll write today to New York for sailing dates and send you a telegram if I discover any possibility. As soon as I receive a telegram from you saying you can get to Lisbon, I can from here at once reserve a place for you on a ship or a Clipper, pay for it in advance and have it confirmed by telegram. It would of course be nice if you could bring dear old Alfi with you. There would be no difficulties at all on the planes, and a reunion with this old comrade of all our joys and sorrows is worth the cost of his fare. I'm not bothering my head at all about the crates and all the other things. Once you are here, I shall be quite content to let the crates with all manuscripts and other possessions sink to the bottom of the sea. If one has learnt anything in these days (and I evidently am still well able to do so), it is that one should not cling to such things.

But take care always to keep me up to date with developments, and it would be better to send one telegram too many rather than too few. If you should run into money difficulties, I can always send you some quickly, you'll have it by cable within two days. Regarding Lisbon, I read that a month ago about 1,000 Americans were there awaiting evacuation. Each Clipper (twice weekly) takes 25, so it would be 20 weeks before a place is available (4 of those have already passed). If ships are sailing, the calculations become simpler, and travel opportunities are perhaps already available. Keep constantly enquiring at the Byrd Institute and I'll do the same here. I have seen the Clippers in New York; they look very reliable.

If your departure still continues to be delayed, I shall go off to Maine in the free month between the end of this present affair and the start at Yale, find some lonely place and there begin to write the famous third volume of the blue book. In view of the lack of advertising, Willy's 1,000 copies are quite a good success, though here we are hoping for a still greater one. In the English version I have added quite a number of things which lessons have shown to be necessary. I had a long letter from Hugo 2 months ago dealing in particular with reprintings. They have republished the piano sonatas there. Voigt wrote a few days ago that he had had a letter from Hugo that was purely business, nothing personal, but from it he deduced that Hugo was still with the firm, at least at the time the letter was sent off. — For Igor's score, Willy will probably have to wait. The good fellow is sitting in Los Angeles and will hardly want to entrust anything to a ship or plane just now. Incidentally, the Pubs have had his symphony photographed and prepared the material for it.

Well, now I have written almost enough to paper your doll's house all over. If only I could now and again telegraph myself across! Here I often look up at the stars and think how, a few hours earlier, all the Bears, Lions, Waggoners, and Orions were there with Pushu. I give them all my love and all my good wishes to take along and offload when next evening they wander past his resting place. You load some Yashny on to them too! Give my regards to all Bluschians and Montanists—I still hope to see it all again one day, if only as a visitor. Regards, too, to all Haennis and the little Bruno. May all the Yijak ghosts that mock Wapuff by the roadside become kind spirits that whisper loving things and remind him how we two often wandered the field and forest paths together and how much we enjoyed all that beauty in each other's company. And let them tell him that he should bear his loneliness patiently and sensibly in the happy and comforting knowledge that we shall come together again at last after all, and in new surroundings enjoy our old pleasant life with surely double the appreciation, after what we have been through, of all that is good in it. Farewell, my beloved little woman, keep on loving me and await the ultimate happy ending. Consider yourself powerfully hugged and kissed and not let go in a hurry.

From the heart, your old   Y

Gertrud Hindemith was finally able to leave Europe from Lisbon on the Greek liner *Nea Hellas*, which arrived in New York on 12 September 1940.

To Willy Strecker   New Haven, Conn.
                                                                    134 West Elm Street
                                                                    27 October 1940

[. . .] Gertrud arrived well preserved on a Greek boat six weeks ago. We spent just a few days in New York and came straight here, where the school soon began. [. . .]

We have found a nice little furnished house in the western part of the town. Everything is now once more just as we wanted it. The position is convenient and pleasant as well. We walk five minutes to the woods and find ourselves amid lovely clumps of oak trees with glorious paths stretching out for hundreds of miles across the country. When you at last get a chance to come here, you can accompany us on our wanderings again. In the meantime, we shall be in training! The school is very encouraging. Not large, but very well equipped (fine library and everything else) and with a good number of talented people. One can work really well here, and the prospects of achieving good results are as good as, if not better than, anywhere else. [. . .]

Gregor Piatigorsky was the soloist in the first performance of Hindemith's Concerto for violoncello and orchestra in Boston on 7 February 1941.

Dimitri Mitropoulos was conductor of the symphony orchestra in Minneapolis, and he gave the first performance of Hindemith's Symphony in E-flat there on 21 November 1941. The orchestral piece "Lazarus and the Rich Man" remained a fragment.

Hindemith's two motets on Latin biblical texts, written just before and just after Christmas 1940, were in the nature of a thanksgiving for his reunion with his wife. They were the first of a series of thirteen written in the following years around the same time.

The Stravinsky work was his Symphony in C.

Weihergarten is the address of the Schott firm in Mainz.

To Willy Strecker   New Haven

16 February 1941

[. . .] The first performance [of the Concerto for Violoncello and Orchestra] was last week in Cambridge and Boston, with the great Gregor on the cello—wonderfully played and with very great success. Three days ago it was mounted in Brooklyn, and yesterday in New York; I heard yesterday's performance, the best so far, but the audience there is abnormally dopey, and it had only a moderate success. All the same, the piece will be played a lot. It is already in another New York programme next winter—with Mitropoulos. A shame that you couldn't be present at the performance; you would surely have greatly enjoyed it. The violin concerto has had six performances, and there are more to come in the near future. The difficulty with this piece is that there is not a single copy available for interested violinists; the Pub is evidently waiting for Hugo.

The symphony mentioned in my previous letters is now happily finished, with five photographed copies in Pub's store. It was originally to have been staged this spring, but the time is too short, so it will be done in the autumn, probably in several places at once. I have begun another orchestral piece but have not yet got very far because I have too much other work; it is a kind of free fantasy based on an old Virginian ballad about the rich man and the poor Lazarus. Chicago has an option on the piece. [Added in margin: I have also written two motets for soprano and piano ("Exiit edictum" and "Cum natus esset").] [. . .]

On rare visits to the big cities one sees more or less the usual sample of old acquaintances. Igor [Stravinsky] with spouse in encouraging form; the gigantic Otto [Klemperer], totally deformed after his operation and still extensively paralyzed and disabled on one side (evidently mentally as well); and the remaining horde of concert givers and goers. . . . Stravinsky's symphony has been mounted in Chicago and Boston. His newest piece is a tango that will be published by some obscure firm. He is back in California.

Things are fine with us here in the provinces, and we are really glad we do not have to live in one of the big cities. Gertrud has become a keen student and performs her housework to the satisfaction of the master of the house. Our house music is again flourishing quite nicely, though so far in reduced circumstances, since we have only violin and viola at our disposal. However, our trunks have at last arrived, at any rate in New York, so we are hoping to put the other long-missed instruments back to work next week. Life is very pleasant and the official work not excessively strenuous. There'll be rather more of it from next autumn on, however. I have drawn up plans for the reorganization of our school and am hoping that it will be carried out exactly as I want it; we shall then have a kind of model school that could set an example for the whole country.

In the summer I shall be teaching in the Berkshires again, and there too I have introduced something new that looks very promising: a historical course for singing and instrument-playing amateurs, six weeks long. It calls for a lot of preparatory work, and once going will keep one very busy, but it is all very interesting and satisfying. So you see, the soil here is fertile, and what it brings forth need fear no comparison with the produce of other zones. (This is true even of the wine!) You too would presumably thoroughly enjoy yourself here, we often feel regret that you can't visit us now and again. [. . .]

The Pub shop in New York is a kind of substitute for the Weihergarten, and whenever I go there Voigt and Bauer show great delight. But nothing can take the place of the original. [. . .] As a prophet you were none too successful, it has all turned out completely differently. I daren't risk plunging into the art of soothsaying myself; I just believe that all things come to an end, and this war will be no exception. This means that a time will come when we shall see each other again, either here or in the probably somewhat battered old world. The former seems to me rather the more promising. [. . .]

To Emma and Fried Lübbecke   New Haven
                                                            17 February 1941

Dear Emma and dear Fried, do not be too cross that you haven't had a single word from me. The intention was always there and occasionally even the necessary free time, but my whole wildly unsettled life, all the new experiences, the establishment of a completely different and newly based existence—so long as conditions remained unstable one lacked the tranquillity for writing. Now they have become stable, as far as one can see. I have once more become a regular school-teacher, am enjoying my new old profession, and feel something like a strong affection for the locality to which a kind fate has driven me. Last year, though I had plenty of work and nothing to complain about, everything seemed somewhat gloomy. I started at the university in Buffalo, gave some 20 lessons a week there, and achieved quite reasonable results. But it was impossible to feel entirely happy, it was a world of little culture that offered too few opportunities for fastidious musicians. The work load steadily increased, for six weeks I was employed simultaneously at three other universities and <u>colleges</u> (Yale, Cornell, and Aurora). Since the distance between Buffalo and Yale is about the same as between Berlin and Heidelberg, you can more or less imagine what that meant! [. . .]

After many difficulties, Gertrud at last arrived in September, and since then we have been sitting here in our new haven, at first being cautiously sniffed over as <u>newcomers</u>, but now already accepted as old settlers. We have a nice little house, motorized of course from top to bottom. It is furnished in the standard American style that neither stimulates nor hurts. The district in which it lies is pretty and quiet, the streets nice avenues of elms; the all-embracing drugstore and the First National store are just round the corner, and in a quarter of an hour we are in the depths of a forest that stretches northwards for a hundred miles or more. The sea is also nearby, but to my shame I must admit we have not yet been there. To make us hundred-per-cent citizens we still need a car. So far we have not felt the lack of one, since the bus service into the city is very good and the parking facilities downtown very bad. We shall get ourselves an old crock in spring, however. We have a little cat that is doing its best to replace Alfi, who unfortunately had to stay behind in Switzerland. [. . .]

The university is a fairly large institution with around 5,000 students. Our music school forms part of it; not very big, but very well equipped—the library in particular is first-class. The university buildings imitate English Gothic, but are nicely laid out, and have what one might call a very pleasant atmosphere all their own. The whole complex is divided into ten colleges in which the students live (the style of life and tuition is entirely English), and one strolls around between them as in a relatively peaceful and carefree retreat. There are symphony concerts and chamber music recitals, a small picture collection and a huge library (something for Fried: it has one of the best collections of Goethe.) If one should feel the need for more normal pleasures, New York can be reached in one and a half hours. "We" have about 160,000 inhabitants. The centre of the town is a large square with three very nice colonial churches. There is not much else worth seeing: the houses are scattered around in the usual hotchpotch way; the newer residential districts further out (such as ours) are all the same, very nice, with detached houses standing in their own gardens. The surroundings are very nice. The work is very encouraging. The land is full of talent, it is just not yet fully developed, and if one is aiming to raise the standards, there is a lot of work ahead. I intend devoting myself energeti-cally to it. [. . .]

During this time my music has made very good progress. [. . .] My things are played often. Mathis has already become something like a stock piece and runs all over the place—not to mention the chamber music stuff.

All in all we are content and thank heaven for having set us down in a place where one can live and work sensibly. Gertrud is busy studying, and housekeeping also costs a great deal of work, especially when we are obliged to entertain col-leagues both close and more remote. We are already beginning to make plans for the summer and are considering whether to go south or west. New Mexico or Ari-zona would not be bad. Ridiculous, isn't it, how here one is worrying one's head about things like that, while on the other side of the globe more or less everything is being smashed to pieces? I hope you are remaining cheerful and in relatively good heart despite all the horrors. We often think how nice it would be to come over for a flying visit, but we shall have to wait a long time before that can happen. Apart from sporadic wishes of that kind, however, we don't miss the things we left behind all that much. Certainly our time in Switzerland was paradise, but it seems one cannot be permitted to live too long in paradises. And what preceded that was so unpleasant that we are thankful for the present solution.

Do write again, and we too shall be rather better correspondents from now on. We send a thousand greetings and trust you won't forget us. Tempora mutantur, but for the present the Hindemiths remain the same, and I hope you do, too. Afterwards we shall drink a glass of our excellent California wine to your good health; the Hochheimer will, I suppose, still be growing as ever, so drink to our well-being too some time.

> Your old   Paul

Das Marienleben, a song cycle on the life of the Virgin Mary to words by Rainer Maria Rilke, was written in the years 1922–23 and performed and published as Hindemith's Opus 27. The composer's feeling that he had done it justice neither technically nor ethically led him to make several attempts at revision, which ended only with the publication of the new version in 1948.

Die vier Temperamente was not staged as a ballet until 20 November 1946. Its first performance, as a concert work for piano and orchestra entitled Theme and Four Variations (*The Four Temperaments*), was given in Boston on 3 September 1944.

The musicologist who collaborated with Hindemith on the "practical-historical course" at Tanglewood, forerunner of the Collegium Museum at Yale, was Leo Schrade, a German emigrant who joined the Yale teaching staff in 1938.

Hindemith made his acceptance of a full-time appointment at the Yale School of Music conditional on changes in its teaching methods. A committee was set up to consider his ideas, and the result was a compromise plan to which Hindemith agreed. His appointment was (at his own request) for three years.

STAGMA is the German fee-collecting agency similar to ASCAP in the United States and the Performing Right Society in Britain.

To Willy Strecker   New Haven

30 May 1941

Dear Willy, your letters arrived, one of them in duplicate and the rest partly in reverse order. They were swallowed with due enjoyment and the sender loudly acclaimed. Your ears must, either via Portugal or Siberia (in this case somewhat later), have been sweetly ringing. [. . .]

After repeated revisions, Das Marienleben is at last completely finished and is now fit to be seen! I perhaps already wrote you that I would much like to publish it in a facsimile version. That would make a volume of 130–150 written pages, with a detailed introduction. Voigt is not keen on the idea, though, after my experiences with him so far, I take that as something like proof that I am right! But I shall not in any case be able to undertake the work for some time. Perhaps I'll hear from you, telling me how you feel about it. For use here, I shall of course write the introduction in English. The material could then be sent to you with the introduction in German, so you could publish it too. I feel it will make quite an impact and duly set the ready pens of the next generation of musicologists furiously scribbling. [. . .]

Nobilissima has been played in NY with success by the mighty Otto. I was not there, since on the same evening I was conducting the same piece here.

Incidentally, have you heard what has been happening to the said Otto? After his brain operation last year, he made quite a good recovery, but he is still a bit cracked, or at least his previous cracks have not improved. He was in a sanatorium, from there he went on his travels, disappeared, was posted missing, searched for by the police, and, with a great amount of hullaballoo, found in a little hotel in New Jersey. Evidently none of all this bothered him very much, and with the aforementioned concert he made an effective <u>comeback</u>.

The little ballet I wrote last autumn for Balanchine (Die vier Temperamente, for strings and piano) is to come out on the 29th in NY, as a kind of dress rehearsal for a tour of South America by the Caravan Ballet. It's said to be very good. I am supposed to conduct it, but as always with these ballet blokes, the final details are never fixed till five minutes before the performance. [Added in margin: Meanwhile postponed until autumn.]

Violin concerto was mounted in Cleveland, Mathis once again in NY, not to mention diverse smaller things that turn up everywhere. Cello concerto will be mounted in August in the Berkshires.

With the word Berkshires we come to the second part of these highly interesting reports.

I have a lot of preparatory work to do for this event (you remember, it is the Boston Symphony Orchestra's summer school, where I was last year). I have my composition class as before, and beside that I am setting up, together with our musicologist here, a practical-historical course, a sort of collegium musicum that will sing and play its way through six centuries. The entire material for it, some 250 pieces, is being prepared here, I have a number of copyists, and I supervise it all. The work there starts in mid-July and lasts till the end of August. We have now spent two days there seeking and finding a home: something that would please you; a former barn, fitted out as a very nice studio, deep in the foothill meadows and far from everything! We also have a car again, a very handsome little vehicle that runs like a greyhound. It is a small Packard.

In the autumn we shall return here to this same house, since we are well used to it and are scarcely likely to find anything more comfortable. The school work is making good progress. I have now become (perhaps I told you already) a "full" professor and in this capacity shall be staying here for the next three years. The school has been totally reformed, basically according to my own plans (cost a lot of work!) and will start in the autumn with a programme of which no one need be ashamed.

Friend Igor is in California. We saw him in NY two months ago and spent a pleasant evening with him and his wife. He was in sparkling form. His newest work is a tango that he has given to some obscure publisher. In a film designed to prove a sensation but doing only moderately well (Fantasia), Disney has filmed, among many other things, the Sacre [du Printemps] with dinosaurs, earthquakes, and so on, truly unedifying. Igor appears to love it. [. . .]

I have received your statement of accounts from last July, and a statement from Stagma has arrived as well. It would be foolish to expect more in the present circumstances—in spite of that, the Stagma soared up to a sum greater than I have seen for years!—and I should be glad if things were to begin to look better for you. Though I am certain that things will work out to the advantage of the publishing firm in the long term, even if we ourselves don't all live to see it, I should not want to win for myself more advantages from the situation than seem reasonable. I should therefore like to suggest that we bring our contractual and publishing relationship more into line with present circumstances. You cannot now be making much out of it, and I am not reckoning on ever coming into the enjoyment of accumulated riches, since I can hardly share Schott's sons' optimistic and idealistic belief in some later "arrangement." I don't of course wish to give everything up, and my suggestion must on no account look as if I am secretly trying to make a run for it— there is no cause for that, and in any case a number of things will continue slowly (but unsurely) to live on, so some kind of connection will always remain. All I wish to do is to make a contribution towards relieving the situation, and I hope you will understand it in this sense. If you care to reduce the payments into my account to a level at which my mother and mother-in-law can continue to live as they do now, taxes can be paid regularly, and my life insurance can continue to run at least until it is swallowed up by some war or civil measure, I shall be content. I get something now and again from the Pubs, so that is yet another reason for a reduction. You will doubtless find the fairest, best, and most practical way for us both. So let me know what you feel about it, I shall regard it all with a friendly eye. [. . .]

After a long silence a letter arrived yesterday from Hugo. He wrote a lot about business affairs, printing matters, etc. He is clearly the same person we know of old. The firm continues to run, somewhat reduced and storm-tossed, and he writes that they will overcome all future obstacles, indeed, he says, he would not have missed the experiences he has gone through for anything. [. . .]

So long, see you later!

Your

Paul, greetings from Gertrud of course

11. In the United States in 1939 or 1940.

12. 137 Alden Avenue, New Haven.

13. Oscar Cox, Gertrud Hindemith, Mrs. Arnold Wolfers, Paul Hindemith, Mrs. Oscar Cox, Arnold Wolfers in Master's House, Pierson College, Yale University, 1953 (Professor Wolfers was the master of the college).

14. Music making with Gertrud Hindemith in New Haven.

15. Karl Bauer in New York, 1945.

16. Travelling to Buenos Aires in 1954.

Beste Weihnachtswünsche 1956
und viel Glück im
Neuen Jahr
1957

Paul und Gertrud Hindemith

17. Christmas Card 1956.

18. Blonay, Switzerland.

Blonay, June 7th, 1960.

Dear Oscar:

Here is the new return, signed — and my face just as brick-red as Form 2555. I am awfully ashamed that I had made such a blunder, can you ever forgive me? Having to do this whole business once over again — the thought of it gives me the creeps ! I swear, it won't happen again (let's see what will happen next year!!). — Only this short note, full with thanks thanks thanks thanks...

I'm terribly busy proof-reading and doing all kinds of editorial jobs. Paul.

19. 1960: Letter to Oscar Cox from Blonay in English.

20. In Vienna in 1963, shortly before his death. Photo: Elfriede Broneder.

The following was Hindemith's last letter to Willy Strecker before the direct mail connection with Germany was severed with the American entry into the war in December 1941.

To Willy Strecker   New Haven

27 September 1941

[. . .] I have not written all that much. A sonata for English horn that we have played a few times at small gatherings and that is very respectable. And just now I am writing one for trombone, with which the whole series of sonatas for wind instruments will slowly near its end. We shall be publishing both sonatas in facsimile. [. . .]

I had already completed three chapters of the third volume of the theory book, but then I hit on difficulties so unexpected that I put it aside again. With my school class I am now getting right down to grips with the newly arisen problems and am hoping to make a big step forward with it in the course of this season. Is it taking too long for you? For me as well, but it can't be helped.

I am glad you have found such a good solution to the money problem. It has taken a considerable load off my mind, and I hope the present arrangement is reasonably tolerable for you, too. Your confidence in future developments is a great comfort to me. As I have seen, the prospects for us over here are very good, and, even if contact between us is beset at the moment with difficulties, you can be assured that my work for Schott's sons and the little business of my own will be pursued with confidence and success. So time is not being lost, and, when, after the war, our mutual work can again proceed unhindered, you are unlikely to find the baby, now cut off from its mother's Weihergartenly breast, returning as a backward changeling! Certainly it will be quite a while before this happens, and the devil knows what pleasant surprises may be sprung on us before then. [. . .]

Warmest greetings from your old fellow travellers,

Your

Paul

Hindemith's pupil Leonard Berkowitz eventually gained a degree in composition at Yale. Ulysses Kay, though a member of Hindemith's major composition class, was not in fact studying for a degree in that subject.

To Leonard Berkowitz (written in English)   The Stevens, Chicago

[Probably December 1941]

Dear General, thanks for your letter, which reminded me very much of the time when I had my military training. It was also No. 81, and I was no good starter either. Anyhow, I think it is good for everybody to be thrown out of his regular trade for a while, and to see other people, live under other conditions and hear other opinions. Music must not necessarily suffer under such conditions, one can construct and solve musical problems without writing one note. I developed quite a kind of virtuosity of this kind and was able to compose while marching or being surrounded by the noisy comrades and later by the still noisier shells and bombs.

Our composition class is working very well. We have more or less the boys you know, only one new addition: a quite gifted coloured boy, Kay. They are working very intelligently. Twice a week we compose, and every Saturday we have a kind of theoretical research work, first with the old theorists (we started with the 10th century and are now in the 13th) and then to-day's problems. I hope you will join in again after your martial career.

I was here in Chicago for a few days and had a lecture at the University. If it would not be so far from here I would have made a short trip to see you in your glory—but to spend 2000 miles and three days railroad for that is not just what I can do in the moment.

Androcles was never finished. He will be entered in the book of History on the same page as Schubert's B minor Symphony.

If you sometime have a pen in your hand instead of the gun (which "in my time" had the official title The bride of the soldier) write a few lines to

Your old music trainer P.H.

My wife sends best greetings!

The first (theoretical) part of Unterweisung im Tonsatz, first published in Germany in 1937, was now at last about to appear in an English translation by Arthur Mendel under the title The Craft of Musical Composition.

A Concentrated Course in Traditional Harmony, the exercises for harmony students, was published in 1943 by AMP.

The "little sonata" for violoncello and piano was written as a gift to Gertrud, who was learning to play the cello, on their eighteenth wedding anniversary. It was not published at the time.

The Sonata for two pianos was commissioned by Celius Dougherty and Vincenz Ruzitska, who first performed in on 20 November 1942 in New York Town Hall.

To Ernest R. Voigt   New Haven
                                                                 8 June 1942

[. . .] Our correspondence just drips, like a leaking tap, but first, it is an old story that people in various parts of the world write to each other more often and more regularly than close neighbours, and second, I always thought you would be paying us your postponed visit. How is it with that?

You already know my opinion of the International Society [of Contemporary Music], and it is not altered by the planned performance of a symphony. All the same, I have nothing against it, but, if the choice is between that and the clarinet quartet, I should prefer the symphony. Go there for the performance? A very friendly suggestion, but in Europe, even if the fare cost only three marks, I never paid to attend performances of my things at any music festival, and I intend to observe this exemplary custom here, too. The whole thing would be a matter of around 500 dollars for each of us, and with all due respect to my beautiful compositions, I should prefer, if I must throw money away, to spend it on more pleasurable things and without an accompanying rabble of musicians. For all that, I naturally have no wish to appear unsociable: I am prepared to conduct the symphony and possibly undertake other things—lectures, lessons—if your friend should chance on someone willing to pay the above-mentioned expenses for me. Incidentally, if the composer is not present, who will the lucky conductor be? I know the musical bunch out there from earlier times and am pretty certain that only in cases of direst peril would I undertake a four-day rail journey on their account.

Fine that the long-protracted theory book is at last on the verge of being published. I believe there will be buyers enough for it. The title you suggest is good. I have put the third volume on ice for a short while, to mature and then to be revised again, but it will be coming to you or to Mendel in instalments before long. Meanwhile, as I told you earlier, I have completed another, smaller book: some exercises for harmony students that emerged in class and are meant for use in schools. It will probably sell like hotcakes, since nothing of this kind has so far existed in this country, and there is a great need for it everywhere. [. . .]

Beyond this book and a little sonata for cello sucklings, I have written nothing. But the machine will start again soon, and it's possible a 2-pianos piece will drop out, though not for elephants, for if (as the New Yorker writes) these beasts have no love for Igor, they will hardly be interested in my things either. What do you think of hippopotamuses? A short adagio for contrabassoon might possibly be the right thing. [. . .]

Fare thee well, noble don.

Thy

Paulus Yalensis

To Gertrud Hindemith   Rose Acres Inn, Cape Cod
[10 July 1942]

Dear Wapuff, today I can do no more than confirm what I told you yesterday—all in all this is a pleasant place. Yesterday I felt and behaved just like an elderly post office secretary on holiday. Having informed his wife, who has remained at home for reasons of economy, of the price of board and lodging, he walks slowly through the streets and acquaints himself with direction, situation, and appearance. Then he lies on the beach in complete idleness and stares dully at the breaking waves and the grass on the sand dunes, waving in the wind. The water is still too cold for him. Then he wanders home to the trough, and afterwards bursts into action with explosive force, helping himself to a postcard of the surroundings and buying postage stamps. Exhausted by these exertions, he makes his way to the little bathing beach behind the house, where he lies in the sun, dozing and reading, almost until supper time, now and again diving into the salty water and swimming out to the nearest diving-board island. It was cold all night long, and now (after breakfast) it is still not warm; the sun is shining, but a really cool wind is blowing. In fact, so cool that there's no sitting out here any longer. Instead I shall go into my house, put on some rather warmer clothes, and go for my morning walk. And that concludes this letter, though not before it is loaded up with best wishes for a peaceful weekend in the lion's den. Mashmu, dear Hasha, and many Yashny greetings from the old holidaymaker.

To Gertrud Hindemith   Cape Cod
                                                    [11 July 1942]
    Dear Hasha, before I get down to my day's work (??) the daily lion's letter must be despatched. There is less to report from day to day, a proper holiday atmosphere prevails, and the less there is to say about it, the more genuine it is. Today, for a change, it's raining, so there's not much one can do. Yesterday was still fine. I was immoderately lazy and did not even go to the big beach, but swam morning and afternoon here in the Oysterpond. All the same, I did do a bit of walking, with my Kepler notes under my arm, and I found a nice out-of-the-way spot on a little hill beside an old windmill. There one can sit all by oneself, looking out over the landscape with its various sea inlets, and can doze, reflect, and write. All these things I did, and with some success even: nothing very significant, but all the same enough to enable me to put together something like a scenario in the not too distant future.
    You will be getting this letter on Monday morning just in time. Within a few hours you will be setting off, and I wish all the lions a safe journey. I shall be waiting for you at the bus stop in the evening.
    Mashmu Hasha, and greetings till the day after tomorrow.
        Y.

Florence Binney owned the house that the Hindemiths were renting in New Haven.

To Gertrud Hindemith   Cape Cod
                                                    [12 July 1942]
    It was very comforting to hear my growling partner at the other end of the line. He will soon be spreading terror through the whole neighbourhood here. Your telephone call came just as I had given up waiting and was about to go to bed (after the

strenuous days here the guests drop off early!), but then I was wide awake again and kept myself amused for the next 1½ hours solving algebra problems with the help of the Binney daughter's mathematics book I brought with me. It had been fine all day, I went walking in the countryside and also swimming. [. . .] I've also done some writing. Today I intend to do quite a bit of keplerizing so that, when the old fellow comes, I shall perhaps (perhaps!) have a scene partly complete.

I won't write to you tomorrow morning, so as not to hold you up in your Wednesdaymorningdeparturepreparations by expectations of a letter. And so: <u>So long</u>, old lion!

    Your

    Y.

To Gertrud Hindemith   Cape Cod

[14 July 1942]

Old procrastinater, so now you won't be coming till Thursday! These lions' dens must be stiff with dirt—no wonder, with these eternal changes of mind.

Holiday life drifts pleasantly and contemplatively along. I scarcely ventured out at all yesterday. I just went for a swim in the afternoon and otherwise strolled through the meadows in the role of a poet awaiting ideas, wandering from one seat to the next. I've knocked together a few lines. It's going slowly, since beginnings are always difficult, but all the same it is a beginning. Besides that I have for the umpteenth time altered that familiar Marienleben song (Mariä Verkündigung), and at the moment I feel the middle section at last has the proper form and shape. [. . .]

It's so windy I can hardly hold the paper down. They are tidying my room and I daren't go along to the common socializing and gossiping pool, since I wish neither to hear for the twentieth time nor remark just as often myself how windy it is today.

So enough, with many little greetings!

    Your

    Y.

To Leonard Berkowitz (written in English)   New Haven

22 September 1942

Dear Soldier:

I was really very glad with your letter. Since I had not heard from you for a long time, I was already a little in sorrows, though I had to consider that you probably would have gone to any strange part of the world, either playing the clarinet or charming kangooroos by other means of musical activity. I am very much interested in what you write about your experiences with primitive players and listeners, it confirms again what everybody has to learn in dealing with amateurs. I learned it in the other war, and I hope our school has finally come to the point, where it seems that students have to be prepared for things they will need in their future life! Till now we are working well and undisturbed, though nobody can know what will happen to such superfluous institutions as music schools!

The composition class last year was a nice and interesting one. We worked every week 12–15 hours, and the result was, that in June we had a performance of about ten pieces of surprisingly high quality. I don't know how the class will look from next month on. Most of the boys are in the army or have to go, so it will probably consist of girls—and my opinions about their creative gifts are not very high. [. . .] A lot of other changes occurred, and probably will occur in the near future, but I think, all such things would sound strange and almost ridiculous to you, having left them behind you since more than a year and being in quite other surroundings.

We are still living in our old house, life goes quiet and I am always working. I have written a great number of things, music and books. With the class together I worked out a textbook on traditional Harmony, which is intended to make work in this field a great deal easier and simpler. Are you interested? Then I can send it. [. . .]

  As ever yours
  Paul Hindemith

Luther Noss was the university organist, choirmaster, and assistant professor of theory at the time Hindemith came to Yale, and he and his wife, Osea, became friends of the Hindemith's. After Noss's departure on military service, the New Haven Symphony played a movement of a symphony that he had written as a graduate student in the thirties.

  Hindemith's new pupil was Kenneth Wolf, a child prodigy who won his degree at Yale at the age of fourteen.

To Luther Noss (written in English)   [New Haven]
                                                      2 March 1944

Dear Luther, you had a great success—well deserved. I heard your piece at the rehearsal, and really liked it very much. It is full of fine and valuable ideas, worked out with the appropriate skill and a remarkable feeling for proportion. Why did you never show these things? I had no idea that you were so good in this field, and I am sure I could have told you plenty of things if I had known you are interested. Osea gave me the other score, and although I read it, I cannot say that I went through it note by note—however, I liked the old piece better. I am sure you came in that strain of forced exaggeration and unnecessary complication (everybody does!), which in itself is not condemnable, especially as it is one of the best ways to collect useful technical material and to get rid of many emotional things, but you should have taken these works as a starting point and should have tried to bring clarity and adequacy of appearance and means in the heap of material. What I cannot understand is that a man with so great a gift for composition (I wished our other composers here had only a quarter of it!) can live without always working and trying to become more and more perfect. Self-criticism is certainly a good thing but it loses all its sense when it prevents fertile and healthy seeds from becoming sturdy flowers. Wait till you come back! I'll see to it that you get to work—and be sure I won't ask very much for permission to put you under pressure!

Everything is going the usual way. I had an offer to go to Chicago with almost twice the salary—but everything is too hectic there, there are no trees, and I don't want to be interested in developing new schools. I have my own problems that I want to develop.

I have a new pupil, a boy, 13 years old. He has more gift as a musician and especially as a composer than all our school put together, and his technical knowledge is already that of a 30 years old man. Sometimes something happens that pleases an old Steisstrommler!

I have to go to town to meet Osea and Gertrud for a spine thrilling movie, so good bye for to-day. All our best wishes and greetings!

> As ever   your
>
> Paul

Following Ernest R. Voigt's death in 1943, Hindemith's main dealings with AMP were through Karl Bauer, who with his wife, Phyllis, were now good friends. Hindemith's form of address in the first letter, "Poet and Karl," goes back to his April Fools' Day joke concerning Suppé's Poet and Peasant, but "Urbanwinterbauers" in the second letter remains unexplained.

Hérodiade was an orchestral work based on the poem by Stéphane Mallarmé; it was commissioned by Mrs. Coolidge for Martha Graham, the dancer, who performed it at the Library of Congress on 30 October 1944.

The French songs were settings of poems by Rimbaud and "The Moon" was a setting of Shelley's poem, all for solo voice and piano.

The String Quartet No. 5 in E-flat was first performed in Washington on 7 November 1943 by the Budapest String Quartet.

The piano concerto was The Four Temperaments, first performed as a concert piece in Boston on 3 September 1944 with Lukas Foss as soloist.

The harmony book to which Hindemith refers is his A Concentrated Course in Traditional Harmony.

Hans Hesse, a former pupil of Hindemith's in Germany, was a prisoner of war in Camp Chaffee, Arkansas.

The overture Cupid and Psyche (German title: Amor und Psyche) was first performed in Philadelphia on 29 October 1943.

Ludus Tonalis, a cycle of fugues for solo piano, received its first performance in Chicago on 15 February 1943. The pianist was Willard McGregor.

Geheimrat Ludwig Strecker was the father of Ludwig and Willy Strecker and former head of the firm of Schott.

To Karl Bauer [West Southport, Maine]
[Summer 1944]

Dear Poet and Karl, many thanks for sending the score and carrying out all requests. Herewith the piano score for "Hérodiade." [. . .]

It's splendid here. We have an old fisherman's house with all modern conveniences. 30 paces from the sea and in complete peace and isolation. Just the right holiday for a composer!

Could you send me something with the next delivery? 3 <u>canvasses</u> for oil paint (and why should one not also do some painting here?) [. . .]

In great haste, but affectionately,

Yours,

P.H.

To Karl and Phyllis Bauer [West Southport]
13 September 1944

Dear Urbanwinterbauers, when somebody sends no word for such a long time, things must be going either wretchedly or excellently for him. The latter is the case, and if silence can be taken as a sign of things going excellently, then you would be hearing nothing either now or in the near future. On the business side, not all that much has been happening, these were proper holidays for once. All the same I have, besides completing Hérodiade at the start, produced 3 French songs and have been pretty much occupied with the text for the new opera, the preliminary work for which you saw in New Haven. Some of it now stands on its own two feet, for the time being at least. Otherwise diversions of all kinds, searching for bilberries and blackberries, swimming in the sea, blazing trails in the woods, building little towns and railways with bits of driftwood, painting pictures, and all the other things people in their dark urges do. [. . .]

All the packages arrived: Moon, Hérodiade score and piano arrangement, quartet, trumpet sonata, and piano concerto. Harmony book as well. I am very pleased with it all, particularly the two pets Hérodiade and the quartet. Both look very nice despite the crabbed handwriting of the moderately gifted copyist. [. . .] I've received no word from Martha Graham, but I have not written either. On the other hand, the Library has acknowledged receipt, sent the money, and had the few misprints put right; so that affair is now done with.

Some of the oil frames and canvasses have already been put to use. I'm sorry to have caused so much turmoil, particularly since these things are so hard to get (something I didn't of course think of), but for us it was worth the trouble. Many thanks!

If you have nothing against it, I should like to ask you to send some more of my things to my prisoner-of-war pupil. He gratefully received the previous package and has performed the "Ludus" and part of the cello concerto in the camp. Perhaps we might now send him: the new songs so far published, quartet score, Cupid Overture. [. . .]

We have had a letter from Frau Strecker in Buenos Aires. The old Geheimrat Strecker has died. Willy was in hospital, having been run over by a cyclist and evidently pretty badly damaged. But he's said to be back in order again. Ludwig Strecker's son is dead—apparently killed in action. Hugo has been married for a year and they are expecting a <u>baby</u> this month, in line with this generation of the Strecker family that seems to be distinguishing itself by the frequent production of babies.

With final holiday greetings,

    Your as-always-ish

      P.H.

The American soldier whose letters are quoted in the following was Emerson Kailey, who played the tuba in the band of the Ninety-ninth Division, stationed in Kitzingen. His first letter to Hindemith, dated 22 May 1945, reveals that he had once visited him in New Haven, together with Hindemith's former pupil Remi Gassmann, his own teacher. William Brown was an army friend of Kailey's whose main instrument was the piano.

Among the "personal things" omitted by Hindemith in his letter to Bauer was the news that the town of Frankfurt had been destroyed, but his mother, although bombed out several times, was alive and well and was living in Butzbach with her daughter Toni. Gertrud Hindemith's mother had died of some illness in Wiesbaden in February 1945. Emma and Fried Lübbecke, whose house in Frankfurt had also been bombed, were living in Bad Homburg.

Kailey's letters were written in English. The dots denoting cuts within the quotations are Hindemith's own, as are the passages in brackets marked "Ed.," which were written in German.

To Karl Bauer   [New Haven]

                                                   15 June 1945

Dear comrades, we have received a number of letters that are quite informative regarding the Schotts. Leaving out the personal things, I quote herewith parts that might be of interest to you.

From a letter sent us by a soldier we know: "I went to Frankfurt and Mainz a few days ago (written on 22 May). . . . I then went to Wiesbaden and there found Willy Strecker. He was very delighted to hear about you. I told him all I knew about your life and activities. His house still stood in Wiesbaden but the publishing house in Mainz is destroyed except for the old building. They did not lose any manuscripts or plates so he considered himself not too bad off. A large bomb hit right in front of his house but broke only all the windows. They have been publishing everything that came through from America. The Ludus Tonalis has sold 1200 copies in the three months it has been out in Germany. He has been most anxious to get the third book of your series. He said that demand for your music grows and grows despite all the bans on its performance. It was played all the time, but more or less in "bootleg" concerts. With the Streckers, the two of them, Willy and the Doctor are in good health. I didn't meet the Dr. The Doctor's son was the victim of a fever contracted in the war against the Russians. Willy . . . told me he bought Universal Edition but was forced to resell it to a friend of Görings under threat of expulsion from the council of publishers. . . . they plan to rebuild as soon as they can. All transport is ruined. He and his brother alternate in going to Mainz. One goes one day and the other the next day. The reason for that is that they have only one bicycle. . . . Herr Strecker asked me to tell you that Germany needed you. I told him that we also needed you and he said 'Yes, the whole world needs him.' (That must be the manpower shortage—Ed.!) He said that he hoped you would at least visit them as soon as possible."

From another letter from the same soldier (25 May): "I returned to Mainz . . . Then I went to the Schott Verlag and got the music I wanted. I got all the things from them that we can do with brass and woodwind instruments. That includes all of your sonatas that they had on hand. I also took them the score to Cupid and Psyche that Bill Brown gave me. Mr. Strecker was quite happy to have it. The presses in the main establishment are gone but they have two or three presses in another Lager. The old building is still intact, the bombs landed behind it. They hope to do some publishing in two or three months . . . I brought back a copy of the Ludus for Bill. He liked Schott's edition very much. It is quite good. . . . Bill and I are going to try to play the four-hand arrangement of the Es Symphonie [Hindemith's E-flat Symphony] which I brought back (the things that go on?!—Ed.) . . . I took the harmony book over but he said that he knew that."

Then from a short note written by Willy himself: "I should not like to let the opportunity of sending you a few personal greetings pass unused. . . . It is to be hoped that direct correspondence will soon be possible. I am burning to hear more in detail about you. When are you coming here on a visit? . . . The old Weihergarten has come through it all more or less intact, the printing works are completely destroyed."

Then we had letters from other friends and from my mother, all sent by this same soldier. But there's nothing in them that would interest you.

All these bits of news, and indeed the situation in general, have left me wondering what can be done musically to meet the apparently very strong demand for important and valuable things. I asked myself whether it might not be the right time to publish the so often postponed Marienleben in the new version, which has in the meantime been revised again. If that were to be done in the usual way, it would take a very long time and also be very expensive (I estimate around 150 pages of music and 10 pages of theoretical commentary. What would you say to a sort of connoisseurs' edition, consisting of reproductions of the manuscript on very good paper, signed and sold at a very high price? Of course the 15 songs could also be sold separately as well in an ordinary edition. [. . .] It would have to be published as it is, that is to say, in German, with just an English translation inserted, though the theoretical commentary itself would be in English. If you are interested in this idea I could begin on the copying soon.

In this connection, would you please inform the enclosed singing goat that, as far as the composer is concerned, one is extraordinarily sceptical and uninterested in her and Herr Goldstein's plans? And please head the Hargail people off. The sonata they have brought out is played in a deadly boring way, and I don't see why it must always be the mediocrities with no invitations to do anything else who try to fish for fame with my things.

So, that is quite enough in all this heat! [. . .]

Oliver Strunk relinquished his post at the Library of Congress in 1937 to take up an appointment at Princeton University. The translations he lent to Hindemith were included in Source Readings in Music History, selected and annotated by Oliver Strunk (1950).

To Oliver Strunk (written in English)   New Haven
                                                                        21 June 1945

Dear OS: if false assumptions cause you to write letters, let me assume the incredible and trust all rumors, no matter how silly they are. Once, at the beginning of the winter term, when your name turned up (I have forgotten in what constellation of questions), some wise guy said he had heard you had left Princeton. There were no reasons given and even no speculations came up about possible reasons (good sort of colleagues, eh?). Don't see anything tragic or important in this; I am glad it was just a rumor. The only effect it had on me, was that I did not write you, after having sent back your more than valuable translations. I always thought: there will be some information about his new place of activity, and there is in the meantime no sense in bothering him. So you can imagine that I was very glad when my worthy introducer in Philadelphia told me about your being and working undisturbed in P.

The translations saved me a great deal of trouble. It would have been too complicated in classes where almost nobody reads a word of latin, to translate the chapters needed all by myself. The main trouble with the selections is that their author doesn't publish them (dammit!). If you don't mind a suggestion, I would say that it would be good to incorporate the chapter of Boetius "Quid sit musicus," since it gives a very clear idea about musicianship in medieval times.

Could you spare for a very short time (3 weeks) the two chapters from Tinctoris, the one of Pietro Aron and of Glarean? I hope to come till Glarean in my next year's course, and if again you permit me to copy them, I would do so right away.

How nice of you to offer me RS's place. But it is as you say: I like it here, and there is no urgent reason to abandon what with some effort and overcoming of obstacles I could build up.

Concerning that thing "Ludus tonalis" I had already a letter from Mr Welch. He asked me about a fellow Goldstein-Herford, and I could not answer immediately, as I had not heard this man's performance. A few weeks later he was here and played it—and then I was too busy with our Perkin etc concert, and did not write to Mr. Welch. I think this letter is an opportunity to straighten this out. Mr. G.-H. plays it well (as many people found) although I would not recognize the pieces as my own—so if you want to hear Goldstein, you may ask him. (You will never have heard such incoherent music in your life), but if you want to hear the right style, I don't know who could be recommended. What about our Bruce Simonds? If you would ask him, he certainly would study it and I could take care of the style!

Oooph, it is too warm! Greetings to both of you from this old couple of dreary villagers, As ever

      Yours   P.H.

Hindemith's "little overture" was *Cupid and Psyche*. The *Symphonic Metamorphosis of Themes by Carl Maria von Weber*, a reworking of music originally intended as a ballet for Massine, was first performed in New York on 20 January 1944. The String Quartet No. 6, written in 1945, was given its first public performance by the Budapest String Quartet in Washington on 21 March 1946.

Hans Flesch's wife, Gabriele, was Gertrud Hindemith's sister.

To Ludwig and Willy Strecker   Petit Manan, Maine

                                                  29 August 1945

Dear brotherly pair,

It was truly a liberation when recently news came through from Mainz, Homburg, and Butzbach. We would have sent you word earlier if the first means of contact had not been broken off: the sergeant who first turned up at your house fell ill and has now been posted to England. Through Bauer a new line seems now to have opened, and I will make use of this at once to bring you up to date with our news, so long broken off. [. . .]

With regard to our old friends, I shall give you just a brief situation report on the question of my relationship with the Pubs (you will no doubt be getting news from more authoritative quarters regarding the latter's other undertakings). Nothing has grown worse since Voigt's death. As he was always somewhat hesitant, too cautious, and in my view very frugal, much is now being done in a somewhat more enterprising spirit. And enterprise is absolutely necessary, for in the uncertain legal situation during the war the ones who found it worthwhile to use their elbows were the ones who did. The main sufferers in this respect, however, were not you, but B. & H., Peters, etc. You have of course already received a few of the more recent things that I published through the Pubs, e.g., the "Ludus" and the harmony book. (The soldiers praised your edition of the "Ludus"!) Both are doing better than expected. The Ludus had to be reprinted in the first months of its existence, and the "Traditional Harmony," which is being used for teaching all over the place, also went into a second edition after just a year. The old 1st volume of "Tonsatz" came out 3 months ago in a new improved edition, and the 2nd volume is due out this winter. I am also hoping this winter to get to the end of the third, so often begun and steadily improved in the rewriting. A string quartet that the Budapest people play a lot is also selling much better than quartets usually do. You have, I know, received the little overture. An orchestral piece that is having a lot of success is the "Symphonic Metamorphosis of Themes by C. M. Weber." In addition we have brought out 8 English songs as well as the 6 little French choruses and the old songs for mixed chorus in a new form. We have reprinted all the sonatas for wind instruments, also the old showpiece, the "Mathis" Symphony. At this very moment a new textbook, "Elementary Training for Musicians," is being printed, and I am just putting the final touches to a piano concerto for the pianist Sanromá. I have written more besides all this, 2 dozen other songs, another quartet, 6 big motets for soprano, etc., etc. This is roughly the <u>output</u> of the past 2–3 years and, considering the large amount of schoolwork, it is not bad.

Throughout this time we were sitting in New Haven, with breaks just for the usual summer holidays and occasional winter excursions. There was always an abundance of work. Domestic servants have long ceased to be available, so Gertrud has had to do all the housework herself. On top of this she studied in our graduate school and recently gained her M.A. in French. They've also dressed me up in a doctor's <u>hood</u>, in Philadelphia.

Dear Willy, the sergeant gave us a detailed account of your situation and the houses in Mainz and Wiesbaden. I am glad the general ruin has not diminished the will to work in either of you. I hope you are giving thought to what might be done later on in regard to a possible international reorganization. Having now seen the matter from both sides, I have a pretty clear idea of what might be necessary. But since it is not my place to talk about publishing affairs, and it would in any case be impossible to do so in the few short pages of a letter, discussions on this subject will have to be put off until we see each other again. When that will be nobody can of course know. Probably neither of you will be able to get away so soon, and for us there is no prospect either, at least not in the next few months. But in any case the situation changes daily.

We are sitting high up here in an isolated farm by the sea close to the Canadian border; it is very lovely here, and the consciousness of having escaped the usual unhealthy summer heat of Connecticut makes it particularly refreshing. As so often during our summer rambles and excursions we are constantly remarking, "If only Willy could be with us too!" Last year we had an old fisherman's house, also by the sea in Maine, and the year before that we went walking in the White Mountains in New Hampshire. School starts again for me in a month's time. We have moved house. The old furnished house we rented has been sold, and from next October on we shall be in a house of our own with a big garden. The address is 137 Alden Ave. New Haven 15, Conn. But please don't give it to anyone else! Begging and toadying letters are already piling up ominously!

Have you any contact with my mother? Or perhaps even with our possessions in store in Berlin? — We should like to hear what happened to Gertrud's mother, how it came about, what she died of, whether she suffered long, why exactly in Wiesbaden, etc., etc. Do you know anything about the Fleschs? About my brother? — We have a pretty lively correspondence with your family in South America. They were recently somewhat concerned when, towards the end of the war, they heard nothing from you; we were able to put their minds at rest. Of Hugo we have had only reports. Willms is back? Thank God! Who else of the old guard is still there? Greetings to all. Write again soon. [. . .]

    As ever,

    Paul and Gertrud

Jean Todd Moran studied at Yale with Hindemith and was awarded a degree in musical theory.

To Jean Todd Moran (written in English)   137 Alden Avenue,

                              New Haven

                           7 January 1946

Dear Jean, decorated all over with your highly appreciated examples of Texan ingenuity I feel almost like a Cowboy—almost, because you did not send the horse to ride upon and the cactus to fall into. But perhaps these are the things that have to be enjoyed on their place of origin, like Bach-cantatas at St. Thomas' Church. Let me thankfully shake your hands, while catching with my lasso a bucking Upright Piano that has broken out of the Corral.

Your report on the introduction of the Trinity-trade-mark-song was highly interesting. By now the waves of excitement will probably have calmed down and you are perhaps one of the most performed composers, as far as performances go in San Antonio. Of course I am by no means an experienced judge concerning theme songs, and the modest range of my knowledge, extending from Deutschland Deutschland über alles to The star-spangled Banner and comprising some oddities in between does not mean too much compared with the wisdom of an old hand like you. If I had to sing it, however, I would think it is too difficult and too high-brow for that purpose. Going into the mental efforts of the 9th Symphony for the stylized praise of Trinity goes a little beyond my power as a theme song singer — but, don't forget, my capacity never went much higher than the Yale Bulldog song! As far as the technical shape of your praiseworthy attempt at musical education by way of the backdoor goes, it's O.K.

Our old Music School is overcrowded. You would not recognize our placid Saturday morning course: The class room is filled to capacity and the teacher has a helluva time to keep them busy. The other activities are approximately as you knew them, with some gifted fellows doing decent work, mostly in higher theory.

I hope you started the New Year well and continue to do so! We are trying to follow the same line. As ever your

    tottering old-timer   P.H.

Die schöne Aussicht was the street in Frankfurt in which the Lübbeckes' house (formerly Schopenhauer's) had stood. In his letter to Hindemith, Emerson Kailey reported the house as having been "burnt to the ground with all of their possessions." As regards Hindemith's Kuhhirtenturm, Kailey wrote, "It still stands and can be rebuilt without too much trouble. The walls are there, but the wooden roof is gone. Dr. Lübbecke said that your piano was still up there being played upon by the wind and rain."

Despite Hindemith's attempts to discourage them, the AMP staged two concerts of his works at the Juilliard School of Music in New York to mark his fiftieth birthday on 16 November 1945; at one of these, Bruce Simonds played the Ludus Tonalis. Emerson Kailey heard Emma Lübbecke-Job play it at a house in Bad Homburg and described her performance as "masterful."

To Emma and Fried Lübbecke   [New Haven]

                                  18 January 1946

Dear Emma, dear Fried, all your letters have arrived, from those forwarded last spring by Sergeant Kailey up to the birthday greetings. But since you never gave an address to which letters could be sent, it was impossible until now to thank you and to send you any reply. Now by chance I have been given an address in Frankfurt, through which this letter may perhaps come into your hands. After our experiences with letters to Butzbach, however, one cannot be certain of that; a few things from there have not got this far, and some letters sent from here have journeyed back here again. A letter from old (81!) Mrs. Coolidge is enclosed. We saw her recently and gave her your letters to read; after that she felt a need to write to you.

It is a comforting feeling to know that you came through all the horrors safely. We have received many photographs from Frankfurt. The portal that is all that remains of Die schöne Aussicht and the beheaded Turm look somewhat forlorn. That worldly possessions are without value need not perhaps be drummed into one quite so drastically, but apparently many people have had to learn it! To us it was demonstrated fairly early by the number of repeatedly struck tents, and a long time elapsed before we were able to settle down again in a reasonably domestic fashion: it was not until recently, after almost eight years of making do, that we once more got a roof of our own over our heads.

We spent the war years working hard. One did not have fewer pupils: as more teachers were called up, so those who remained behind had more work to do. There were some restrictions, and one could not travel around as freely as before, but otherwise there were no difficulties. Both professionally and personally we were treated here with a friendliness that probably no other country would have shown with a war going on—and even towards enemy foreigners! This was particularly heartening after our experiences in our so often lauded fatherland.

A lot of appeals from there, reminders of national obligations, artistic exhortations, have landed up here. I am very well aware of my so-called historical mission (seems to be quite a mouthful!), but, leaving aside the view I have always taken that a work of art is more important than the person who produces it, and therefore in my case I preferred to let the music speak for itself rather than appear in person, it seems to me that no discussion of this question is at all possible yet. There has been no official enquiry so far, and I even have the feeling that there will be none, since after the first wave of enthusiasm many people will be of the opinion that music in Germany must be provided by those who "were there at the time." Even if I should be mistaken, it still seems to me inadvisable, just on the urgent exhortations of many friends, to abandon a laboriously built-up existence all at once. Many people over here are of the opinion that I have a building job to do in this country of at least equal importance. I must abstain from making a decision on this question, but (mindful of the above-mentioned national obligation) I shall be prepared to enter immediately into serious discussions if and when an official enquiry comes. Quite apart from our own and our friends' personal wishes, no one can know for sure how the future will turn out. Things may develop in a way totally different from what we imagine, and any kind of influence there may be on musical events in Germany may assume forms that nobody perceives at the moment, or it may emerge from totally unforeseen motives and tendencies. I feel it is not yet time to make decisions, though this does not stop us thinking seriously of a trip to Europe. So far there has been no prospect of anything of that sort, even in pipe dreams, but it is possible that the realization of such plans might not be so very far away.

We have received countless reports, letters, and newspaper reviews of my things in Germany. A lot of them seem to have been very good. You of course know how little store I set on public success, and so you will understand that, while gladly appreciative of such efforts, a person who was not too severely put off his stroke by state-supported condemnation cannot raise more than token enthusiasm for a wave of success that looks pretty much just like an attempt to make amends. I feel it would be best to do what we did when everything was being clubbed down and, in view of its waxing fame, concentrate our efforts all the more diligently on the music. As you can imagine, that is proceeding at full speed!

In any case, I am glad not to have been obliged to take part in all the celebrations. Here something of that nature took place too, but things are done here in a quieter and more sober way. There were three very fine concerts in New York, of which I conducted one (I have long given up playing, no longer being good enough), and I also wagged the stick in Chicago and Detroit. Here in New Haven everything was passed over in welcome silence — other former fifty-year-olds in the faculty have not been celebrated either — so all in all we came through fairly undisturbed. Our dean, an excellent pianist, played the Ludus superbly in New York. Nonetheless, we should of course have loved to hear Emma's version, for which many letters were so full of praise.

It feels funny to be talking so much about ourselves — it is anyway not all that important, and to us it seems humdrum, past and done with. But presumably this is exactly what you are interested in. So here is some more from the same stable.

Gertrud has a lot to do in the house. Servants are hardly to be had except at an exorbitant price, and for people in our circumstances the new house is somewhat roomy. It has a fine music room facing south that reminds us a bit of its Berlin predecessor. We frequently indulge in house music — not to mention an althorn! Gertrud did a lot of study last year, and the outcome was a <u>Master's Degree</u>. My writing progresses merrily, interrupted unfortunately by much schoolwork. The school is interesting: the quality of the classes varies of course from year to year, but just now I have an intelligent group, particularly as regards higher theory. My work on this subject has developed quite considerably — so much so that I am now hoping to be able to write the third volume of the Unterweisung, which is always being put off. I have written a lot of music, The Marienleben has been entirely renovated and much improved. I have done sonatas for all conceivable instruments, many songs, two quartets, orchestral works, and much else. Much of it has been printed here, and the things are being performed all over the place. So many pupils are applying that I am unable to admit any more. We have spent the summer holidays up on the Maine coast in very lovely and in part completely untouched areas. Otherwise we sit quietly here at home, often wandering through the surrounding hills and now and again taking part in university activities. Because of the petrol shortage during the war we sold the nice little car we had bought, but cars should be easy to get again before very long. We have heard from people coming from over there that trains are slowly beginning to run again, and that life in general seems to be returning to something like normal, as far as that is possible after so much destruction. You seem, under the circumstances, to have struck it tolerably well in Homburg. From all we have heard, the lack of electricity and heating seems to be the worst of all the evils. But the days are getting visibly longer, and winter will pass! A modus vivendi for the whole country will surely evolve in the course of time. I am assuming that everything is in a state of flux and nobody knows in which direction the ship is steering. Here, anyway, everyone is filled with the best intentions and there is no trace of any hostility, although the war has cost the lives of many young people. That means more here than anywhere else, since playing at soldiers is loathed, and war in a far-distant country seemed to most people to be thoroughly unjustifiable. Still, most of the lads we were reluctant to see go have returned safely, and life here is slowly getting back to normal. We are hoping the same for the old homeland, and at times it seems to us that faint rays of light are becoming visible on the horizon. [. . .]

Write soon and let us know an address where you can be reached. It can after all be some time before postal connections with private persons become possible again.

Your old

Paul

When Lilacs Last in the Door-Yard Bloom'd, a Requiem "For those we love," for mezzo-soprano and baritone soli, mixed chorus and orchestra, was first performed in the New York City Center on 14 May 1946 by the Collegiate Chorale under the direction of Robert Shaw. Hindemith began work on it a few days after being sworn in as an American citizen on 11 January 1946. In his book Paul Hindemith in the United States Luther Noss writes: "Hindemith had been deeply saddened by the death of President Franklin D. Roosevelt in April 1945 and by the terrible casualties suffered by both sides in World War II. He greatly admired Walt Whitman's poetry and felt that this tribute to the memory of President Abraham Lincoln and the Civil War dead, with its eloquent plea for peace, brotherhood and the reuniting of former enemies in a spirit of humanity and democracy, was an ideal text for the musical expression of his own reflections."

Heinrich Strobel's biography of Hindemith, first published in 1931, was reissued by Schott in a third fully revised and expanded edition in 1948.

Hindemith conducted the National Symphony Orchestra of Mexico in two concerts of his own works at the invitation of its musical director, Carlos Chavez.

Hotel Guardiola, Mexico, D.F.

15 July 1946

Dear Willy, two short letters from you arrived yesterday together, a slow one of 14 May and a fast one of 28 June that went via Mr. Singer. Your complaint about a standstill in our correspondence is of course justified, but the reason is to be sought less in any dwindling desire to write than in the fact that since my last letter to you I have had, besides my very demanding schoolwork and a few journeys, to compose a complete oratorio and prepare the necessary 180 pages of score and 65 of piano arrangement for photocopying. On top of that there was my class's school concert (music of the 14th and 15th centuries) with daily rehearsals and finally the work here, which has taken a full week of strenuous rehearsal time for two symphony concerts. In such circumstances, little time for letter writing remains for even a keener epistle producer than myself!

We wanted at various times to send you the works you asked for, but several things stood in the way. In the final months before the general opening of mail connections it was no longer possible, since the necessary soldiers were always changing and many letters came back undelivered. Since then we had no address of that kind to make use of. Though it is now possible to send clothes and food packages (Bauer says he does so regularly), no other parcels or even printed matter are allowed through. I shall give the Pubs Mr. Singer's address, then you can try sending things off again.

You will then get the Weber-Metamorphosis, but I doubt if they'll be able to send you a big score, since we have photographed only 5 or 6, and the piece is constantly out on its rounds. So you will probably be sent the pocket score, which has been greatly reduced in size and can serve as copy only with the help of a magnifying glass. And even then, with all the writing from here to New York and from there to Mainz, it will probably arrive too late for September. I don't know what the festival is for which you want the piece, but anyway I should advise you first of all to arrange performances of the orchestra pieces which you have already got and which have either never or hardly ever been played in Germany (Nobilissima, Symphonic Dances, symphony, cello concerto), since there is, after all, a lot of ground to be made up before the latest things are released.

Since you already have the string quartet score, there's no longer any need to send it, but the remaining newly published things can of course be sent, though you will hardly find them of any use (some 10 English songs). The same goes for the oratorio, since it is in English (When Lilacs Last in the Door-Yard Bloom'd) and I know of nobody who could fit a translation to the music (I could myself, but it's an awful grind and there are so many other things waiting to be dealt with). Meanwhile yet another new quartet has been given its first performance in Washington (also by the Budapest people); I didn't hear it, but it is said to have been very good. [. . .]

The oratorio was launched in mid-May in New York with a truly capital performance. The Collegiate Chorale, which performed it, is by far the best chorus in the world, and the success was corresponding. Last week it was broadcast over all the Columbia stations throughout the country. You must surely know Whitman's poem. It was originally written on the occasion of Lincoln's death, and some parallel happenings at the time of Roosevelt's death make the whole thing a moving experience for everybody.

The Marienleben, although it is finished, I would frankly rather not publish just now. Or, if after a short while, then only here in the States, and later—but only when it has become sufficiently well known, in Germany. My reasons for this may seem somewhat strange to you, but I have no doubt that you will understand and approve them. This is the situation:

As you rightly assumed, I have received hundreds of letters since the war ended, and the stream shows no sign of ending. After the years of separation, we waited in suspense and longing for any scrap of news. The very detailed newspaper reports had of course prepared us for all the misfortune, destruction, and misery, but all the same the tragic personal fates with which we were confronted aroused our deepest commiseration. Our feeling in general was to return at once and help wherever we could. More and more news came in and, once the accounts of past or present situations had lost some of their novelty value, it became more and more apparent that the gist of practically all the letters was: we want this, help us with that, you could after all do this or that, we expect the following . . . Well, that is understandable, and as far as the fulfilment of such wishes relates to purely material things, it is only a small teacher's salary with very scant additional earnings that puts a brake on one's spirit of enterprise. (The publishing rights in the few things that sell well, such as the Harmony book, belong to Mainz or to London and are consequently controlled by the Alien Property Custodian, who won't release a single penny). The continual requests for testimonials to the effect that the writers had never been Nazis can also be settled easily enough, though the worthlessness of such evidence should be obvious to everyone since it is not and cannot be based on any sort of personal knowledge during the last critical years. Besides these, there are still numerous requests to provide affidavits, to advance travel money, to arrange jobs, etc., etc.—but these matters solve themselves, thank goodness, on account of the above-mentioned financial situation. As I say, this is all perfectly understandable, and it has my fullest sympathy, though there is little I can do. But where, unfortunately, my sympathy threatens to dry up is in the field of music.

What emerges from the letters is quite simply sickening. I have always seen myself as a private individual who happens to be a musician, and what the public does with the music I deliver has nothing to do with my private life, just as with this music I do not aim to affect the private lives of others. Now, however, I am beginning to feel like a cornerstone against which every passerby passes the water of his artistic opinion. Even that one could be prepared to accept, since it is after all the inevitable consequence of being well known and successful. But what is quite unacceptable is when even your best friends—and these in particular—shout out loudly in public everything they know about you. It is done under the guise of "promoting art," "making amends," "old loyalties," but it needs only a cursory glance to see that all each of them is doing is trying to turn the existing situation to his own best advantage. To make matters worse, one must also listen to repeated accounts of how this or that person is performing this or that work, always with the blatant aim of drawing attention to himself or interesting the composer, even of putting him under an obligation. (The same thing happens over here of course, but without such a fuss, nobody pushes himself forward quite so crudely, and probably—as various recordings that people have sent me from over there suggest— the performances here are very much better.) And then everyone knows exactly what it is I have to do! In Germany the musical demands of the moment are paramount and have instantly to be obeyed! The fact that horizons change, that people who have been pitched out cannot and do not wish to build themselves a new life every few years, and that there may be other tasks beside the rebuilding of a shattered musical life—however big and fascinating a task that might be—and that finally the person of whom demands are being made may also have an opinion of his own based necessarily on physical and spiritual developments of a very different kind—nothing of this seems to occur to anybody. For all of them one is just a piece on a draughtsboard that in their egoism they are trying with all their strength to push into the position best for them, in order to gain as much as they possibly can for themselves. And all this under the banner of artistic idealism! I should be idealistic enough to give up at once all that I have built up for myself with so much effort, solely in order to further the personal manipulations of others. God, what consideration has one not given to the question of starting up again over there, how much thought, concern, and love has been spent on ways of helping to restore order there! But it has become all too clear that one-sided idealism can be of little use. One must simply wait until the waves of artistic egoism, which seem to be breaking with particular force over my head, subside and are replaced by the clearer voices of a more levelheaded musical outlook. You will now understand how repulsive I should find it to fling my Marienleben, a work that lies particularly close to my heart, into this quagmire. There is no doubt that it will flourish much better in the atmosphere over here, which is also not ideal, but is certainly healthier.

I do not care much for the idea of getting Strobel to bring his old book up to date. What does he know about me? As good as nothing. And he can hardly write about the pieces, since hardly any of the printed material is easily available to him, and on top of that, much of the new stuff is not yet in print. And if I should first have to tell someone about all the things I have done and how they should be taken, I would choose a person of higher intellectual standing than a journalist (however good he may be). Such things were possible twenty years ago, but today conditions are different, and consequently other ways must be sought—or (and this would please me best) the whole idea should be dropped entirely!

I had hoped perhaps to be able to come over in the summer or autumn of this year, at least in order to see my mother—not to mention all the other things piling up that are in need of settlement—but there seems no possibility of this happening. I myself have not the money to pay for the journey (about $1800–2000 for the two of us there and back with a short stay) and so far I have found nobody who might pay it for me. There was indeed a discussion with Tompkins two months ago. As you know, there have long been talks of a new ownership for A.M.P. and Tompkins is the leading prospective buyer. I personally would see amalgamation with a large organization in the same line as of great importance from a business point of view, though the Pubs in its new form (since Voigt's death) has been working very well as far as publishing is concerned. Apparently they cannot agree on the price, and the present stockholders, now they have suddenly realized the value of the thing, are obviously screwing it up. If the deal had gone through, it would perhaps have been necessary (this was Tompkin's opinion) for an envoy to go across to talk with you and other European participants, and it seemed sensible to choose someone who could be seen as a friend rather than a business representative. I might then have been sent in that capacity. But as I said, nothing of any significance has yet occurred, and I don't know if it ever will.

We have had good news of my mother. Apparently she has come through all the horrors reasonably well in spite of her age, and she seems to have treated all the 50th birthday fuss, to which she was repeatedly dragged, in her usual way and exactly as the birthday boy would have wished. Of others the news is less good. Rudi Heinisch is sitting in Hamburg with a baby, doing his best to make ends meet. Another poor wretch, [Edgar] Rabsch, is cooped up with seven children in Itzehoe, at the moment thrown out of everything, since at some time or other he had been obliged to join the party in order to save his kids from starving—and if there is anybody who could never have been a Nazi, that was Rabsch. If you have any idea how one can help such fellows, please leave no stone unturned.

My brother also seems to be somewhat out of favour, at least that is what some letters suggest. How is it with Gieseking? He could give us a sign of life sometime. I am so glad that our good Willms has come back safely. I was often worried about him. Dr. Böttcher, one of the best, was killed in Berlin right at the end, and Genzmer has written me that Spittler has also been killed. What incidentally has happened to Schnell?

Pretty whacked by all the hard work mentioned at the beginning (to which can be added all the end-of-term exams, etc.), we made our way in very slow stages down here at the beginning of June. One can do it by plane in 1 ½ days, but we took a whole week, with pleasant stop-offs in New Orleans and San Antonio, Tex. After the two very successful concerts here (Metamorphosis, Cupid & Psyche, Nobilissima, Mathis) we travelled a little around the country (you know it, don't you, if I remember correctly?), were in Puebla and surroundings, in Taxco and Cuernavaca, and we are now going on to a small hotel near Morelia in Michoacan. We'll be back home at the end of August.

Your family in Buenos Aires writes often. The last letter urged us to keep you well supplied with food packets. The Pubs have in the meantime arranged a regular packet service, and I am told that it covers everyone as far as possible, so that I can devote whatever my restricted finances allow to other persons in need. But if there is anything you lack, let me know and I shall of course always gladly jump in.

Well, that will be enough for today. [. . .]

To Willy Strecker   New Haven
                                                                20 January 1947
Dear Willy, your long letter with the report on Mathis in Stuttgart has just arrived, and since today is in any case a letter-writing day, I shall answer it at once. I had already heard about the performance from various other quarters, and I can well imagine how it was. On the whole it is of course praiseworthy that among all the rubble people should put on a work such as this, and one can hardly grumble about technical deficiencies, let alone the intellectual skylarkings of conductors, producers, and stage designers. Your description of the Hamburg Nobilissima and reviews winging in from elsewhere about the Berlin performance create roughly the same impression. Though I am in general glad not to have to live through all the socializing, the outbreaks of enthusiasm, and probably equally well concealed or not yet clearly defined resentments, I shall perhaps find myself in a position to see one of the later performances—perhaps in Frankfurt. It depends how long the Frankfurt opera season lasts. The fact is that our European tour is now beginning to take more definite shape. Though there are not yet all that many firm dates, we do know that the first concert will be on 14 April in Rome. Directly after that there will be a few more things in Italy, then various other bits and pieces in Austria, Belgium, etc. that will take us through to May. The visit to Frankfurt and surroundings could follow, and then we shall retire to our old Valais for a well-earned holiday. There will be a further series of concerts in September, and then we shall be returning to our Connecticut home for the beginning of term. But please keep this entire timetable to yourself. I wish neither to fall victim to the whole pack of so-called friends, nor to become officially involved in anything in Germany, musical or otherwise. Even on this projected basis of keeping things as utterly private and discreet as possible,

there will be more fuss and confusion than a harmless New Englander can happily take.

Your remarks about Kepler, Freischütz, and Fidelio recall the problem that naturally arose very forcefully the minute we made our final landing here. In the beginning I came to more or less the same conclusions as you, but today I feel quite differently about it. It is possible that in one's younger years landscape, atmosphere, upbringing, and personal identification with objects and events may provide an important stimulus for one's artistic work, but now I find that the chronicle of people, events, and experiences, as well as their interpretation and portrayal by artistic means, are no longer tied up to the same extent with these external factors. The main concern is how to put one's experiences to use, rather than to keep on collecting new ones on the spot. If it were otherwise, one's urgent desire to treat a German subject would have vanished entirely in the course of the past twelve years. For the working out of deep-laid plans, somewhat more settled minds should find the Rhine no more important than the Mississippi, the Connecticut valley, or the Gobi desert. So the Kepler opera, though put off again and again, will sometime see the light of day. That it didn't happen long ago is due to the same causes that have kept the theory book ten years in the making: first, its author's perpetual hope of achieving greater maturity, knowledge, and creative strength, and second, the major curse of this earthly existence, a permanent lack of time. The first has absolutely nothing to do with surroundings, and as regards the second, over there one would probably be forced by the need for restoration, vital though that is, into compositional suicide. And this is something I wish to put off as long as possible—particularly now, just when everything is going so well! [. . .]

Here at home everything pursues its ordered and peaceful course. The school is as usual causing much work, but the results are very gratifying and acknowledged on all sides. Since we shall need to leave before the school year ends, the final turmoil with graduations, etc. is being concentrated into these remaining two months—we shall be glad when we are able to stretch out our legs for a few days in complete idleness on the ship's deck!

We have heard that poor Willms has died. How sad! If anybody had deserved a peaceful and contented old age, it was he. But some people seem to be pursued throughout their lives by misery and want, and, in order that they shall not be allowed to enjoy to the full all the good things their talent could give them, they have in addition to die too soon. Was it heart trouble? The list of those one will not see again grows longer every day, and strangely enough it is always the best who are thus extinguished.

I have heard from Bauer that parcels are now being regularly sent to you, and I recently saw a mountain of things piled up waiting to be despatched. Unfortunately, a lot seems to get stolen. Of all the packages we sent off scarcely more than half apparently reached their destination. Before Christmas we sent you a tobacco greeting, and we are hoping someone else didn't smoke it up! [. . .]

> The Hindemiths left New York for Genoa, Italy, on 2 April 1947 on a visit to Europe that lasted until September.
>
> William Steinberg was the regular conductor of the Pittsburgh Symphony Orchestra at that time. The offer was for an orchestral work in connection with the second centenary of the town of Pittsburgh. Hindemith did not write his Pittsburgh Symphony until 1958.
>
> M. E. Tompkins had now assumed complete control of AMP. The clarinet concerto for Benny Goodman was written in 1947 but first performed in 1950.

To Karl Bauer   Sierre

30 June 1947

Dear Bäuerle, we are back again in our old Valais district, and your letter reached us immediately after our return from Vienna. Everything here is as it always was, and after the extensive travel from one end of Europe to the other, interesting though not always easy, we are greatly looking forward to the coming holiday weeks.

The concerts all went well and were in all respects very successful—particularly in Vienna, where people behaved tumultuously and clapped for a full 20 minutes. The concerts were in Trieste, Milan (2), Turin, Genoa, Naples, Amsterdam (2), Brussels, London (2), and Vienna (2). Lucerne will follow in August. [. . .] I spent a week in Frankfurt (looks awful!), saw my mother, who is as lively as ever, and had frequent and long conversations with the Strecker brothers. They are both well, and the firm is functioning perfectly. [. . .]

As for Pittsburgh $1000 can be answered only with hahaha. Demand 2500 and go down as far as 2000 if you must; less than that and we won't do it. If the orchestra lacks money, let the more powerful conductor, if he's really interested, pay for it out of his own pocket. [. . .]

Greeting to Mr. Tompkins, who by now will, I suppose, have moved in. The clarinet concerto for his protégé B[enny] G[oodman] is already being worked on. [. . .]

> Henry Kaufmann, a former pupil of Hindemith's at Yale, was now teaching at Milton Academy in Massachusetts. He sent Hindemith the correspondence in which the father of one of his pupils complained to the headmaster about the Hindemith textbook Kaufmann was using in his class, describing it as "restrictive, artificial, entirely technical and mathematical." It is not recorded whether the father carried out his threat of withdrawing his son, but it is worth noting that the headmaster gave Kaufmann his full support.

To Henry Kaufmann (written in English)   New Haven

                                                            8 December 1947

Worthy seducer of American youth:

Thank you for your very illuminating letter. What kind of mathematics and modernisms did you put into those harmless books of mine, that Thayer's father had to become so terribly enraged? Nothing of the kind of poison he mentioned was ever found in the books as long as we used them here. Poor Thayer, having to steer between the Scylla of his father's musical convictions and the Kaufmannian Charybdis of musical mathematics and artificialities! And no wonder that you had to go to the infirmary. Don't you think back to the peaceful days in your teacher's protecting lap here at Yale, far away from the cruelties and realities of life, as demonstrated by the fathers of the boys at Milton?

We (that means the collegium chorus) were supposed to come to Boston and sing at some teachers' convention or something of that kind, but the class decided that they would prefer to enjoy their Christmas vacation. Right they are. Instead of going to Boston we (the Hindemiths) are going down to Washington for a few days. In January the chorus is starting rehearsals for the spring's concert (Josquin, de la Rue, Isaac e tutti quanti). How about helping us? We could use an experienced tenor.

Have a good Christmas. And don't take too serious father Fremont-Smith's attempts at correcting the musical situation. He is not the first father in history that made this attempt, nor will he be the last one. We can be glad that he is not given the power to decide on un-american activities. If he had, we both probably would meet very soon in some hard labor camp. Let's face it and prepare in time for such eventuality. As ever, your co-convict to come

    Paul Hindemith

> *Apparebit repentina dies*, a setting of a seventh-century Latin text for a chorus of mixed voices and ten brass instruments, was written for a symposium on music criticism at Harvard University and performed there by the Collegiate Chorale and members of the Boston Symphony Orchestra under Robert Shaw on 2 May 1947.
>
>   The Sonata for cello and piano was given its first performance by Gregor Piatigorsky in New York, but not until August.
>
>   The reference to Hugo Strecker was connected with the prolonged and (from Hindemith's point of view) somewhat bitter tug-of-war between Mainz, London, and New York regarding the publishing rights in his works that was now in progress.
>
>   Mainz University wanted to award Hindemith an honorary doctorate.

To Willy Strecker   [New Haven]

                                                            22 February 1948

[. . .] Towards Christmas you were sent the German version of Traditional Harmony and about two weeks ago the new Marienleben. It lacks the last song (no.

15), however, and this will be despatched from New York in the next few days. Das Marienleben will then be ready for printing as far as the music is concerned, though for the final production several pages of detailed text are still to come, since I wish to see the piece published only with a very comprehensive report and analysis establishing its link to the "Unterweisung."

The "Apparebit" proofs have not yet arrived but will be dealt with immediately on arrival. This piece can hardly be played with strings. It is, after all, a very primitive and drastic depiction of the Last Judgment, and only brass can really suit it, not a soft string sound.

I am just putting the finishing touches to a sonata for cello and piano that Piatigorsky will play next month in New York.

The "Hérodiade" is not to be spoken! The melodic lines in the orchestra (only 11 instruments, no doublings) are themselves the recitation, following the poem word for word. As a ballet (two persons only) it is likely to suffer the dismal fate of being presented in the most idiotic way, for what nowadays hops around on the stage is, for the most part, not up to tackling a genuine artistic task calling for the highest degree of concentration and dedication. The whole thing is admittedly a very esoteric affair. To read the text and listen to the music at one and the same time is an impossibility even for experienced connoisseurs, and one cannot demand from ordinary listeners a study of each single factor and the way they interact. So you will not get very much joy out of this particular article, since nobody can really discover what it is about—though I myself believe it is something out of the top drawer. A further drawback is that it is enjoyable only in a very good and clear performance, and the experiences I have had in this connection in Germany last year were not very encouraging.

Hugo seems in the meantime to have left the stage. As I said to you last summer, I was already convinced at that time that this would happen. When someone feels he is not the right person for the job, the best thing is of course to give it up. What I find less pleasing is that up to the last moment, up to mid-January, he always gave the impression in his letters that he would be remaining in his post for the next 50 years. I feel I deserved rather more openness on his part (I had known it already in any case!), after I had fallen out with everyone here for his sake. If one had known then how it would all turn out, it would probably have been better for everyone to leave the publishing rights here. I assume that Tompkins, who will be going over [to Europe] soon, will again be making proposals to you to this effect. [. . .] The AMP business is not going quite as satisfactorily as I had expected. Tompkins is certainly a good and very agreeable fellow, and he has the best intentions. But, unfortunately, of music he has *not the slightest idea.* [. . .] He is, as in the years before 1939, always very nice to me, *particularly* now in fact, since he had expected nothing at all and now sees that I am the firm's only solid supporting pillar. He regards sales and performance figures of my things, of which he is informed daily, as simply incredible. The whole concern is now being run more or less on the intellectual level of a potato business. [. . .] The economic basis for a very successful publishing firm does exist here; but, if things go on like this, it will be wrecked by a lack of artistic understanding. [. . .] Bauer is very good and is even virtually irreplaceable in the hiring department, since every conductor in the country knows him. But he can make no artistic decisions. [. . .]

With regard to your news about the Mainz University plans, you of course know how little I care for such things. But maybe it's even sillier to give the affair more significance than it really has by refusing it, and so it will be best, I suppose, to swallow the pill when I am next there.

That brings me to our travel plans. Nothing has so far been fixed. We would both prefer not to leave here at all, but apparently it can't be avoided. So we must now slowly begin to work out our travel plans and costs. In this connection I should like to know soon whether and to what extent the American authorities in Germany are interested in any activities on my part. The big noise in Berlin (one Benno Frank) appears to have been over here a short while ago and to have engaged some players to give performances. To judge by this, there does not seem to be very much interest in my appearance, otherwise he would have approached me, since he does of course know where I'm to be found. In point of fact, I have no great interest in making a tour of Germany that would probably be more than wearisome and disagreeable, but we need to know roughly what we should have to reckon with, for, if taken altogether it doesn't amount to enough, so that (as last year) we should land back here broke to the last penny, we would perhaps have to call the whole thing off. However, if we do come to a positive decision, we should be leaving here, as I think I have already told you, in July or at the beginning of August and remain over there to the end of January. [. . .]

Now I have surely said everything that one can manage on a Sunday evening in the grip of a heavy cold and snowed in for the umpteenth time this winter. I hope you haven't had it so cold as we have since Christmas. It is the worst winter experienced here since 1888. On account of the shipping lanes being frozen over, heating oil could not be brought in from the south, so we sat around in a somewhat cool house, even without any heating at all for part of the time. Things are now rather better, and in a couple of weeks we shall probably see the first crocuses creeping out. [. . .]

A new financial arrangement between the publishers in Mainz, New York, and London resulted in payments to Hindemith that enabled him to embark on a second visit to Europe. He was able to make it longer than the first trip since Yale had granted him sabbatical leave for the first term of the academic year 1948–49.

The summer school in Dorset (England) with which the tour began was Bryanston; founded in 1948, it later moved to Dartington. Hindemith was familiar with Samuel Courtauld, the eminent arts patron, through the Courtauld-Sargent concerts in London, at which some of his works were played in the thirties.

To Willy Strecker [New Haven]

15 July 1948

[. . .] Das Marienleben arrived, was corrected and started its journey back to you yesterday. It is the old familiar Schott typesetting, which makes an old composer's heart jump for joy as he reads the proofs. Please compliment your compositors on my behalf. I don't know which of the old ones are still there (is old Schmidl still around?) but, if new ones have been working on it, they have learnt well. [. . .]

I have managed to survive all my honorary title ceremonies. Of the Frankfurt one I have heard nothing except in roundabout ways. I suppose something in the nature of a notification will arrive some day. I don't wish to appear impolite by not sending a letter of thanks or something, but it would of course be even stranger to send one before having ever been notified (importance!) Columbia has also put a collar round my neck. The new president, Gen. Eisenhower, was very nice, and I had a long talk with him about his experiences in Germany. He was then himself given a degree by us here at Yale in the following week.

We shall leave here at the beginning of August. Ship to England. There I shall be teaching for a week in a summer school somewhere in Dorset—a kind of legacy apparently from Mr. Courtauld. Then we go via Frankfurt to Lucerne. August 24, 26, and 28 I shall give lectures on musical theory at the music festival there. Then a few days rest in the Valais. Beginning of September, concert in Geneva. Then I hope to spend three weeks in labour with some writing, and perhaps get my mother to come to Switzerland. Beginning of October I shall be conducting in Baden-Baden. Then a week of classes in Salzburg, then Lilacs and other things in Vienna. Later, in November, there are some things in Italy, and in January, Amsterdam and Zurich. End of January or beginning of February we return home.

Please say nothing about these plans. Unfortunately, I am once again being approached by all old friends, those who wish to become friends, and others who claim they once were. And I'm not in the mood for any of the three kinds, since I am anyway more than fully booked up and don't want just to remain for ever the sucker for others. Besides, I had hoped to spend my sabbatical in peace and do a lot of writing, but you will see from my timetable what has become of that. [. . .]

If I don't see you in Switzerland beforehand (how nice, if you could come to Lucerne!), you will, I suppose, be coming to Baden-Baden. This time Gertrud will be with me, so we can sit together again as in old times and perhaps even manage a walk in the surrounding hills. We shall perhaps also want to go to Frankfurt, and

Gertrud has been thinking of visiting Berlin in order somehow or other to free the possessions of ours that still lie there, virtually undamaged. But that prospect seems now to have become entirely hopeless.

Now just quickly to let you know that things have been going very well for us. For the first time we enjoyed summer in our own house, and it was really worthwhile. We may perhaps spend a few days next week in Pennsylvania, in the district where the Pennsylvania Dutch and the Amish live — these are mainly 18th-century settlers from the Rhineland — in order to see whether the people there still understand the Frankfurt dialect. And then we shall begin slowly to pack. [. . .]

Let's hope the complicated political situation won't put paid to it all. [. . .]

Hindemith's piano concerto, composed in 1945, was first performed on 27 February 1947 in Cleveland by Jesús Maria Sanromá, to whom it was dedicated.

To Willy Strecker   Chateau Bellevue, Sierre
                                                     16 September 1948

Dear Willy, I found several mountains of proofs awaiting me on our arrival in our familiar Sierre yesterday, and I herewith send two corrected loads back (cello sonata, piano concerto solo part). Both pieces have again (as always) been set well and conscientiously. [. . .]

"Cardillac" in Venice was well performed, musically at least, and it enjoyed a big success. Scenic designer ([Caspar] Neher) not good, director ([Oscar] Schuh) so bad that it could almost have been Strohbach. The music has worn quite well. Most of the pieces are still enjoyable, so the score could be rescued musically with only relatively minor changes. Unfortunately, however, the text is so idiotic that, in order to make the piece viable for the future, the action would have to be changed completely. That too could be done, and I also know how — but where is one to find the time to carry out all one's plans? [. . .]

We shall probably he coming to Frankfurt around 2 October. Please keep this secret, for we want to try and get to Berlin for our things, and in connection with that will have to visit all imaginable official departments in Frankfurt, in which activity the usual retinue of friends and acquaintances would be an immense hindrance. [. . .]

Your intervention in regard to Mother's journey was successful, and we thank you very much for your efforts. She is now at this very moment sitting opposite me in fine holiday spirits. We went to the airport in Geneva to meet her, but the plane from Frankfurt arrived without her, since on account of the bad weather and the overcrowded airfield the pilot hadn't even landed there. We were somewhat worried, since she didn't know our address. After a lot of telephoning we eventually discovered that she had been flown with other air passengers to Zurich and there put on a train. In the evening I found her at last on a train halfway between Bern and Lausanne. After Geneva we spent a few days in Nyon, and the day after tomorrow we shall again be striking our tents. We are leaving my mother here in this district till we return from Perugia. Then we shall send her back home. [. . .]

> At this time, Bruce Simonds was dean of the School of Music at Yale. Rosalind was his wife.
> Tam Shan-Kwong had attended Hindemith's composition class at Yale.

To Bruce Simonds (written in English)   Hotel des Palmes, Palermo
                         15 November 1948

Dear Bruce, your long letter was received with all the joyful appreciation it deserved. I didn't trust my eyes, seeing a handwritten letter of yours, and mentally I counted all the sighs and curses that went into it when you forced yourself down to the writing desk after all your school work!

Tam's death is a very sad affair, but the posthumous efforts of his friends are merely ridiculous. The man who wrote you sent me about ten letters of similar wording through different channels. A good deal of important letters gets lost every day, but postal connections with China seem to be pitifully reliable! I wrote the preface he wanted for Tam's complete works—which as far as I can see will only comprise one single Tome of about 15 pages—without saying that Tam was China's greatest genius since Kung-tse, but doing justice to his efforts—and I hope this will be my last official utterance concerning Chinese affairs for a long time.

Now to my own problems. So far things are going well. So well in fact that every day I'm receiving new offers and demands. I am supposed to conduct and lecture all over Germany, in Austria, Italy, and six weeks in Palestine. I declined all these offers because I am not too keen to travel. But there are some other requests of importance. They are: (a) Frankfurt (my home town) University put in an application at U.S.Government for me (without telling me in advance) as Austauschprofessor (Exchange) for one year. I did not like to discuss such a plan and talked it over with the Military Govt's man in charge of Universities in Hessen, etc., a Professor Montgomery from Minnesota University. Obviously there is now a new kind of policy of better cultural relations with the Germans, and instead of putting all the power of cultural decisions into the hands of little Jenkinses one is now sending people with experience and unselfish devotion to their task. This Mr Montgomery thought it of the highest importance to do some thing of that kind—and after a long talk I offered him a much shorter time, possibly one term. He may have sent in a request to Yale University by now, and he thought this would be a good opportunity for Yale to participate in this new plan of German recovery (which, in general, is since last year going on at an unbelievably fast pace!), since many other Universities have already done so—the Frankfurt "Rector" is now as a guest professor for one year at Georgetown. Seeing the situation as it now is, I would be willing to spend two weeks lecturing etc. at Frankfurt. (b) The Military Government of Bavaria asked almost the same thing, and it seems even more important to do it there because of the proverbial stubbornness of the Bavarians. For this I would like to consider another two weeks. — (c) The "Magistrat" of Berlin sent many telegrams asking for the conducting of one Concert with the Berlin Philharmonic Orchestra, which would mean an additional week.

Now comes the $64-question. Do you think these things important enough to delay my return until the last days of March? There is a boat the 25th of March which I could try to reserve instead of our original boat on the 2nd of February. [. . .]

You know very well how much I dislike irregularities and changes in established schedules. Only the fact that I know both points of view, the american and the german, so well makes me consider the proposition in the above told form. I'm sure you see that I boiled down a year's or more work to 5–6 weeks and about 2 additional travel-weeks, which is—considering the relative importance of the job—a very short time; but if you think that even that time cannot be afforded I shall be glad to cancel everything and take the boat February 2nd. Of course I would be very grateful to have your reaction as soon as possible. [. . .]

Give all my greetings to the faculty! With one weeping and one laughing eye I am thinking of the faculty meetings I am missing! If the idea of plenty of sunny south, old Europe and success comforts them, please give them this resumee of my adventures. After I wrote you last we prepared for another trip. My mother had come to Switzerland and we put her up in a tiny Pension high up in the mountains. In the meantime we went to Perugia (Assisi, Spoleto etc included) where I conducted the oratorio "Lilacs" of mine, sung by an excellent Viennese chorus in a German translation I had made. Back to Switzerland where we picked up Mother and sent her home to Germany by plane. We ourselves went by train to Wiesbaden and Frankfurt, where I had many talks with the authorities and with my old friends, the publishers Schott. Then by car through the Rhenish countries to Baden Baden for a concert to which people from all over Germany had come. The French as the sponsors of the concert were delightful and made every effort to participate and show their good will—which (where ever you come) is quite obviously out of the question as far as the Americans are concerned! The success was correspondingly enormous. Then to Freiburg for a lecture at the Music School, which was a very moving event. Back to Switzerland, the turntable of our baggage. Then to Salzburg for one concert with the Mozarteum Orchestra and a one week's course on composition. Then three concerts (twice the "Lilacs" again) and two lectures in Vienna. Back to the baggage in Switzerland and down to Rome. Business talks there and trip to Naples. Seven (!) rehearsals and one concert at San Carlo theatre. And now we are here in Palermo again for many rehearsals and a concert.

The trip so far was, as you can see, rather strenuous, but after the concert here (at the Teatro Massimo) we hope to go for a two weeks' vacation to Taormina where we want to enjoy the wonderful spring weather and all the flowers, orange trees, and no concerts. During this time I want to rewrite an old opera of mine (the one they played in Venice) for its new performance in Zürich which will take place late in the spring. The 8th of December there will be a concert at the Sta. Cecilia in Rome, then some other concerts and once at Milan. In January I'll have to go to Switzerland for two concerts and to Holland for three. Italy is wonderful, most of the ruins of the war are already rebuilt or will be shortly—coming back to places where we roamed in our younger years is partly pleasant, partly funny and partly sentimental, but always interesting and full of life.

Now I think I've told you enough of our events. We would be glad to hear something about New Haven and the activities at the School. Please give Gertrude's and my love to Rosalind. (In Vienna I performed some of the old Collegium-songs, and I missed her very much!) Greetings to the Traffic Regulators, to George Hart's slumber songs, and to the already married and the not yet married members of the School. As ever,

Yours   Paul

Hindemith's request for an extension of his leave was granted, and he returned to New Haven in April 1949. It was for only a single term, since Harvard University invited him to deliver the Charles Eliot Norton lectures in the winter of 1949–50, and those involved residence there. Yale, well aware of the high honour of this appointment, which comprised six lectures followed by a teaching course, felt obliged to grant Hindemith a further period of leave.

During this period he and his wife lived in a hotel in Boston, and there he received news of his mother's death on 23 November 1949 at the age of eighty-one.

The lectures, which were delivered in English, were published by Harvard University Press in 1952 under the title *A Composer's World*. Hindemith translated them himself for publication in German (*Komponist in seiner Welt: Weiten und Grenzen*).

To Willy Strecker   Hotel Fensgate, Boston
                                                    2 December 1949

Dear Willy, this letter should have gone off some time ago, but during these last days I had no time for anything beyond the lectures here, which right to the end turned out to be a tremendous drag. It all went off well, and now I have just the one course remaining, and that is one I always teach at Yale. Of course the news of my mother's death kept me feeling somewhat dopey, so that I couldn't really think properly. She went downhill fairly swiftly, thank God, after she had the first stroke. It would have been terrible to see her lying there helpless for months or even years. Fortunately one was able to give at least her final years a rosier look, thus compensating her for much earlier hardship and enabling her to take her leave in peace. We were glad that we were able to see her at least a few more times in recent years. Our warmest thanks to you and Ludwig for your telegram. You are of course better informed about the last few days, since I assume my sister will have kept you up to date, at any rate I asked her to. I at first thought of flying over for the cremation, but I should not have arrived in time, since we received the telegram announcing her death a whole day too late, we were once again on the journey to New Haven around this time, and the telegrams followed us back here. I couldn't anyway have been of any help, and here it would have been very difficult to postpone the final lecture. So I gave up the idea. [. . .]

I shall be preparing the English version of the lectures very soon and the German one later in the spring. For the German and possibly other language rights, you will have to contact the Harvard University Press. I have already spoken to the people here about it, and there will be no difficulty. [. . .]

In a long talk with Tompkins about three weeks ago, we discussed the situation at great length. Since in all these controversies regarding sales and payments I am always the main selling and earning article, I am naturally very depressed by the eternal discord between Mainz, London, and New York (I am of course talking, not of the percentages the AMP receives, but of the operations insofar as they affect me personally). [. . .] Basically it comes down to the fact that London pays and all others earn—that is certainly somewhat exaggerated, but in principle it is so. [. . .] Would not the most sensible solution be to place my contract with you on a new footing, so that we won't be fleecing the poor Londoners quite so much? AMP's direct payments to Mainz have by now become such that they could more easily take on the costs in relation to me. For the triangular concern Mainz-London-New York the result would be the same, but the weakest link would then not have to bear the whole burden while enjoying relatively few advantages. This need not be decided right away, but perhaps you can think it over. [. . .] It is obviously all the same to me who pays, but it is an unpleasant feeling to be the constant cause of difficulties that could perhaps easily be avoided. [. . .]

Nylon shirts have been sent off, purposely somewhat crumpled so that you will have no difficulties with customs. I hope you have as much joy with them as I—joy with shirts, think of it!—one does literally just throw them in the water. The next invention will be a shirt that one will just have to look at sharply for it to become clean. [. . .]

To Willy Strecker   [New Haven]
                                                5 December 1949
Dear Willy, your detailed description of Mother's funeral has just arrived. After your earlier news I did not think you would have been back from Paris on this day;

it was all the nicer of you to have taken such loving care of everything. For me it has been a strange feeling to be so far away and to have left all the trouble to others, but in this instance I had no other choice. It must all have been very moving, and the last reflected glory of so-called fame which this world has to offer and which in her own way she shared <u>whimsically</u>, but not without some enjoyment, was surely sincerely intended by all who contributed to it, and it was a parting salute she well deserved. Once again my deepest thanks to you and Ludwig for your sympathy and active help, from Gertrud too.

    Your   Paul

Hindemith conducted the first performance of his Sinfonietta in E, written for the Louisville Symphony Orchestra, on 1 March 1950 in Louisville, Kentucky.

    The revised version of *Das Marienleben* was first performed in Hannover, Germany, on 3 November 1948. Its first performance in the United States was given by Jennie Tourel at a New Friends of Music concert in the Town Hall, New York, on 23 January 1949. The performance "last week" to which Hindemith refers was either another one or a lapse of memory on his part.

To Emma and Fried Lübbecke   New Haven
                                                   23 December 1949

[. . .] We were very moved to receive your letters about Mother's death. We heard from many people how noble and consoling the funeral ceremony was and how you, dear Fried, kept the farewell in word and deed so entirely in line with what she was and would have wished. You can imagine how painful it was for me to leave all this to my friends, and also to know that Toni was quite alone, but it was impossible for me to get away from here quickly, and I should have arrived too late even with the fastest air connection. [. . .] It was very sad to see Mother so swiftly fade away. We knew it could not be very much longer. Last summer in Switzerland I found her already much reduced in some respects, despite her usual good physical and mental condition. [. . .]

We always considered the few times we were able to see her in the last two years a great gift, having during the war reckoned on never seeing her again. Despite the difficult times, we were able to make her final days as comfortable and pleasant as possible; much that she had had to endure in earlier times was thus justly compensated for, and so she could on the whole be well content with her long life. [. . .]

Christmas will be a quiet series of days spent writing letters. The weather is just made for that: warm, dark, damp—like in Brueghel's Gloomy Day—no snow and nothing in the least Christmassy. This time last year we were in Rome; now I am happy to be able to sit at home in peace for a few weeks and, when the letters are done, to write again for once on music paper. My lectures at Harvard went off well. The usual thinning of audience numbers during a lecture series did not occur on this occasion; six times my lecture room was well filled, always with the same people. Now I must slowly begin adapting the lectures into a book, first in English, then in German. Besides the lectures I still have a course on the history of music theory, and to follow that I shall be preparing an illustrative concert of old music (13th and 14th centuries) with the class. Immediately afterwards (in April) we shall once more be boarding a ship for Europe—Gertrud as concert manager is already busy working out our next tour. Germany will figure in it again. Otherwise, where we shall be going is not yet finally fixed; but there's plenty of time still.

Before this I shall be performing another new piece of mine—in Louisville, Kentucky (of all places—there's nothing there really but bluegrass and horses), it is—or rather, will be, for I've only just begun it—a Sinfonietta.

Das Marienleben was sung last week in New York; one of the best-known singers (Jenny Tourel) did it entirely off her own bat and at her own expense. It was very well attended and is said to have been very fine—Gertrud told me about it; I prefer to stay at home when my things are being played. In Cambridge recently old Mrs. Coolidge gave a party in our honour. She had just had her 85th birthday, but she's as lively as she ever was. She asked about you both several times and basked in reminiscences. [. . .]

Incidentally, Emma, have you received the new (well, it's no longer quite so new) piano concerto? I'm sure Willy Strecker has sent it to you. He probably always gives you everything as it appears. If he should have forgotten, you only need to remind him. [. . .]

I'll leave the rest of this page for Gertrud. I must anyway begin slowly to decorate our miniature tree. With electric lights, haha; we were conservative with real candles long enough, but the wooden houses here catch fire all too easily, and it's not worth burdening the days of Christmas with an unnecessarily high degree of fire-phobia. [. . .]

To Darius and Madeleine Milhaud   [New Haven]
(written in English on Hindemith's self-drawn Christmas card for 1949)

California is too far away, otherwise we would jump over and look how you are. Sometimes people come from the West Coast and tell us they had seen you and talked with you. They praise unanimously your different activities and we in our small village listen in amazement to these stories from a distant a miraculous world. On your next trip to the Eastern Centres of Culture (?) don't miss New Haven and at least two of its inhabitants, who would be very glad to see you again. (It was so easy in Europe; now, since we are in the same country, there is at least the railroad fare which is strictly opposed to feelings of friendship!). The only thing we can do in this moment is to send you a few thousands of good wishes and greetings! As ever your old

Paul and Gertrud

In a letter to Willy Strecker dated 21 January 1951, Hindemith explained that his dissatisfaction with his publishing arrangements had come to a head with the discovery that, since 1946, both AMP and Schott in London had been paying money earned by performances of his works to the Alien Property Custodian (APC) without supplying him with any records of the payments. The APC was now prepared to reimburse him but required proof of his entitlement. His enquiries to Schott in London had been met with complete silence. As for AMP, Tompkins, he complained, not only offered him no help in carrying out a time-consuming search of the firm's files for the necessary evidence, but afterwards presented him with a bill for $68 to cover the cost of photocopying the documents. "It was this famous straw that finally broke the back of the equally famous camel." Hindemith sent Willy Strecker a copy of a letter he had sent Tompkins, giving notice of his intention to break off relations with AMP entirely. "This letter," he told Strecker, "is of course not meant as notice of ending my contractual relationship with Schott in Mainz or Schott in London, but rather to give you a basis for any legal steps that may be necessary for setting up a new practical and worthy working relationship."

To Willy Strecker   New Haven

12 February 1951

[. . .] After his arrogant behaviour Tompkins has now become very subdued, and in two letters so far he has promised to do all he can to rescue what can be rescued. He intends to engage an artistic manager—that is to say, one who is acceptable to me—and he speaks seriously of his impending retirement altogether. He is coming here next week for a discussion, then we will settle everything in detail, and then I hope at last (and definitively) to establish order in this wretched affair. Bauer was here 2 weeks ago with the <u>accountant</u>, and we completed all the balance sheets. I enclose two statements from which you will see the sums involved. From the APC it is almost $25,000 and from Schott in London 13,000 I am owed!!! None of this sum would I have seen in the foreseeable future, and it would have continued to mount up if I had not gone into the matter myself. I consider it an utter disgrace, and I feel that publishers who do their best to hold back someone's well-earned money should be skinned ruthlessly, especially when they are as greedy for their own advantage as the AMP are. *Well, it won't happen again!* [. . .]

Don't be surprised at my business zeal. I hate all money matters as much as ever, but my peasant miserliness, evidently inherited from my mother's side of the family, simply cannot allow ten thousandsworth of dollars to vanish on account of a negligence bordering almost on sharp practice. Rather than that, I prefer to sit myself down and learn to do my sums—and successfully, as you see!

In response to the pressures for a return to Europe, Hindemith accepted a teaching appointment at Zurich University, to alternate on a yearly basis with Yale. From August 1951 to September 1952 he lived in Glattfelden, Switzerland, spending two days a week during each term teaching in Zurich.

Balanchine's ballet *Metamorphoses* was based on Hindemith's *Symphonic Metamorphosis of Themes by Carl Maria von Weber* and was first performed by the New York City Ballet in the City Center on 25 November 1952.

Shriners are members of a masonic order in America.

Following Tompkins's departure, Charles Wall joined AMP, of which he became president.

The Sonata for four horns was in fact given an official first performance in Vienna in June 1953 by members of the Vienna Symphony Orchestra.

The Septet for wind instruments was chosen by the New York music critics as "best chamber work of the year" after the performance given by the New Friends of Music, though it had had its first performance in Milan in 1948.

To Willy Strecker

New Haven
28 November 1952

Dear Willy,

Election is over, <u>Thanksgiving</u> is behind us, it's gradually getting cold, we were in New York—after this shattering profusion of events the turn comes for the letter to Schott's sons. There's quite a lot to report.

First of all, the most topical. Balanchine's staging of the Metamorphosis was a great success. We were there. He did it very amusingly. Just comical dancing around without any concrete action—unless one likes to accept that a beetle winding itself laboriously around a young lady counts as that—excellently performed. The City Center has a rather curious atmosphere, a former masonic temple full of Shriner frippery, and thoroughly provincial. But B. has indeed established something like a national dance culture here. They have now been dancing for weeks, the Metamorphosis and also the Temperaments are in the programme six or seven times. He is mad on getting a new ballet from me, if possible a full-length one. I shall think of it.

At the AMP a new spirit reigns. Tompkins has in actual fact disappeared, and since then everything has been going better. Wall shows goodwill, though he probably does not yet wholly grasp what the whole amounts to. I have had long negotiations with him and the others, and for the first time since Voigt's death I feel I am back with a sensible publishing firm. All the mishandled finance matters have at last been put back on the rails. It's incredible, all the things T. left undone—and he calls himself a <u>businessman</u>. All outstanding payments are now being settled. The Custodian will get nothing more—everything is being paid direct to me. All accounts with Schotts in London, which showed manifold divergences from my balance sheets, have also been settled. In short, everything is being put right. [. . .] And so after all the years of folly something sensible appears to be emerging once more. [. . .]

I have got Bauer to send you the sonata for four horns. It has been photographed white on black, and you will be able to transform the black into white without any difficulty. A piece like this is of course no business proposition, and you don't have to pay me for it, all I care about is seeing it published, since it is a nice piece. Please don't grant any first performance rights, anyone can perform it in any way he likes, first or not. I wrote it for the Salzburg horn players, who early one morning greeted me in my sleeping car with a serenade. [. . .]

Next Sunday I have a concert in New York with the <u>New Friends of Music</u>; the Septet for Wind Instruments, the old cello concerto, the Concert Music for Piano, Brass, and Two Harps, and the old Kammermusik with the siren. This Kammermusik has a part for a harmonium of a kind that no longer exists. I have rewritten it for an accordion. I'll send you the part after the concert, so you will have it on hand if needed. With it the piece will be easier to perform. I found several mistakes in the score—the composer must at that time have been a lamentable proofreader. [. . .]

In the interests of his composition work, Hindemith decided to settle permanently in Switzerland, and the academic year 1952–53 was the last he spent at Yale. During this period he was approached by Jack Bornoff, the general secretary of UNESCO (United Nations Educational, Scientific, and Cultural Organization), who invited him to write a work for an international conference on the role of music in the education of young people and adults that would take place in Brussels, Belgium, in July 1953. Gertrud Hindemith appears to have suggested the venerable French writer Paul Claudel as a possible collaborator. The following is the draft, written in English, of Hindemith's letter to Claudel, which Gertrud Hindemith translated into French before it was despatched from New Haven on 2 March 1953.

To Paul Claudel (written in English)   [New Haven]
                                                        [2 March 1953]

Since I never had the pleasure of meeting you, I am grateful for the opportunity of approaching you in the matter of which Mr Bornoff of the Unesco office talked with you. He wrote me that you would not be too adverse to the idea of providing the text for a kind of choral composition which would emphasize the aims and ideals of the United Nations.

May I be permitted to briefly outline what I had in mind: four short movements, each built on a quatrain which is to serve as the basis of a short hymn-like tune. The four hymns to be used as thematic material for a prelude, a fugue, a passacaglia, and a rondeau—in each of which the respective tune is played incessantly and subject to continual variation, joined towards the end of each piece by a solo singer whose rendition of the tune is to prompt the audience to participate in singing the final presentation of each quatrain-hymn. The general idea of this structure being: to reward the participant morally for his part in building up a musical form, as opposed to the more epicurean intake of music in an ordinary concert.

I know it is rather preposterous to ask you for a poetic formulation of miniature size, but who else would be able to compress within a few lines ideas of great importance and general validity? You may perhaps find in your desk some forgotten little poems which would be at all suitable, and which would permit to try out on a smaller scale of collaboration the ability of this composer—who would be extremely grateful and honored if you would entrust him with the musical re-formulation of some of your poetic ideas.

Looking forward to an early reply and thanking you for your willingness, as expressed in the preliminary talk with Mr Bornoff, I am

very sincerely,   yours

Also, Mr Bornoff wrote me about your planning an oratorio. Would it be immodest to ask you for some information about its subject and form? In case you find the firstmentioned project too insignificant and not worth your attention, I would be glad to be at your disposal for a work of a larger scale.

Claudel responded by sending his *Cantique de l'espérance* (English title: *Canticle to Hope*), which was designed as the third part of the oratorio to which Hindemith had referred. The following draft, written in English, was translated into French before being despatched from New Haven on 16 March 1953.

To Paul Claudel (draft written in English)   [New Haven]

[16 March 1953]

Dear Mr Claudel, your extremely friendly letter which reached me only several days ago—I had a concert in the Midwest and it was forwarded—together with the Cantique d'Espérance, was the most pleasant and encouraging surprise. The poem is a marvel and just seems to wait for its music. I am touched and happy at your confidence with which you call me your collaborateur eventuel and I hope that I can find musical formulations worthy of your poetical visions. I would have liked to start right away with the draft of the piece, but your remark that the "cantique" is the final third of the entire piece forces me to wait till you give me some further information concerning the two preceding parts. Your plan, as I understand it, seems to call for a gigantic paraphrase of the 17th psalm as the first part, and the Easter-piece as the second (just thinking of their musical possibilities makes me shudder!), and for this second part, you say, personal discussions are necessary. Alas, no musical architecture can be planned for one part without knowing the measurements of the complete building. Could you not send me the first part as far as you have it, and for the second give me some outline as to its contents, length, dynamics, and kind of expression? This might help me to draw some blueprint of the whole piece and on its basic proportions build up the third part which, as a kind of preview, could be performed at the Unesco's Brussels meeting—after whose success or failure you could still be free to decide whether you want me as your composer or if I would be permitted to penetrate your summer holidays with musical questions and suggestions. For today nothing more than this: thanks, many thanks for your willingness and for the wonderful poem; and an expression of hope that out of your inspiration and its transmutation into a musical organism something will arise that will be comfort and elevation to many.

> Claudel sent Hindemith the first part of the projected oratorio (a version of the seventeenth Psalm) but explained that the second was based on a personal experience that they would have to discuss in person. At this point Gertrud Hindemith took over the correspondence on her husband's behalf, requesting permission, as time was pressing, for Hindemith to begin composing the *Cantique de l'espérance* as a separate piece for the UNESCO conference. Claudel agreed and supplied an additional final verse to the text at Hindemith's request. Hindemith completed the composition in New Haven before leaving America on 2 June 1953.
>
> Oscar Cox, a Washington lawyer, was a friend as well as Hindemith's legal adviser, and from now on he was a regular correspondent. He and his wife, Louise, had attended the lavish farewell party in the Hindemith's Alden Avenue home (now sold) on 2 May.

To Oscar Cox (written in English)   The Biltmore, New York
                                                          2 June 1953

Dear Oscar: Of course you know that my silence is not an expression of a neglect of business matters, nor that my appreciation of all the work you have done for me has diminished. The ending school year with its exams and concerts, our dissolving of the household combined with the constant flow of buyers, sellers, and farewell-wishers—and on top of all the obligation to finish the Claudel piece—it was just too much. To-day we are leaving, and the next six days will be spent in plain laziness. I decided to actually do nothing at all, which will be a novum in my life.

We signed the Power and our druggist confirmed the signature. Enclosed are the three copies. I think we should accept the $150 tax adjustment, whatever the ways of arriving at this sum may have been. Frankly, I expected even more than that!

The $3969.35 arrived and I gave them to the bank. The bank's trust man, who is very much on the cautious side, finds that now is a bad time for buying stocks, as apparently everything is sliding (up or down—I was too inattentive to really find out what the direction was!), so he is buying Government bonds, which seems to me in principle a sound idea.

I hope Mr Barker finally agreed to my statement of foreign expenses. He must not forget that I am working in three different full-time jobs, and that, as he well knows, busy teachers in this country have their secretary, so have composers with a more than busy workshop, and so have conductors. I am using only one secretary for these different activities, and furthermore I am married to her. On a regular basis my expenses would of course be much higher. As for the car: if we had not had the car, a higher amount of travel expenses would have gone into railroad fares. So we saved quite some money for Mr Barker. This may by now have become theoretical and academic, provided he sticks to his $150.00 which I hope he will do. I suggest that he get my tax return from Mr Carr and audit the problem in its entity; otherwise the New Haven agents will unroll the whole question again, will have the same old objections and must again be defeated only to arrive at the same result that we have now. [. . .]

Of course you will always have reports and demands coming from me, although sometimes several months may pass before I can find the time to write. But before I settle down to a new chapter in my life I would like to pay old debts: please prepare a nice bill for me and I shall be glad to send you an equally nice cheque. — Auf Wiedersehen for awhile to you, Louise, and the boys. I hope Warren will be happy and successful in Yale. We were so happy that you came to our silly party and we plan to have similar performances the next time we will be here. [. . .]

Greeting to all of you, also from Gertrud,

As ever Yours   Paul

Hindemith's first musical engagement in Europe was the performance of the *Canticle to Hope*, which he conducted in Brussels on 9 July 1953. Claudel, whom the Hindemiths had visited immediately after arriving from America, was present at the performance.

Their new home was in Blonay, near Vevey on Lake Geneva, but shortly after taking possession they went off on a tour of Italy.

To Willy Strecker   Blonay

7 October 1953

[. . .] We arrived back from Perugia on the evening before last, having driven slowly up through Italy. The entire material did in actual fact arrive in time, after having for some unexplained reason been two weeks en route. Both concerts went well, and the final piece, the Claudel cantata, was a big success. Not everyone joined in the singing, but anyway the spirit was willing, and it was something entirely new for the people. Above all, it was a good thing that we could make up for the fiasco in Venice. It seems the piece was completely bungled there. The conductor was Rossi from Turin, and evidently he aimed only at loudness, crudity, and ruthlessness—in the Teatro Fenice, where the thing doesn't in any case belong—and he didn't permit the audience to sing either. [. . .]

Our new house is coming along very nicely. It is a real pleasure to have all one's things together again after so many long years. Of course there's still a lot to do before everything is in good order, but getting to that point is fun too. The address is just: Blonay—but that is only for publishing and private correspondence. If my address has to be given to any outsiders, then always just: Vevey, poste restante. This place swarms with so many famous and pseudo-famous people from whom I should like to keep my distance.

In two weeks' time the university begins, which will mean extra work for me. We shall probably find somewhere to stay there, so as not to have to travel to and fro. [. . .]

Following his revision of *Cardillac* which was first performed in Zurich on 20 June 1952, Hindemith turned his attention to *Neues vom Tage*, which he decided to revise for a production at the Teatro San Carlo in Naples. Hindemith himself conducted its first performance on 7 April 1954.

Hindemith gave the following letter two dates, probably simply the result of uncertainty.

To Ludwig Strecker [written in a train between Vevey and Zurich]
10 (12) January 1954

Dear Ludwig, Willy wrote that he would be in London till next week, so I shall now have to burden you with the NeuesvomTage affair (I hope you can read this scribble, I am sitting in a train and it is rocking terribly).

As you probably know, some attempts have been made to rescue the old crock in some way or other. Weigel in Vienna was supposed to be seeing to what extent it could be done by changes in the text, but he has produced nothing. I didn't want to change anything in the music, at the most just write a few small inserts if necessary. It was indeed clear to me from the start that the vocal parts would need to be changed completely (above a completely unchanged orchestra), for the exaggerated floridity of the old version was one of the main reasons for its never more than moderate success: it was stylistically at odds with the lighthearted story, and it was too difficult for the singers. During the Christmas holidays I sat down and revised all the vocal parts, and at the same time, in one big spring-cleaning, brightened up the story and the words. It could not have been offered to the Neapolitans as it was; there more than anywhere it would have been a flop—now it all seems to me more fluid and funnier. Above all, there are no more dead spots. The story remains basically the same, however; the order of scenes also. So apart from the vocal line, the score and the orchestra parts remain untouched, only a couple of newly composed pieces need to be inserted and, in addition to that, an intermezzo from another of my pieces (piano concerto).

But the piano arrangement! The piano part itself is untouched (except for the inserts), but its appearance is totally altered by the changes in the vocal parts. [. . .] I shall be sending you the first half of this new arrangement when I arrive, the other will follow on Saturday at the latest. [. . .] I am in Zurich for 2 days of lectures till Tuesday afternoon, but on Tuesday evening I shall be back in Blonay, where I shall finish the rest of the arrangement. [. . .]

I hope your New Year celebrations went off well. There was not much festive joy here, owing to the unceasing scribbling of the piano arrangement. Hardly a moment could be seized to wander out into the splendidly snow-covered countryside for half an hour or so. The whole year seems to be unrolling in the same fashion—it is already jam-packed; I'm dreading it. [. . .]

When writing in English, Hindemith always called his wife Gertrude.

Under the 510-day rule Hindemith, now an American citizen, would remain liable for U.S. income tax on his total income if he returned to the United States within 510 days after taking up residence abroad.

The clipping from the London *Daily Mail* has not been preserved, and, since Hindemith gave no date, the article cannot be identified.

Cox was an amateur poet, and Hindemith set two of his poems, "Image" and "Beauty touch me," to music in 1955.

To Oscar Cox (written in English)   Zurich
                                                     7 February 1954

Dear Oscar:

You are well acquainted with my standard opening of letters—accusing myself of having not written earlier—so that I can spare you that old routine. . . . Gertrude at least thanked you for all your lovely and heartfelt gifts, and I hope you know that she expressed my feelings, too. What she did not say was that I sipped, like a connoisseur of old Burgundy, your manifold legal instructions, Schott contract, tax information etc etc etc—I only regret that I could not go to Washington and get all that instruction personally. Thank you ever so much for all your kindness.

The Schott contract I left with them when I saw them two weeks ago. Willy Strecker—the one you know—was very much impressed with the whole affair. I thought it would be good if he and his lawyer brother would be given time to study the opus so that at our next meeting they can discuss it. Of course, I shall let you know what the outcome will be.

In the meantime I got busy with the tax problem and enclosed herewith you will find the result of my efforts. You will see that I made a tax return as if I were still residing in the USA, the reason being, that it is difficult for me to see what falls under the Swiss tax and what under the USA. However, I explained all the income from European sources, too, so that it should be relatively easy to tell the different parts apart. Of course, you are not supposed to bother with these questions; what I mean is merely that you glance through my work of art and give it to Mr Carr with your instructions, if at all necessary. There is one point which may decide the whole question in a favorable or unfavorable sense: I probably will not be qualified to use the 510 day rule. We left New York on June 1st and plan to be back after the South American trip, which means about the middle of November. This would mean that my Swiss salaries etc would come under USA tax which is considerably higher than the Swiss tax, or we would have to come to the States after December first and stay for a while in some southern Island. Actually there is no urgent reason for our going north, much as we liked to come back to the old hunting grounds, and if there does not show up any engagement for an important concert or something alike it would almost be wasted money to make the detour. Well, so far we really don't know what to do. I hate to mingle sentimental questions like coming home and seeing old friends with tax considerations. On the other hand the differences between Swiss and American taxation are so evident that they must be considered in planning long trips.

If all the tax goes to USA, there might [be] a difficulty in the fact that I gave, in my last return, a low estimated tax which turned out to be much higher. The reason was, of course, that for the purchase of the house in Blonay I used some of the money in New York instead of Swiss money, which I could not know in advance. Perhaps the development of political things will be so that the question whether one wants to go to America or not will be decided by higher powers. The enclosed article from the London Daily Mail will explain what I mean. We went through all those lovely events once before and we know that it always starts with the persecution of political opponents and ends up with the condamnation of the arts. Music that does not sound like Tchaikovsky will have no chance of surviving and if the composer happens to be a subject of the country in question his music will be banned and he personally can be glad if he does not end his ambitions in a concentration camp. I wonder what your reactions to all those happenings are!

Your poem was a great success. It is of the same high quality as its predecessors and as far as my modest judgement on English verse goes it is great poetry. I think you should not hide behind a game with the boys and frankly call it what it is: the true expression of a truly poetic mind. Or is such a confession against the legal attitude? I wonder if you would care to see it set to music. If so, I would at first suggest that you look in your drawer for some poem which is somewhat less didactic, because the abstraction of thought in the two poems you sent so far will lend itself only to equally abstracted musical forms, e.g. to formulations which in spite of greatness and profoundness will always have some soberness, too. But it can easily be done, and if you don't have anything else or don't write a whole new Liederkreis and—of course—you are not adverse to the idea of being cooked and stewed in a musical gravy, I will be ready to go to work as soon as the high tide of concert and writing obligations will be over, which means on the trip to South America.

We wondered if you were up in Maine during the Christmas vacation. We thought of you at that time when we were completely snowed in down in Blonay. I was kept very busy, though, as I had to rewrite an old opera of mine which will be done in Naples in April. With all the concerts in Vienna and Berlin (better success than the conference so far), University and Writing I had not had one single day off since November. Today we are going to Bonn for a concert, next week I am finishing up my semester at the university, after that two more concerts in Holland and then—finally—two weeks at home. Hereafter again, concerts in Germany and recording sessions, then the performances in Naples and a longer trip to Vienna. By that time it will be summer and after a few weeks of rest and un-hectic work at Blonay preparations for the America trip will be made. And soon after that we shall meet you in Washington. Time runs fast . . .

This is all for today, since we have to pack the suitcases. [. . .]

    With love

    Paul

To Willy Strecker (written on a picture postcard depicting Vesuvius)   [Naples]

    April 1954

Dear Willy, on the reverse side, another puff in memory of Sancarlosian eruptions. We were up there yesterday in the finest weather. — The opera has steadily grown into a real success. We had the final performance yesterday—enthusiastic audience with only a single (though very good) hisser, who only encouraged the persistent clappers and in the end gave up. So the initially somewhat dismal aspects have cleared up completely, and it was all as good as could have been expected. Naturally, the quality of the performance has in no way improved, either musically or theatrically. [. . .]

Hindemith's revisions of his two early operas aroused considerable criticism, and at some time in 1954 he wrote to a friend in Tübingen, Professor Walter Gerstenberg, defending his actions. Gerstenberg quoted the following extracts from this letter in his obituary of Hindemith that was published in December 1964 in the periodical *Universitas*.

To Walter Gerstenberg   1954

[. . .] When I provide a new version of a work of my own that lies close to my heart, I should be allowed enough credit for the alterations to be taken seriously. I am talking of the music, not the text. If this represents something special to my friends of those earlier times I, who wrote it, understand and am grateful. But if today, after a development of which I am very well aware [. . .] I undertake a revision, it is my friends in particular who should pause to reflect. I have the impression, however, that a large number of my former supporters, and, above all, those who are concerning themselves for the first time with Cardillac, have not taken the trouble seriously to compare the two versions with each other, but are playing off my former work against me for historical reasons. I am confident that I shall in the end, for artistic reasons, be seen to have been right. [. . .]

Paul Claudel died in February 1955, shortly before the complete choral work in three parts, Ite, angeli veloces, discussed at the time of the composition of the Canticle to Hope in 1953, was given its first performance in Wuppertal, Germany, on 4 June 1955 under Hindemith's direction.

Theodor Heuss was president of the German Federal Republic from 1949 to 1959.

To Oscar Cox (written in English)   Hotel Schlicker, Bochum
                                                                         9 March 1955
Dear Oscar:

I should have written right after the arrival of the moving letter you wrote on February 9th, but during the two weeks we had been at home I had to write one of the missing parts of the Claudel cantata—he died, as you probably read; and he wanted so much to hear the finished piece before his end!—and that kept me busy every day from morning to night. Now we are on tour again (on our way to London, and with two concerts here) and this is the first opportunity to write letters, although time is short and writing facilities are poor.

Although in your letter you somewhat overdid the praise of my little gift, I am awfully glad that you accepted the two little things with so much grace and benevolence. The photostats arrived—the photographer has done a very good job—and I shelved them with all the other productions. (You received the AMP-PH catalogue, so you can see in what kind of mixed company they are.) If I ever come down to translate the ten other English songs I published in New York into German I would like to add the translation of your two opera, too, and publish them with Schott's. Do you mind?

In a recent letter from AMP they told me about some kind of German Day in Washington, with playing of German Music (Mathis der Maler included), and an exhibition of manuscripts, pictures, letters, etc. etc. This obviously is some kind of propaganda enterprise of the German embassy. Needless to say that nobody asked my consent, nor that anyone wrote early enough so that I could have uttered an opinion. I don't like too much this kind of over-emphasis of the German side of my existence without ever referring to the American part. Of course, their attitude is understandable: they think that something had been done wrong—perhaps not so much against myself personally but rather as a representative in the field of the arts—and that they do some acts of recompensation whenever the opportunity shows up and without asking the poor victims. Only the other day when I had a concert with the Cologne Symphony Orchestra, the president of the republic, Mr Heuss, had come over from Bonn with his whole entourage. He was extremely nice and we had a very good time for hours after the concert, but nevertheless . . . . as said above.

Something else showed up. Mr Wall—the president of AMP, as you know—came with suggestions for a grand representative concert (or concerts) in New York, for which they wanted to invite me, expenses and everything else paid. If this plan can be realized—and for its realization we suggested April next—this would be the opportunity to re-appear over there, and you can imagine how much we are looking forward to such an event. The only questionable point in this plan is its suddenness: AMP never so much as said moo to all suggestions in the direction and now they arrive with a complete worked-out plan! In your last letter there is a phrase (although in another context) which says, "So, I do my little to make what I know meaningful." Am I to suspect that you had your saying in this, too?? [. . .]

To Oscar Cox (written in English)   Blonay
                                                                    13 April 1955
Dear Oscar:

You certainly kept me informed during the month of March with the tremendous amount of letters you sent. I am feeling like a poor swimmer in the high waves of a stormy sea: he tries to keep going in spite of the onrolling breakers, but to no avail; hardly had he some time to breathe, on rolls another one. They are agreeable ones, though, and I feel very comfortable with this kind of massage. Were it not for the feeling of remorse that I have in face of so overwhelming an activity I would always be prepared for more.

Your elaborate discussions both of the tax problem and the Schott contract were particularly interesting and illuminating. But I feel that, in spite of such illumination, complications are growing steadily and, with my work and income stretched over many countries, are already by now almost out of proportion to the objects of the contracts and tax returns. The crux of the matter seems to be—at least your instruction makes me see it that way—the question of residence, i.e. if I had a permanent residence in the USA, almost no problem would exist. Nowhere do I find a consideration of the status of non-residence. Either there ain't no such animal or that name is reserved to expose the unfaithfulness of citizens who simply cannot be (or perhaps sometimes do not want to) in permanent touch with the country. This is strange, as in other countries a citizen abroad (Auslandsdeutsche, Auslandschweitzer) are looked at as the best advertisement of their homeland's culture and produce, and nobody ever thinks of calling them back periodically; if they love their country they will be back whenever they feel like. I thought that with the application of the 512 days rule one is automatically made a non-resident. What else could the sense of that rule be if one has to go on with taxes just as before or even has to pay double taxes in different countries?

In my particular case there is no doubt that I have to be in Europe. My two main activities are composing and concertizing (I hope to get rid of any university duties after the current term), both of which I cannot do in the States: for composing there would not be any time left over, as for making a living one is obliged to have a college job—and this, as I had amply time to find out, is practically the end of composing, not to mention the rather hopeless situation of a music teacher whose only obligation seems to be to produce hundreds of mediocre students, write again hundreds of recommendations for them each year and as for highlights in his career waits for a Guggenheim or other fellowship every second or third year. As for conducting, the situation is more than hopeless, as the conductors in the USA more than anywhere else are a kind of brotherhood worse than those of the locomotive engineers': they prevent any outsider to come into their realm.

Here in Europe with the cost of living still reasonably low and travel distances short, I have plenty of concerts (next year's season is already taken care of) and once I have no more university work I can finally come down and write all those things I wanted to write since years. I hate travelling around, but here I can keep travelling a relatively minor affair and concentrate on the main business. Another point is artistical reputation. Here I am a famous man (whatever that means—but it is part of a musician's existence) while in America in spite of the many students scattered all over the country I was just one of many teachers and nothing else. That beside that I did some composing as a side line, was recognized, to be sure, but what does that mean in face of all the native talent that has to be taken care of and pampered—there is hardly such a thing as free competition, except in a very small way, as far as solo or chamber music playing goes. The best proof for this statement are your clippings which you sent on so kindly. What do they show? Mostly performances of minor importance, never an opera, almost never a symphonic piece—of course one may think they are not worthy of being performed, but over here one thinks differently and I think a musician cannot be blamed if he grasps one of the few chances that life can possibly give him.

How this american non-reputation works in other countries I told you many times when I wrote you about the situation in South America. Here in Europe it is no better. In Cologne the other day the Bundes President came over from Bonn (as I wrote you); pleasant as it was to have him there it was rather embarrassing not to see any of the Americans, not even a third rate cultural attaché, and it would have been a fine and cheap opportunity to show some interest, and claim that the successful conductor was something American. Same in London: I had an extremely spectacular concert with the Royal Philharmonics in the new Festival Hall—nobody showed up (besides the sold-out hall!). I am sure you understand: I do not complain, and basically I am glad if beyond concert duties I do not have additional social obligations. I mention these things just as further illustration to my statement that I am forced to do my work here in Europe.

When I left the States I thought it would be easy to have four or five concerts each year to make annual returns worth while. Last year not even two of them showed up so that the travel expenses would have been higher than the income. Now with the AMP's proposition for next year (I wrote you about), which I thought would be a basis for a trip overseas, it seems to have faded out like McArthur's old generals: nothing any more after the first fanfare.

So much about the reasons for non-residence. Now some technical questions about the same problem. Does non-residence mean that taxes on German and Swiss income which I paid in these countries will not be credited against US taxes? Or can by handing in some application such credits be obtained? So far it seems that the US-Swiss and US-German agreements are not made to make the life of any of the respective countries' citizens any easier, but on the contrary to catch the poor worms more safely than ever in an ever narrower net of taxation.

If it thus appears as if a US residence would be a better solution of the problem, your suggestions will have to be discussed. You propose that in some way or other we make your Maine home our place of residence. Heartwarming as such an offer is and touched by your endeavor to assemble more and more fiery coals on my head I would be afraid to accept it. Even the most pleasant people are a bore once you have them around the house and in my opinion musicians are particularly disappointing at closer scrutiny. Furthermore we probably would never have the opportunity to sit out at your premises the time required by law.

Buying a house somewhere in the States and rent it would in my opinion hardly be a favourable solution. First, it would add more complications to my already rather muddled affairs at a time when I try to reduce all unessential things in favor of the more important enterprises. Besides, it would be difficult to get rid of the tenants when we want to get in and to find new ones when we get out. Further, it means that I spend quite some money for the only purpose of saving some taxes. It seems to me that a double taxation is still cheaper, with Swiss taxes being low anyway and

German taxes being greatly reduced as of this year. The same goes with having a permanent apartment in a New York or other city's hotel: it would be more expensive than any tax gain. Of course there remains the moral question of a citizen's US residence, and he may be expected to pay rather dearly for that. I would be inclined to regard this possibility as the last way out. The best solution would be, if each year or every second year enough concert offers from USA would make it possible to appear frequently over there and show that I am always willing to do something for my citizenship. If then some kind of permanent headquarters would have to be established we could perhaps hire an attic room in our old New Haven house, as a legal base, and stay most of the time in a New Haven hotel, if that is possible.

All these questions should be cleared up if I could sit down with you and discuss the problem thoroughly. If finally our trip next year will materialize, this can be done. It seems that up to that time I have to become a non-resident and pay double-taxes (if that is the main effect of non-residence) or, if you find that—besides the moral side of the problem—it is more practical to stick to some kind of US residence, a way to do so has to be found. In the meantime I shall go on paying German and Swiss taxes as before. [. . .]

Next problem: Schott contract. [. . .] The main problem here again is the question of residence. I wonder if this could be avoided by omitting entirely the English firm Schott and Co. They had to come in as long as the Schotts needed a British foothold, the situation in Germany being unstable; but now there is no real reason against a contract with the Mainz Schotts. It would, in my opinion, simplify matters by having only two countries involved instead of three, one of which seems to be particularly fancy in respect to her tax laws. There is one question: if I am a non-resident in respect to the USA, would I have to pay British taxes only, from a contract as it is drafted now, or would there be a double taxation, in England and in America? [. . .]

I think it would hardly be possible to increase the amounts of payments due me from Schotts. They pay a decent amount of money which can be maintained during times of ebb without hurting them—in fact, they paid monthly sums to my mother during the war when I could not reach her—and personally I prefer to have regular payments of a certain stability instead of going up and down with the market fluctuation; this is done anyway with the royalties. [. . .]

Concerts are over for this season, as I have to go back to the university in two weeks, which means some preparation of the material for the courses. There will be one more concert in June, when the new Claudel piece will have its first performance. Just now I am writing the orchestra score of its last part which means about 50 elephant-size sheets. The lake of Geneva at this time of the year is unbelievably beautiful. Why don't you come over for a short visit with Louise and have some Canton de Vaud for a change? [. . .]

To Oscar Cox (written in English)   Blonay

23 April 1955

Dear Oscar:

Today we have something different.

I received the following telegram from the Finnish consulate in New York:

Confidential information Wihuri foundation Finland desirous to grant 1955 Sibelius award 7.500.000 finnmarks to you provided you travel to Finland at own expenses to receive award october ninth and conduct at least one concert in Helsinki prompt reply prepaid finlandia

New York Artturi Lehtinen, Consul General of Finland.

Now in this case I need your advice more than ever. This prize is after the Nobel one of the highest available; and for the poor musicians the only one of greatest international fame. Stravinsky got it last year or two years ago. The sum mentioned seems to be the equivalent of $30.000, which is quite something. Of course, there is—personally and artistically—not the slightest reason why I should not accept, and I sent a telegram saying so.

BUT: I looked up the income tax table . . . . As you know, I am now in the bracket of about $30.000 which means that I have to pay about $13.000. If $30.000 will be added to my income and this sum is not taken as earned income (how could it be) my taxes will go up by about $30.000, that means the sum of the award. In other words: the Finnish government would pay the US government $30.000 and I would be in the same situation, prize or no prize. This goes absolutely against my sense of justice. If furthermore the Finnish government deducts its own taxes the end will be that with travel and hotel expenses and the loss of other things the award may cost me a few thousand dollars instead of giving me something. If the taxes of this windfall (or basilisk's egg—whatever it turns out to be) would go to Switzerland, everything would be all right, as something would be left over for myself, but with the taxes going to the US I doubt if it is worth while to accept it. It really is a disgrace that well-meant actions turn out to be a burden and expense instead of a benefit.

What do you think about this problem? [. . .]

To Oscar Cox (written in English)   Blonay

13 May 1955

[. . .] Many thanks for your Wihuri inquiries. In the meantime they wrote from Helsinki, too. Even there the award seems to be tax free, and also here it is not likely that they will take away taxes—Mr. Decombaz is tracking down the legal side of it, although he said there might not be too much of a clear information, as cases like this one did never show up around here. . . . The thing seems too good to be true. Anyway, the month of October will probably be seeing us way up in

Finland—häälipuuoovioyakainnen, or whatever they say for hallo, good luck, and how are you.

We called Stravinsky when he conducted in Lugano, and Gertrude talked with Vera (Mrs. S.). [. . .] He did not receive the Wihuri money two years ago. It was given the first time in that year, and to Sibelius. [. . .]

In order to cope with all his conducting engagements, Hindemith gave up his teaching work in Zurich in July 1955. Although having initially refused the invitation, Hindemith did in fact tour Japan with the Vienna Philharmonic Orchestra in April 1956.

To Karl Bauer [Blonay]
[after August 1955]

UNFAITHFUL MAN !*&%"§ç+?:äää!!!!!

How come we never caught a glimpse of you??????? As we informed you, we were travelling around all the time, thought, however, you could come to Edinburgh, since it seemed you had to visit London anyway. *Shame on you.* There would have been so much to talk about, but it seems it wasn't meant to be.

As so often before, AMP has again apparently forgotten to send me a financial statement for the year. Well, I have written off all hopes of ever seeing orderly conditions there. My friend Mr. Cox will look after all questions of business with them.

In present circumstances it is hard to say when we shall next be coming to the USA—there, too, it had all been planned quite differently. . . . . . There can be nothing better than loyal friends who stick to their word.

Can you deal with the enclosed mail? I don't like doing it from here, for it becomes never-ending and the people keep on writing back.

In December I shall be doing Neues vom Tage in the Vienna Volksoper, the concert schedule for the winter is filled to overflowing—mainly Mozart and PH—I have just turned down a big engagement with the Vienna Philharmonic for a visit to Japan on account of too much work. So, as you see, everything is going well.

Quick warm greetings. Let us hear from you again soon, himmelherrgottsakrament und Zwirn...§!!&%*_)"⅙+?öööööö ö ö ö

To Oscar Cox (written in English) Hotel Breidenbacher Hof
Düsseldorf
26 February 1956

Dear Oscar,

We are again in Düsseldorf; I remember that the last time I wrote you it was from here, more than a month ago. Gertrude kept you posted about the events of the past weeks. I was sick in Frankfurt; food poisoning which started some kidney and other chain reactions. Afterwards I was very weak, was in Blonay for a few days like a poor reconvalescent, and it is only now that life seems to proceed the normal way. Here I am amidst the rehearsals for the Bach B minor Mass which will be on Friday next. After that there will be one more concert in Bielefeld, a week at home, another concert in Switzerland (Winterthur), then the rehearsals with the Philharmonics in Vienna must be done and right after we are on our way to Japan—about the 2nd of April—directly from Vienna via Istanbul and Bangkok. It seems that we shall miss you when you come over to Europe. Can't you come later? We will be back the last days of May.

All your manifold gifts reached us. Ladle and book middle of February, as Gertrude wrote you. I wish I had ideas to fill the book with, but as my talents as a writer are of no value and my ambitions in this field are nil, it probably will end up filled with drawings (perhaps with little funny poems attached) which, I hope, will not be contradictory to the intentions of the noble spender. The author-inscribed book arrived just the moment when we left the house, starting the present concert trip, so I just had time to see the title page and had to leave it for further scrutiny when we come back. The mathematics book followed me to here; it really is a nice opus. I adore this kind of popular or semi-popular dealings with difficult subjects. It is somewhat on the same line as Hogben's Mathematics for the Millions, but less presumptuous, less boasting, and free of politics—thank heaven. Thanks for all these, and for the different issues of the Long player.

I am profoundly moved, if not rather embarrassed, by your efforts in making my music and/or person palatable to American conductors, trustees, and the like. I do not want to discourage you, but I am sure that after a while you will find out that nothing can be done. In case we see you when you come over to Europe we can talk about these problems, it is of no value to write too much about them, they are not that important. After all, it does not matter whether there are a few concerts in the States or not. From next season on I have anyway the intention of curbing my concert activities in favor of composing. Nevertheless, it seems that via our friend and manager [Walter] Schulthess some American engagements seem to take shape.

As far as business is concerned, I feel somewhat derailed, owing to that sickness which obviously left my brain in a state of nebulosity. I don't remember which of your questions I have answered and which not. I remember, though that I sent you the draft for my income tax return. Did it arrive, or did it land in the stomach of a whale causing him pains? [. . .]

Well, I think this is all for today. Let me add a few under-zero greetings (it really is cold! the Rhine is solidly frozen down to Coblence; it is a strange sight to see people walk on the river's bed). [. . .]

Hindemith's Symphony *Die Harmonie der Welt* was performed for the first time in Basel on 25 January 1952. He used the music from the symphony in the opera he was now beginning to write.

To Oscar Cox (written in English)   Blonay
                                                          6 June 1956

Dear Oscar:

this is just a very short note, full of gratitude and admiration—both of them in the reversed proportion to the length of my few sentences. Gratitude for the amount of work you did with the preparation of the income tax return, and admiration for the skill with which that was done. Looking at it I got rather dizzy and my last few hairs stood on end at the idea what I would have done if I would have been left alone for solving that puzzle—it really is a nightmare!

The reason for my brevity is, that after all the concerts of the past season and the oriental trip I got down to the brass tacks in the form of the libretto of my new opera. I want to finish it now, have the brain full of ideas, and if everything goes well, the book will be ready in about two weeks, so that after that I can start with the music. (In case you are interested: the opera is "Die Harmonie der Welt," a symphony of which is already rather common place in concerts and on records). Gertrude, who is well instructed about all the problems, will write you in the next days—about the trip; our sorrow of having missed you in Europe; Americans in Japan; possibilities of seeing you; a faint possibility of doing Mathis der Maler (this is another opera of mine) as a concert performance in New York next spring; and about preliminary considerations concerning the questions of residency and citizenship.

Thus, permit me to end this note here and now and to go back to my writing and rhyming. Thanks again! Love to all of you!

     Yours acceleratedly
      Paul.

Hindemith wrote the first page of the following letter, up to the signature "Paul and Gertrude," by hand and attached to it five typewritten pages under various subheadings, beginning with "Activities."

The Concerto for horn and orchestra was first performed in Baden-Baden on 8 June 1950. The same soloist (Dennis Brain) and conductor (Hindemith) made the gramophone recording in 1956.

"Harvard book" was *A Composer's World*. Anchor Books eventually published a paperback edition in 1961.

Cox had warned Hindemith that, unless he paid a visit to the United States before June 1958, his American citizenship would lapse. Rather than accede to Hindemith's fatalistic reaction ("the best thing to do now is just to leave everything as it is"), Cox went to the secretary of state, John Foster Dulles, and persuaded him to grant the Hindemiths honorary American citizenship, which had no residency requirements.

To Oscar Cox (written in English)   Blonay
                                                              14 December 1956

Dear Oscar, thanks for your birthday greetings, thanks for all things you did for me again during the past year, thanks for your good will and thanks for your patience with my shortcomings, mainly my rough way of sometimes simply not agreeing with things done or proposed. I am sure you understand all that. Besides, it is Christmas time now, and I hope your few little thoughts you have on our behalf will be friendly as are our rather melancholy memories of all the Christmases we had in America. For old people like ourselves with no younger folks or friends around Christmas means just another year passed by—a pleasant year, though—and looking back on the many preceding years with all their events and old friends gone forever makes the heart heavy; heavier from time to time, till the weight is full. I hope the little bell from Vienna will tinkle with some faint tones some little song of the Hindemith's love and devotion to all of you. Be happy, all you Coxes, be embraced, and don't forget these old hermits.

   Yours, as ever   Paul and Gertrude

   Activities

After a beautiful fall with a very good apple harvest—no pears or other fruits this year—we packed our suit cases again and went for some concerts in Germany. Then London with one week full with recording sessions. Every day two of them, which is quite strenuous. We did seven orchestral pieces of mine, among them the little Horn Concerto of which you have the score. It will be sent to you as soon as it is published, so that you may check if we played the right notes. Thank heaven, no official invitations came; it would have been impossible to accept them, as during the day we had hardly time to eat and at night just dropped exhausted into our beds. After London we enjoyed several days here and went to Vienna. There I did the tape recording of an opera of mine (Cardillac) for the Austrian radio—have you ever heard of an American radio doing a complete modern opera?—which again meant a full week with two sessions daily and the corresponding fatigue.

At the same time the score of the new opera is progressing, rather slowly though, but nevertheless, I am almost halfway through. Right after Christmas we must go for a concert to Berlin (an oratorio of mine [*Das Unaufhörliche*]) but after that the whole month of January we can stay here and that time will be reserved for composing and writing the rest of the score. In February and March there will be concerts in Germany and Italy, and April and May will see the final touches of the opera. In June the rehearsals for it will be under way and after the Munich opera's summer recess towards the end of August the performance will take place. I hope you can manage to witness it. It will be quite an event and the performance ought to be good, as their personnel is fine and is not, like many others, always travelling around.

Harvard book

Thank you for the Stravinsky book and for the memo on mine. I have not heard from the Harvard press people recently, but as the book sells rather regularly—annual royalties being rather stable at about 160 dollars—they might still want to keep it for themselves. I remember that they had printed 5000 copies which except for a few hundred seem to be sold. To cover this year's sale they probably made a reprint, and this, too, may be an obstacle for a transfer of the book. In general, I would think there is not such a demand for a book of this kind that a popular edition would be necessary. With Stravinsky the case is different. He is more agreeable, anyway, and if he offends people it is only the composers and other musicians, while grouchy old Hindemith cannot keep his mouth shut and offends almost everyone on earth.

Citizenship

I hope you are not too cross about my reactions to the Passport Division's suggestions, as reported to you by Gertrude. As a last word in this case let me just recapitulate: If the procedures suggested—whiningly offering one's services, making propaganda for American music in America Houses, concerts, lectures, etc., etc., indulging in cocktail parties and other nonsense—are the conditions for keeping one's passport, one should have been warned at the time the application for citizenship was filed. I never would have applied. Certainly we, like many other artists and other people, escaped political oppression and were grateful for American political etc. freedom (although I still remember some of our jewish friends who, after having been spared Hitler's ovens, never found any place in New England where they could spend their holidays, because of the "restricted clientele"), but, to be quite frank, in our art we did not find any freedom. In music freedom does not exist in America; the musician, especially the composer, lives in medieval slavery, being the serve [serf] of all kinds of Managers, union bosses, conductors, professional societies, against which no individual can do anything, unless he has millions to spend and has the background of his musical activities in old Europe. I think you saw glimpses of this deplorable situation in my own case. Of course I have no complaints, as the whole world is still open to me and gives me more than the US with their one and only resource of college teaching ever will, but people in America should learn to see the difference and should not think that they have created and maintain the ideal conditions for creative musical work. Nothing can be said against the above mentioned conditions, as long some little singers or their likes are concerned: they may, even ought to, climb up the ladder of success by offering services, play and sing in all the America Houses possible, and drink all the cocktails offered. A musician's services can be had by the government for the asking—but I have the experience, that your doings and sayings will be ignored if ever you dare having a different opinion from the general "we are perfect" one. I was fourteen years in America and did my best to collaborate in the development of American music. Nobody ever bothered to call me an American musician, I always remained for them a foreigner, although I even wrote the piece that in due time and after the waning of that musical ignorance may well become one of the few musical treasures of the nation ("When lilacs . . . ."). As for the America Houses and parties: why did they not send the Toscaninis, Walthers and other distinguished new citizens first through this mill as an encouragement for the lesser crowd? I think, nobody would have dared.

Oh, let's finish up this dreary chapter, it is too dull for words. Besides, I am afraid I shall never change my mind, and if stubborness of this kind prevents me from being regarded an asset for American culture, I cannot help it and must prefer to travel with a stateless passport, as do so many other artists. I think, the best thing to do now is just to leave everything as it is. It seems rather certain, that in June 1958 we have to go to the States. If by that time bureaucracy wins, some other solution will easily be found, otherwise we shall be just as happy and proud as before to retain our citizenship.

It may interest you, that of all the composers, that in the thirties went to America, all—except those that died and except Stravinsky who cannot find any better climate for his health than California—are now back in Europe, not to mention all those Americans (singers, players and hundreds of other musicians) who found Europe a better place to live musically and are a commonplace sight as was the once immigrant European artist in New York.

Let's forget all this stupidity.

Why Hindemith called himself the dairyman (Meier) in the following letter is not clear. His opera is Die Harmonie der Welt, which was first performed at the Prinzregententheater in Munich on 11 August 1957 with Hindemith conducting.

To Karl Bauer   [Blonay]
9 June 1957
Dear Kallche [. . .] It's now a year since we were together in Nuremberg! Time goes too fast, and on top of that the weather is atrocious. Morning walks to the Wertheimer Castle in continuous rain are not recommended; the most one might do is ring a few bells—it should be dry in the bell towers, if perhaps a bit cramped.

The dairyman has his opera all tied up, 350 pages of score and 400 piano arrangement, on top of that the complete text (completely altered). He is now going with his dairyman's wife to Munich to join in the production preparations. In the midst of that comes the Vienna music festival with the cantata [Ite, angeli veloces] as in Nuremberg and Reger's 100th Psalm. Powerful audience-singers wanted! Likewise voracious first-night tigers for the 11th August— or for the second performance on 16th, which I am myself conducting. I recently did the complete Mathis twice in Wiesbaden.

Hasty greetings

Hindemith returned to Zurich University from 3 to 21 December 1957 to give two courses on Gesualdo and the string quartets of Arnold Schönberg and to conduct a seminar for advanced students. These were in fact his last courses.

The first performance of the Canticle to Hope in the United States, in Hindemith's English translation, was given in Woolsey Hall, New Haven, by the Yale School of Music on 19 April 1958, together with Brahms's A German Requiem. The conductor was Howard Boatwright. The concert was repeated the following evening in Carnegie Hall, New York.

To Karl Bauer   Blonay
                                                                  31 December 1957
Dear Karlchen,

The year is being ended, as you see, with you—all's well that ends well.

First of all, warmest thanks for your Christmas gift. If we had intended to give up drinking, it would certainly not have been the right thing. But, since we have no such intention, the two bottles were a pleasant sight and will in the course of the next few days find an even pleasanter inner appreciation. At Christmas we spent just three days sitting here quietly, had then to hasten to Milan, where the Scala was doing Mathis (a good success), and now we are burying the deceased '57 here. Tomorrow touring starts again, Cologne, Kassel (concerts and Cardillac), and England. We spent December in Zurich with university courses (my last ones, I hope). [...]

Regarding the City Center, they should not be given an option on Mathis. I have just seen once again in Milan that there's no point putting on this piece unless it's very well done, and I don't see how this somewhat brittle 57th Street institution can do that. They have hardly any regular personnel, and the orchestra will not be exactly first-class. The conductor, whoever it is, may be all right, but there has never been any sign there of an acceptable stage director or scene designer—and in this piece a lot depends on them. On top of all this, Böhm is bringing out Mathis in Vienna in April, and so the first chance of a performance in New York should be given to him anyway. It should of course be AMP's job to raise things like this with the Metropolitan. The man there who prepares those exciting monthly reminder stickers for radio stations could also turn his attention now and again to publicizing opera. After all, both Mathis and Cardillac are being done all over the place, as well as continuously throughout Germany (even East), and Die Harmonie der Welt has been running successfully in the repertoire of two theatres since summer. A publisher's representative worthy of the name could achieve something with facts like this, but I suppose that calls for a bit of imagination. . . .

Concerning the Canticle to Hope and the complete piece (Ite angeli), it would of course have been best to have waited until I myself had performed the piece over there somewhere, since there is always a slight problem with the audience joining in the singing, and the whole piece crashes to the ground if this is not skilfully handled. You were there when we did it in Nuremberg last year, perhaps you can tell the people who want to do it without the composer's participation roughly how it should go. I presume it will be Boatwright or [Fenno] Heath taking charge of the performance at Yale, and I don't know what conditions and which people have to be reckoned with in Aspen.

We are still reckoning to come over towards the end of summer or some other suitable time. So, if there is any suggestion of performances (important ones) anywhere, you can indicate that I could possibly take them on myself. However, not in the way Little Symphony-Sherman offered: that I should do one of my own pieces in the programme and he the rest (haha). There are a few irons in the fire. [. . .]

That you are overworking is not very clever. For whom, in fact? Is anyone thanking you for it? AMP perhaps? [. . .]

Hindemith mistakenly dated the following letter 1957, but the contents show it to have been 1958. The compositions on which he worked in 1957 following the completion of Die Harmonie der Welt included his Octet for clarinet, bassoon, horn, violin, two violas, cello, and double bass, which was first performed in Berlin on 23 September 1958, and the Twelve Madrigals for five voices a cappella, first performed in Vienna on 18 October 1958.

From the reference to Lambretta and Fiat it can be assumed that these Italian car manufacturers were among Cox's clients.

Mathis der Maler was performed at the Viennese Staatsoper on 17 May 1958 under the direction of Karl Böhm. Its first performance at the Metropolitan Opera, New York, was not until 1968 (a guest performance of the Hamburg Opera).

To Oscar Cox (written in English)   Blonay

24 February 1958 [1957]

Dear Oscar:

Well, centuries went by since I last wrote you. Gertrude tried to overbridge the gap, but as far as this poor composer is concerned, he entangles himself only today from his mass of staff paper, sketch books, musical ideas etc. etc. etc. to come down to the brass tacks (about tax, see later!!), i.e. to the long overdue letter to you. My last letter was written at the end of November (think of it!) before we left for Zurich. The few University weeks in Zurich were quite strenuous, as I tried — rather successfully, I think — to pack a whole term's work of three courses into three weeks. One day before Christmas we landed here again, just in time to bestow hundreds of little gift packages on all the local recipients. After one day of relaxation we went to Milan. At the Scala theatre they premiered Mathis der Maler, which we had to attend. The performance was just so so, but made more success than contemporary things usually do at that barn, as is shown by the fact that they played it once more than planned. Having again arrived at home we had just time to pack new suit cases and hop onto the next sleeping car. Concerts in Cologne and Kassel. In Kassel, furthermore, they did another opera of mine ("Cardillac") which was performed very nicely in spite of the fact that their theatre, bombed to pieces during the war, has not yet been rebuilt and they are playing in an old hall with almost no stage facilities whatsoever. Then we were in our old Frankfurt and Mainz for two days and from there went to England, where I was one of the conductors of the Hallé orchestra's centennial. The concerts were very pleasant (all in Lancaster and Yorkshire), but with snow storms, dirt, and general English winter conditions we got all H.R.M.'s mid-England coal dust, bleakness, and grippe bacilli into our lungs, brains, and stomachs, so that on the way back we came down with a pretty nice sickness. I had to make a layover in a Paris hotel bed, and Gertrude managed to reach her own den here in Blonay. Ever since, we have recovered, and we are enjoying the ever changing aspects of either premature spring weather or an all-over blanket of snow. I fell back to my old bad habit of composing if there is nothing better to be done, and I really got involved! The staff paper I covered with music during the last three weeks weighs at least a pound. So you see why I did not find any time for letters!

We will be leaving for Italy the 9th of March — I think Gertrude wrote you about it. The concert in Torino is on the 14th, one in Rome the 22nd. It really would be wonderful if you could be in Italy at that time. Let's pray to all the motorized deities and to those special ones at Fiat's, Lambretta's or whatever other wheeled powers will bring you over — sacrifices to these idols probably consist of a can filled with extra gas (contains lead), with perhaps some oldfashioned olive oil added. And don't forget to bring Louise with you!

The plans after Italy will be: first Vienna where the State Opera is doing "Mathis" (Böhm conducting), and some new concert pieces of mine and 16th century madrigals under my direction. The second or third performance of the opera is also for me, and in May I am doing the "Harmonie der Welt" in Bremen, together with a concert in connection with a choir festival (25000 participants only). As you see, there are right now three operas of mine running in German Theatres; the fourth one (Neues vom Tage — News of the day) is again announced for next season in Mannheim. I heard that Böhm (see above) has put "Mathis" onto the next year's Metropolitan Opera's season, but I don't believe it before it is over! I assume that at first he will see how it comes out in Vienna — he hasn't done it before!

Concerning your idea of doing one of these things in Washington: I think the most suitable one would be "Cardillac," as it is quite handy, rather pleasant and without the grand opera apparatus that is needed for "Mathis" or "Harmonie." "Neues vom Tage" would be good, too — but a success of this piece depends very much on the ingenuity of the Regisseur; it is a harmless and funny comedy which so far, always having been produced as a hideous satire on contemporary life, never had the success it deserves — except once in Naples where I did it three years ago. [. . .]

With all your Christmas presents, with which your attempts at spoiling the Hindemiths reached new climaxes and which kept coming in from mid-December until the last days of January, you wrapped us into such a layer of warmth and heartfelt pleasure that we felt very much ashamed in receiving all those treasures. The wonderful leather bag went into service right away, so did the little silver gadgets and their big brother, and so did finally everything except the books which so far remained unread — the reason being, of course, the long-stretched disease of compositis — see above. But they will be tackled during the next days.

Your last shipment of clippings showed me that your songs have again been done in Washington. Are you still feeling comfortable as a "composer poet"? At least you have the advantage of having heard those two songs and thus knowing them, while for the other party of the production team they still are nothing but music written on paper — but they are in good company! [. . .]

At the beginning of March 1958, Willy Strecker died suddenly of a stroke. He was seventy-four.

Hindemith conducted the first performance of his Pittsburgh Symphony, commissioned for the second centenary celebrations of the city, on 31 January 1959 in Pittsburgh.

To Karl Bauer   Blonay

Easter 1958

Dear Kallche, news trickles through now and again, but there's not much to report anyway and work leaves little time. A lot of concerts, a lot of composing, a lot of carting manure in the garden. . . . my time is well ordered.

You will have heard no doubt of Willy's sudden death. This was an awful blow. He had been somewhat run down over the last two or three years, and his eyes got steadily worse. I was fearing that he would soon become blind; however, it seems his unexpected death had nothing at all to do with his eyes. In his will he asked for some music at his funeral (among other things my Music of Mourning), and I played at the funeral. I don't yet clearly see how things will develop at Schotts. In my opinion they are facing almost insurmountable obstacles, for everything really hung on Willy.

Otherwise all is well here. Mathis was at the Scala and is now coming out at the end of this month in the Vienna State Opera. We're going there for it. You will no doubt have heard about Pittsburgh. I am writing an orchestral piece for them (please keep this secret) and we shall be coming over at the end of January next year for it. I expect there will be other things as well.

That's all for today. It's snowing here!

Hasty greetings to all good people (the others can . . .)

    Your   Paul

Hindemith played one of the two viola parts at the first performance of his Octet in Berlin on 23 September 1958.

The Bremen production of *Die Harmonie der Welt* in November 1958, with fifty curtain calls on the opening night, enjoyed much greater success than the first production in Munich.

The American tour began in Pittsburgh with concerts on 30 January and 1 February 1959, at which Hindemith conducted his new symphony and works by Schumann and Reger. On 8 February, in Waterville, Maine, he conducted the Colby College orchestra and chorus in his *Five Songs on Old Texts*, Bruckner's Mass in E Minor, and orchestral works by Handel and Mendelssohn. The final concert before leaving America on 21 February, was in the Town Hall, New York, and consisted of the Bruckner Mass, Hindemith's Octet, and six of his madrigals.

To Oscar Cox (written in English)   Blonay

24 July 1958

[. . .] We are sitting quietly in our enclosure, doing garden work, writing music, and enjoying a complacent sort of life not clouded by concerts, public business and official obligations. We plan to go up to Montana (not Montana U.S., but Montana, Valais) a nice place where we lived before we went to America—my god, that was hundreds of years ago! We felt that we needed some high mountain air. If the weather is not quite as bad as it is here right now we hope to do a lot of hiking, breathing cow dung and eating raclettes.

Since I last wrote you we have been rather busy. Mathis in Vienna was a good success, if one can believe the reports. We did not go to see the performances, the reason being their shifting around the date of the première and not getting together a good group of musicians for the concert I was supposed to have. The cast obviously was excellent, but I am afraid the decorations and staging were not quite what they ought to be—the two fellows who did that had already staged the Milan Mathis last December, which I saw and did not like. Very soon I shall see what it is like: they asked me to do the next performances in October.

Wouldn't that be a good time for you to come over and bring Louise with you? When this letter reaches you it will be exactly one year that you were here. We spoke so many times of your visit, and whenever I am sitting in one of the easychairs on the terrace (weather permitting) Gertrude always mentions [an illegible word] your having taken a nap there—which shows that (1) people need to be prompted into their well-being, (2) that glorious events will not be forgotten. As for the current year the dates for a congruent repetition are over, it really would be good if you could arrange something with the almighty Fiats. Concert life for us begins in September again, so if we would be on the way we could always meet you somewhere else in tiny Europe. If not Vienna, perhaps Berlin would do. We shall be there towards the middle of the month. They have their annual music festival at that time, and I have a concert with one or two new pieces of mine; I'll even appear as tamer of my old viola.

The Pittsburgh piece is well under way. It will be a larger symphonic whale (or rather a whalley) for full orchestra and I hope it will be worthy of all the pits and Pitts with all their coal dust and smog atmosphere.

Before we settled down here in Blonay we travelled in Germany—through the part of the country where my mother came from. We knew only vaguely that beautiful hill country near the river Weser and were grateful for the opportunity of exploring it somewhat more carefully. In Bremen I did the Harmonie der Welt, which again was a tremendous success. And then there were concerts, again in Bremen, and in Detmold, Goslar, Bern, and Konstanz. Well, that was that.

As Gertrude wrote you, there is one of my former students who offered the only concert possibility besides Pittsburgh (although I have the feeling that he, too, got cold feet in the meantime); he is the music teacher at Colby College which is up in Maine (I think it is Brunswick). So if by any chance—or better unchance—we cannot see you in Europe and you are perhaps just here when we are in Pittsburgh there will always be a chance to have a meeting in Maine!

I think I'll stop this letter before I start writing more nonsense. Music paper is waiting anyway, impatiently and reproachfully.

Thus, kurz und bündig: Lebwohl and love to both of you.

As ever yours

Paul.

Shortly after Hindemith's return from a second conducting tour in the United States, which included on 19 February 1960 a concert in New Haven of choral works by Buxtehude and Gabrieli, Stravinsky's Symphony of Psalms, and six of his own madrigals, he began work with Thornton Wilder on the one-act opera *The Long Christmas Dinner*. Hindemith completed the opera in August 1960 but held back its production in the hope of receiving a companion piece from Wilder. When this failed to materialize, he approached other possible librettists, among them the English poet, Dame Edith Sitwell.

The Latin songs to which Hindemith refers in the first letter were the Thirteen Motets, which he had begun in 1941 and completed in 1960.

Hindemith made no settings of Edith Sitwell's poems. Her prose works included *English Eccentrics* (1933) and *A Notebook on William Shakespeare* (1948).

To Edith Sitwell (written in English)   Vevey, poste restante

12 May 1961

Dear Dame Edith,

the letter which Mrs. Hindemith has written a few days ago has explained, I hope, my long silence after having received your very kind letter. The books we found only when we returned from a long Concert Tour through Italy, and I want to tell you that I was overjoyed when I began to read them. A good deal of the Anthology's poems I knew of course (although your wise comments present them in a new light), but of your own marvelous creations everything but Façade (via William Walton) was new to me. I am still reading, rereading and digesting them, and I feel this will keep me busy for quite a while.

As for your suggestions of composable poems, most of them could be done as Lieder with Piano (and very impressive ones), but as I just got rid of a series of 13 extended and profound Latin songs (from the Vulgate) I feel somewhat exhausted as far as songs go. May I tackle them later? "Dirge for the New Sunrise" can be worked into a fine Baritone Aria with Orchestra, but the one that fits best my current problem of writing a piece for the Glee Club (men's chorus with orchestra) of my former University (Yale), is "Heart and Mind." I hope that during the summer months I shall have time and ideas enough to write it.

Would you not be interested to write a sort of one act musical comedy? I am always looking out for librettos of this kind, and it would be wonderful if an opera could be created without the usual operatic nonsense — perhaps in the spirit of your "English (or any other) Eccentrics."

> With gratitude for your kindness
> and respectful regards
> Sincerely yours
> Paul Hindemith

To Edith Sitwell (written in English)   Vevey

                                                                12 June 1961

Dear Dame Edith,

I am, as usual, late with this reply to your kind letter. The reason is, that we were again on a concert trip (to Prague and Germany), and with journeys, rehearsals, and performances there was hardly any time left over for other things.

I considered and reconsidered your suggestions of a libretto derived from your splendid account of Carlyle's domestic sufferings, and I hope you will not be too cross with me if I voice some doubts as to the feasibility of this theme. The charming essence of your narrative is, of course, that we know: here is a great man, with whose achievements as a historian and philosopher we are acquainted, and that now we see him in incongruent and unexpectedly akward situations. This contrast can hardly be shown in a short opera—nothing can be implied; Carlyle would, for instance, have to clear the situation by saying (singing): "I am Th. C. who wrote about heroship etc. etc" or something to that effect, which would neither dramatically nor musically be interesting, and it would need some weighty development. So we would merely see a queer and grouchy old anonym whose peculiarities appear magnified and made disproportionally important by the music. This would probably have a rather distressing effect, the more as one would find it somewhat disrespectful towards the memory of a great man. Furthermore, music as a highly stylized and elevated form of acoustical manifestations (even if it is used as a comical means of expression) can hardly serve as a vehicle transmitting low-grade acoustical facts, as noises, crashes, crowing, and barking of dogs etc—they cannot be stylized and therefore would be in uncough contradiction to the musical organism. Another weakness of the piece would be, that in a sequence of scenes only one single trick, e.g. the reaction of a neurotic towards external vexations, would be the contents of the piece. Although by some technical means a more convincing arrangement of this could be found and other scenes could, as you suggested, be interspersed (Mrs. Carlyle's death etc.), the question remains if that warrants the employment of singers and at least 30 musicians.

Now you will probably think: P.H. is an old fastidious, wisecracking bore, worse than Mr. Carlyle as shown in the "Eccentrics," with whom no collaboration is desirable—but with the same fastidiousness I have the faint hope that you will have some further suggestions. If so, please don't think of any music or of acoustical effects, but only of visual action; the musician will find out how music can be amalgamated with it, and for this some very sketchy notes only are necessary at the beginning—the better if in multiple form . . . Needless to say that, besides musical considerations, I greatly enjoyed your jotted down scenario.

We found your Shakespeare book when we returned, and what we have read so far (not much, to be true) increased our already existing amazement and admiration. With your friendly assistance we musicians will end up as real erudite people! Many thanks for your thoughtfulness.

Warmest greetings, also from Mrs. H., and heartfelt thanks for the dedication,
Sincerely yours
Paul Hindemith

The first performance of The Long Christmas Dinner was given on 17 December 1961 in Mannheim under Hindemith's musical direction. Entitled Das lange Weihnachtsmahl, it was given in the German translation Hindemith himself made as he was setting the original English text to music. In the absence of a companion one-act opera, it was accompanied by two of his ballets, Hérodiade and Nobilissima Visione.

The first performance in English, also conducted by the composer, took place at the Juilliard School of Music in New York on 13 March 1963. The companion piece on that occasion was his early ballet (1922) The Demon (Der Dämon).

The performance in Berlin was in September 1962. Milhaud's Opéras minutes are L'enlèvement d'Europe, L'abandon d'Ariane, and La délivrance de Thésée.

To Darius and Madeleine Milhaud (written in English on Hindemith's self-drawn Christmas card for 1962)

Dear Darius and Madeleine, we celebrated the 70th birthday (Darius', of course) in Berlin with a fine performance of the 3 Opéras minutes (billed together with this [The Long Christmas Dinner]). I had the Mannheim Opera's singers and orchestra, and the success was great and well-deserved. There was a project, to bring the whole production to Paris, May next (without me; we'll be in Chicago at that time) but I have the impression that the plan will collapse, for financial reasons. After the performance in Berlin everyone wanted to send a birthday card with all the names of those present on it, but obviously the liquids served were too good and plentiful, thus the present combined birthday-Christmas- and New Year's card is all that is left over from the glorious enterprise. — We came through Paris several times, either you were in America or we were in the through sleeping car from Switzerland to Calais or vice versa, which is in Paris at 7 a.m. Let's hope for the next time. — Hope you both are the same as always—as are we, except for the approaching senility, which seems the right state of mind for our ceaseless concert life.

Love   Paul

Greetings from Gertrude, she in in Montreux right now, shopping.

General Index

—in Great Britain, 53–56, 59–62, 67–68, 75–76, 90–91, 118, 227, 233, 238
—in Switzerland, 3–4, 87, 90, 120, 122–23, 215–44 passim
—in Turkey. See Cevat Bey; Conservatory for Music and Drama, Ankara
—in United States of America, 95–105, 110–16, 126–36, 148, 240, 242; residence, 152–218 passim; on American citizenship, 195, 225–28, 231, 234–35
Hindemith, Robert Rudolph (father), xii, 7–8, 9–10, 97
Hindemith, Rudolf (brother), xii, 3, 18, 20, 27, 30, 49, 191, 199
Hindemith, Rudy (cousin) and wife Eunice, 97–99, 103, 105, 126
Hindemith, Sophie (mother), xii, 49, 94, 97, 177, 186–87, 199, 202; reunion in Switzerland, 207–9; death, 210–12
Hindemith, Toni (sister), xii, 49, 186, 211–12
Hitler, Adolf, 62, 81, 84–85
Hoch Conservatorium, Frankfurt, xii, 3–5, 8, 10
Hochschule für Musik, Staatliche, Berlin, 49, 69–70, 86, 88, 92, 97, 106
Hoffmann–Behrendt, Lydia, 110, 126
Hurok, Sol, 118–19, 122, 143–44

International Society for Contemporary Music (ISCM), 29, 36, 179–80

Jagel, Frederick, 100
Jöde, Fritz, 43, 50, 51; letter to, 43–45
Jones, Parry, 67, 68

Kägi, Werner, 146–47
Kailey, Emerson, 186–87, 189, 190, 192
Kampfbund, 69, 75, 76
Kaufmann, Henry, 202; letter to, 203
Kay, Ulysses, 178–79
Kepler, Johannes, 129. See also Harmonie der Welt, Die in Index of Works
Kielmannsegg, Graf von, 14–15, 17–18, 21
Klemperer, Otto, 42, 52, 134, 172, 176
Korngold, Erich, 30, 74
Kortschak, Hugo,. 112
Koussevitzky, Serge, 52, 110, 127, 138–39, 154, 161, 167–68
Krenek, Ernst, 74
Kulenkampff, Georg, 94, 95
Kulturgemeinde, 82, 83, 93

Ladwig, Werner, 47
Lange, Hans, 11, 103–4, 113–14
La Scala, Milan, 236, 238, 241
Leigh, Walter, 53, 54, 67, 68
Library of Congress, Washington, 95, 100–101, 184–85
Liepmann, Klaus, 112
Lindberg, Helge, 27
Lion, Ferdinand, 35
London String Quartet, 55
Los Angeles Philharmonic Orchestra, 134–35
Louisville Symphony Orchestra, 212
Lübbecke (-Job), Emma and Fried, 18, 24, 27, 37–38, 54–56, 58, 92, 186, 192; letters to, 22–24, 40–41, 42–43, 63, 142–43, 173–75, 192–95, 212–13
Luftwaffe, 92–95

Mainardi, Enrico, 94–95
Martinu, Bohuslav, 53
Massine, Léonide, 106, 116, 121, 131–34, 154, 161, 168
Mechanical music, 41, 42, 48, 51
Meissner, Hans, 78–79
Mendel, Arthur, 139, 179–80
Mendelssohn, Arnold, xii, 3, 5, 61
Mengelberg, Willem, 7, 11, 89, 137
Mergler, Betty, 164, 169
Mersmann, Hans, 50, 51
Metropolitan Opera, New York, 237, 239
Milhaud, Darius and Madeleine, xiii, 50, 244; letters to, 51, 87–88, 213–14, 244–45
Miracle, The (Vollmoeller), 5
Mitropoulos, Dimitri, 171–72
Monteux, Pierre, 129–31
Moran, Jean Todd, 191; letter to, 191–92
Museum concerts, Frankfurt, 7, 11, 16
Musikantengilde (Musicians' Guild), 43–45, 50
Muzak, 115–16, 117–18, 119

Nabokov, Nicholas, 132, 139–40, 151–52, 155, 166; letter to, 141–42
National Symphony Orchestra of Mexico, 195, 200
Naumann, Hans Heinrich, 70–71
New Friends of Music, New York, 212, 215–16
Newman, Ernest, 75–76
New York City Ballet, 215
New York City Center, 195, 215, 236–37

Tompkins, M. E., 97, 103–4, 115, 119; as
   AMP chief, 199, 202, 204–5, 214–16
Tourel, Jennie, 212–13
Tovey, Donald, 59, 60–62
Turkey. *See* Conservatory for Music and
   Drama, Ankara

UNESCO (United Nations Educational,
   Scientific and Cultural Organization),
   216–18

Vienna Philharmonic Orchestra, 202, 230–31
Voigt, Ernest R., 95, 97, 128, 140, 142, 151,
   165, 173, 184, 190; letters to, 95–97,
   116–19, 122–23, 139–40, 143–44,
   162–63, 179–80

Wall, Charles, 215, 225
Walton, William, 53–54, 121

Weber, Gustav and family, xii, 3; letters to,
   3–10
Webern, Anton von, 33
Wells College, Aurora, 132, 141–42, 151–52,
   153–57, 165
Whitman, Walt, 27, 28, 195, 197
Wilder, Thornton, xiii, 242
Williams, Harold, 67, 68
Willms, Franz, 78, 92, 191, 199, 201
Wittgenstein, Paul, 34; letters to, 34–35
Wolf, Kenneth, 183–84
Wood, Henry, 53, 54, 60, 67, 68

Yale University, 112, 156–57, 158–61, 163,
   168, 169, 171–218 passim, 236–37, 242

Zuckmayer, Eduard, 106, 108, 110
Zurich University, 215, 220, 228, 230, 236

Index of Paul Hindemith's Works

56; for violin, viola and cello, 37, 38, 66, 67, 75, 76

Tuttifäntchen (fairy play), 28–30, 38–39

Unaufhörliche, Das (The Perpetual, oratorio), 63, 67, 68, 81, 168, 233

Unterweisung im Tonsatz (The Craft of Musical Composition): I, Theoretischer Teil (Theoretic Part), 82, 83, 87, 92–95, 97, 100; additions to, 131; English translation, 139, 170, 179, 180, 190; II, Übungsbuch für den zweistimmigen Satz (Exercises in Two-Part Writing), 116–17, 131, 133, 136–39, 164, 168, 190; III, Der dreistimmige Satz (Three-Part Writing), 160–61, 170, 178, 180, 190, 194

Vier Temperamente, Die. See Four Temperaments, The

When Lilacs Last in the Door-Yard Bloom'd (Requiem "for those we love"), 195–96, 206, 209, 235

Wir bauen eine Stadt. See Let's Build a Town